Liberty in Their Names

Also available from Bloomsbury

Portraits of Wollstonecraft, edited by Eileen Hunt Botting
Becoming Beauvoir, by Kate Kirkpatrick
Dying for Ideas, by Costica Bradatan
The Philosophy of Anne Conway, by Jonathan Head

Liberty in Their Names

The Women Philosophers of the French Revolution

Sandrine Bergès

BLOOMSBURY ACADEMIC

LONDON • NEW YORK • OXFORD • NEW DELHI • SYDNEY

BLOOMSBURY ACADEMIC
Bloomsbury Publishing Plc
50 Bedford Square, London, WC1B 3DP, UK
1385 Broadway, New York, NY 10018, USA
29 Earlsfort Terrace, Dublin 2, Ireland

BLOOMSBURY, BLOOMSBURY ACADEMIC and the Diana logo are trademarks
of Bloomsbury Publishing Plc

First published in Great Britain 2023

Cover design by Louise Dugdale
Cover images, left to right: Madame Roland at the Concièrgerie
© Bibliothèque nationale de France.
Sophie de Grouchy / photograph taken by Jérome d'Aboville,
and owned by Madeleine Arnold-Tétard.
Olympe de Gouges © Bibliothèque nationale de France.

A catalogue record for this book is available from the British Library.

A catalog record for this book is available from the Library of Congress.

ISBN: HB: 978-1-3502-2712-5
PB: 978-1-3502-2713-2
ePDF: 978-1-3502-2714-9
eBook: 978-1-3502-2715-6

Typeset by Deanta Global Publishing Services, Chennai, India
Printed and bound in Great Britain

To find out more about our authors and books visit www.bloomsbury.com and
sign up for our newsletters.

Contents

Figures

All the illustrations included, unless specified, were retrieved from gallica. bnf.fr / Bibliothèque nationale de France.

Foreword

This book took five years to write. It feels longer. I have been steeped in the Revolution, the political thought, the theatre, the guillotine, Paris, but especially the lives and works of the three women I was writing about – Olympe de Gouges, Manon Roland and Sophie de Grouchy – the entire time. I progressively lost myself in the late eighteenth century, and, for all intent and purposes that don't include Wi-Fi and word processing, I am still there.

The journey started when I was ten, and I read an account by the popular historian Alain Decaux of the fate of the royal family during the Revolution. There was some exciting mystery regarding the son – Louis XVII: I was hooked. Then my mother took me to visit the Concièrgerie, the last prison of nearly everyone who died at the guillotine during the Revolution – and I came back, enthralled, with two postcards: a portrait of Danton and one of Marat. The obsession lasted – my husband may not know to this day that our two children are named after Charlotte Corday and Maximilien Robespierre – but it took a back seat when I became a philosopher. Until, that is, I discovered that there had been women philosophers in the French Revolution.

History of philosophy is not history – at least it's not supposed to be. As philosophers, we look for ideas and arguments that we can engage with (code for disagree) or that we can apply to our own times. We're not here to reconstruct the details of what these ideas meant to those people, at that time, in that context. But increasingly, historians of philosophy agree that to get the most out of past philosophical writings, it helps to understand the context in which they were written. Knowing that Hobbes wrote the *Leviathan* during the British civil war helps makes sense of the idea that for him any strong leader will do – whether king or Cromwell. And that is even more true when it comes to texts by women. They are not well known, so they don't belong to a well-established narrative of the kind Socrates-taught-Plato-taught-Aristotle. We don't know how they fit. Their texts – as complex and deep as those of their male counterparts – don't represent a familiar step in the rehearsed history of the discipline. So knowing the context helps.

And when it comes to the revolutionary period, when French philosophy was being performed in speeches at the Assembly or Convention, posted on the walls of Paris, published in newspapers or acted out at the theatre, it really helps to know what was going on. So the project of recovering the philosophical thought of three women of the French Revolution was the perfect excuse to indulge my childhood passion.

One reason why philosophers don't do history proper is that they don't know how. So please bear with me, as I do my best to set the context necessary to understand the powerful political thought of Gouges, Roland and Grouchy. I've provided plenty of titles in the biography where you can go and check out my references. And for those who are no more French Revolution experts than I was when I started, I have provided a timeline and a glossary of important people and places.

There are many people who deserve thanks for their help. If you are one of them and I forget to name you, please know that this preface was written during the last (hopefully) severe Coronavirus lockdown in my adopted country, Turkey. So it is distraction, not ungratefulness.

This book was made, as much as written. It involved several walks through Paris streets and visits to monuments and cemeteries. My mother, Anne-Marie Chaput, accompanied me on most of them, as did my daughter, Charlotte Wringe, and my son, Max Bergès. We went down into the catacombs where I put my claustrophobia to the test, we chased cats with my niece, Roxane Gobé, in the Père Lachaise cemetery, and investigated a lost infirmary with her brother Alexandre in the Concièrgerie. Charlotte, her friend Melisa Erişen and I walked all over Paris, following the route described in Chapter 2, and ended up locked in to the building where Sophie de Grouchy once had her studio. My mother drove me to Villette castle, where Sophie de Grouchy was born, and we persuaded the lovely manager, David, to take us for a guided tour of what is now a luxury hotel for movie stars. We found a great little restaurant nearby and the owner told us that Tom Cruise had been helicoptered in when he was filming in Paris.

A lot of the making of the book was also writing. And there is no writing without reading. I want to thank my writers Coven, Eileen Hunt and Alan Coffee, who read and commented on several chapters and supported my project by asking about it and referring to it in their work when it wasn't yet under contract. We met throughout the Covid-19 months on Zoom to discuss each other's work, and I can't thank them enough for their support and friendship.

My husband, Bill Wringe, has also read draft after draft and listened to me going on about the revolutionary women philosophers for the last five years. And yes, he does probably know that our children were named after revolutionary characters.

Kemal Sağbaş, my graduate student, asked if I could give him some research assistant work. I suggested he read my manuscript. He did – with a vengeance – and returned eleven perfectly annotated chapters, with his observations on the content and structure, notes on the narrative flow and typos (how do I still not know how to spell 'cemetery'?). So, thank you Kemal.

Earlier on in the process, when I still didn't know whether this was a viable project, I sent a proposal draft to Eric Schliesser and Lena Halldenius, both of whom sent me comments that led me to reshape the project in ways that would make it much better: I hope I succeeded in following their advice.

Lisa Shapiro read a later proposal as well as several chapters and gave me detailed and creative feedback, designed to improve not only the content but also the style and the tone. And then she read another two versions of that same proposal and kept on commenting. Lucy Randall also read part of the manuscript and offered generous and insightful comments. I'm very grateful to them both as well as to any anonymous referee who gave their time to comment on the book. Many thanks also to Stephanie Palmer and Alexandra Abranches, who read my glossary.

Gina Luria Walker and Penny Whitworth welcomed me to The New Historia team at The New School, where I learned a lot about writing women's lives. My friend and colleague Saniye Vatansever helped me spread The New Historia project in Turkey.

Jacqui Broad invited me to try out the central ideas for the book in a special issue of the Australasian Philosophical Review. Her invitation gave me the confidence that people would want to read about women philosophers of the French Revolution. Writing the lead article, reading the fantastic responses sent in by Martina Reuter, Lena Halldenius, Patrick Ball, Karen Green, Spiros Tegos and Martin Fog Lantz Arndal, and responding to them were great ways of focusing my ideas and figuring out a new approach to these women's thoughts.

Martina Reuter invited me to lecture about Olympe de Gouges in Jyvaskyla in 2016. Ruth Hagengrubber and Mary Ellen Waithe invited me to do the same in Paderborn in 2017. These classes were probably the best way of figuring out what people didn't know about Gouges and what they needed to know. I'm grateful to all three of them for trusting me to do a good job when I was just starting out my research on Gouges.

I also want to thank my students and the members of my department, who listened to me going about Gouges, Roland and Grouchy even at times when it wasn't entirely relevant. My departmental chair also contrived to make my life easier on occasions when I needed to hunker down and write, for which I'm very grateful.

I'm grateful to anyone who offered me comments on the draft – on submitted papers or at any of the conferences where I presented on the women of the Revolution over the past five years, and to all those who facilitated research, in archives, libraries and monuments, and to Madeleine

Arnold-Tétard who always answered my questions about Sophie de Grouchy and to Millicent Churcher who shared the results of her research on Grouchy with me.

I'm grateful to all the people who read my blog 'Liberty in thy Name', all those who 'liked' my watercolour pictures of the French Revolution on social media and to my friends, especially the ones who were part of my 'Covid bubble' Ceren Sibel Sayın and Valerie Kennedy.

Finally, I am grateful to my editor at Bloomsbury Philosophy, Colleen Coalter, who trusted that this would make a good book.

Timeline of the French Revolution

January 1789: Louis XVI calls a meeting of the Estates-General: nobility, clergy and Third Estate as a last resort to try and save France's economy.

January–April 1789: Campaign and elections of the members of the three estates.

5 May 1789: First meeting of the Estates-General in Versailles.

4 June 1789: Joseph, oldest son of Louis and Marie-Antoinette dies and is buried on 13 June.

17 June 1789: The Third Estate, led by Mirabeau, invites the clergy and nobility to join them in one united Assembly.

20 June 1789: The meeting room for the estates is found closed, but the newly formed Assembly finds a new room to gather in: the king's Tennis Court.

The members of the Assembly swear an oath not to part until they have written a constitution for France.

11 July 1789: The king dismisses Necker, his secretary of finance.

14 July 1789: Camille Desmoulins stands on a rostrum in Paris and calls for the crowds to take arms. The crowds take the Bastille.

26 July–6 August 1789: This was the period known as the Great Fear when the French countryside witnessed panics and riots.

4 August 1789: The Assembly produces the first article of a constitution which abolished aristocratic privileges.

26 August 1789: The complete draft of the *Declaration of the Rights of Man*, a preliminary to the constitution, is approved at the Assembly.

4 October 1789: Parisian women walk to Versailles to protest against the price of bread, and they bring the king and his family and most of the Assembly back to Paris.

20–21 June 1791: Attempted escape of the king and his family, disguised as a bourgeois family. They are stopped and recognized in Varenne and brought back to Paris.

13–14 September 1791: The king is forced to endorse the Assembly and swear allegiance to the sovereign nation.

5 October 1791: The Constitutional Assembly becomes the Legislative Assembly. The king is stripped of his executive power.

10 August 1792: The people attack the Tuileries, where the king and his family are held, and massacre their private army, the Swiss guards.

2–6 September 1792: Refractory priests, aristocrats, Swiss guards, but also prostitutes and disabled patients are pulled out of their prison cells and massacred by the crowd.

22 September 1792: The republic is declared and the National Convention replaces the Legislative Assembly. Its members are elected – the Reign of Terror begins.

3 December 1792: The trial of Louis XVI begins.

21 January 1793: Louis XVI is executed.

9 July 1793: Charlotte Corday kills Jean-Paul Marat, stabbing him in his bath.

17 July 1793: Charlotte Corday is executed.

16 October 1793: Marie-Antoinette is executed.

31 October 1793: Jacques-Pierre Brissot and twenty-one other Girondins are executed.

3 November 1793: Olympe de Gouges is executed.

8 November 1793: Manon Roland is executed.

29 March 1794: Condorcet dies in prison.

5 April 1794: Danton and Desmoulins are executed.

27 July–24 October 1794: A political group enacts a coup d'état against Robespierre and Saint-Just and forms the Thermidorian Convention.

28 July 1794: Robespierre and Saint-Just are executed – end of the Reign of Terror.

17 January 1795: New constitution drafted.

25 October 1795: The Directory is formed and attempts to create a stable government.

9 November 1799: Napoleon stages a successful coup d'état.

Note on the revolutionary calendar

On the day France was declared a republic the National Convention decided to adopt a new calendar to mark the occasion and break with the past.

Year 1 started at the end of September 1792.

The first month, starting 22 September, was called Vendemiaire (referring to the grapes harvest). Months lasted thirty days. Thermidor (from *thermos*, or heat), as in the Thermidorian Convention, runs from mid-July to mid-August.

Each day of each month also had its own name – after a plant, animal or mineral. 14 July was *sauge* – or sage.

The calendar was abolished during its fourteenth year, in 1805.

Glossary of people and places

Amis des Noirs, Société des: Abolitionist society founded in 1788 by Brissot, Grégoire, Condorcet and Etienne Clavière, under the patronage of Mirabeau. Olympe de Gouges was an honorary member.

Bastille, la: A medieval fortress used, from the reign of Louis XIV onwards, for political prisoners and personal enemies of the king. A person could be incarcerated there without trial on the authority of a *Lettre de Cachet*, that is, a letter with the king's seal. The Bastille was also a depot for gunpowder, which is why it became a target on 14 July 1789 as the Parisian people sought to arm themselves. By the time the Bastille was taken, there were only seven prisoners left. Some, including the Marquis de Sade imprisoned for seditious writings, had been evacuated to other prisons. The Bastille was destroyed during the Revolution.

Beccaria, Cesare (1738–94): Milanese criminologist and philosopher, who wrote the very influential *On Crimes and Punishments* (1764), a critique of European penal practices, especially torture and the death penalty, and an argument in favour of more humane punishment. Beccaria's penal thought was consequentialist and was influential in the development of utilitarianism through Jeremy Bentham. Beccaria was also very popular in France: his work was translated and introduced by Voltaire. Beccaria frequented the salon of Madame Helvetius, as did many Girondin revolutionaries a decade later.

Brissot (de Warville), Jacques-Pierre (1754–93): Journalist, who edited the revolutionary newspaper *Le Patriote François*, co-founder of the Société des Amis des Noirs and prominent member of the Girondins (sometimes called the Brissotins). Executed in October 1793 alongside twenty-one other Girondins politicians.

Buzot, François (1760–94): Deputy of the National Convention, a friend of Brissot and Roland, and later lover of Manon Roland. He committed suicide after her death.

Cabanis, Pierre-Jean-George (1757–1808): Doctor, politician and physiologist, adopted son of Madame Helvetius, he was a close friend of Condorcet and his wife, Sophie de Grouchy with whom he collaborated. He married Charlotte de Grouchy, Sophie's sister.

Capet, Louis (1754–93): Name given to Louis XVI during the last month of his life, after he was stripped of his title. Capet was the name of the dynasty he was issued from.

Commune de Paris (1789–95): Governing body for Paris during the Revolution. Under the rule of the Jacobins (especially Robespierre, Marat and Danton), it became one of the principal organs of revolutionary power after 10 August 1792.

Concièrgerie, the: A medieval palace converted into a prison which became famous during the Revolution as the Parisian antechamber of the guillotine. Adjacent to the Palais de la Justice, where trials were held, it was used to imprison Parisians just before and after their trial – often only for a few days.

Condorcet, Marie Jean Antoine Nicolas de Caritat, Marquis of (1743–94): Mathematician, philosopher, economist and politician, Condorcet worked with Turgot and then Necker in the Finance Ministry. In 1788, he married Sophie de Grouchy, and together they became involved in the Revolution, publishing the journal *Le Républicain*. Condorcet was one of the founding members of the Société des Amis des Noirs. He was also an advocate of women's rights. He died in prison in 1794 after spending several months in hiding.

Constituent Assembly of 1789: In June 1789, the Estate-Generals were shut out by the king from their meeting place. They regrouped in another location and decided to work together and become the National Assembly. In July, after deciding to draft a constitution, they changed their name to Constituent Assembly.

Constitution of 1791: In the summer of 1789, the National Constituent Assembly began to draft a constitution. The resulting *Declaration of the Rights of Man* served as a preamble to the first constitution, which was accepted in September 1791.

Corday, Marie Anne Charlotte d'Armont (1768–93): Girondin sympathizer who came to Paris from her native Normandy to murder Marat, whom she saw as responsible for the Terror. After the assassination (by knife while he was working in his bath), she gave herself up and was executed.

Cordeliers, club des: A revolutionary society founded in 1790, meeting in the refectory of the Convent of the Cordeliers in Paris' Latin Quarter. Its most famous members were Danton, Desmoulins, Fabre d'Eglantine, Marat, Hébert, Robert (husband of Louise Keralio-Robert), Choderlos de Laclos and Théroigne de Mericourt. More popular than the Jacobins, its membership was free.

D'Aelders, Etta Palm, baroness (1743–99): A Dutch spy who settled in Paris before the Revolution and became invested in its reforms, especially those concerning women. She founded the women's revolutionary society 'Société patriotique et de bienfaisance des amies de la verité' in 1791 and published several tracts arguing for women's civic and political rights.

Danton, George-Jacques (1759–94): Lawyer from the East of France, known for his physical strength, Danton's fame as an orator rose from the early days of the Revolution when he gave speeches at the Cordeliers. He claimed to be responsible for the massacre of the king's personal guard on 10 August 1792 and was accused by Madame Roland of having started the September Massacres. Danton worked with Robespierre at the Paris Commune, but as he came to disagree more with Robespierre's policies, he was decapitated in April 1794.

Declaration of the Rights of Man (1789): Drafted by the Constituent Assembly in August 1789 and published that same month, this served as a preamble for the Constitution of 1791. The Declaration asserted the 'natural, unalienable and sacred rights' of all citizens, with political rights for 'active' citizens only (free men).

Desmoulins, Lucie-Simplice-Camille-Benoît (known as 'Camille') (1760–94): Lawyer by training, Desmoulins became a journalist during the Revolution, writing often inflammatory articles. On 14 July 1789, he jumped on a café table and harangued the crowds, urging them to wear a 'cocarde' – a green ribbon (later tricolour) – and arm themselves to defend the Nation against the king's private army. Close to Robespierre, with whom he had been at school, and Danton, his Paris neighbour, he was decapitated together with Danton in April 1794. His wife, Lucille, followed ten days later.

Directory (1795–99): This was the first government after the fall of the National Convention, and it set up a bicameral system of legislation, with the lower house, known as the Council of the Five Hundred, and the upper house, Council of Ancients, which consisted of men over the age of forty. This government was predominantly Girondin. The Directory lasted until Napoleon took power in 1799.

Dumont, Pierre-Étienne-Louis (1759–1829): Swiss author who worked with Mirabeau during the first years of the Revolution and later moved to England where he worked as a translator and editor for his friend Jeremy Bentham. A moderate republican and a close friend of the Condorcets, he collaborated with them on the journal *Le Républicain* for a short while.

Equiano, Olaudah (aka Gustavus Vassa) (1745–97): Native of Eboe (southern Nigeria), he was captured and sold as a slave in his childhood and purchased his own freedom at the age of twenty-one. In 1777, he travelled to Britain, where he became involved in the abolitionist movement. He toured the country to talk about slavery and the slave trade and, in 1789, published his memoir *The Interesting Narrative of the Life of Olaudah Equiano, or Gustavus Vassa, the African*.

Estates-General of 1789: In January 1789, the king sent out a letter of convocation to all provinces to ask them to elect representatives for the three estates: nobility (First Estate), clergy (Second Estate) and the commoners (Third Estate). The estates had not been called since 1614. The purpose of gathering the estates was to help resolve France's national debt. The estates gathered in the spring and by the summer constituted themselves into the first National Assembly.

Free people of colour: French colonies were populated by white colonists, slaves, a white underclass ('les petits blancs') and 'gens de couleur' men and women who were free, and had mixed black and white ancestry. Older families had plantations of their own and were sometimes slave owners. At the outbreak of the Revolution, white colonists belonging to the Club Massiac argued that free people of colour should not be classified as 'active' citizens and thereby should not benefit from political rights. The Société des Amis des Noirs fought on behalf of free men of colour.

Gironde, la: A name given after the fact to a group of Jacobin politicians who disagreed with the Montagnard faction (Robespierre, Danton, Marat). The name 'Girondins' was given to them because a number of their members came from the department of the Gironde (Vergniaud, Gensonne, Guadet). During their lifetime, they were sometimes called the Brissotins or the Rolandistes, after two of their most famous members, Brissot and Roland. Many of them died during the Terror: twenty-two were executed on 31 October 1794, and several others died in exile shortly afterwards. Among those who did not die, some served as part of the Council of the Five Hundred during the Directory.

Gouges, Olympe de (1748–93): Born Marie Gouzes in Montauban in the south of France, illegitimate daughter of the local gentry, she came to Paris as a young widow and mother in 1767 and developed a career first as an actress, then a playwright and a political writer and philosopher. She defended abolitionism and women's rights, and more generally, republican values. She was arrested in the summer of 1793 for a text in which she attacked Robespierre and the Commune, and she was executed in November 1793.

Great Fear, the (Summer 1789): After the fall of the Bastille, there were some peasant revolts throughout France, targeting local aristocrats and their properties. This turned into a general panic, with France unsure whether they were under attack from England or brigands or French protestants. Many landed gentries sought refuge in their townhouses.

Grégoire, Henri (Abbé) (1750–1831): A provincial Catholic priest with a solid philosophical education, Grégoire represented the clergy in the meeting of the three estates and was one of the men responsible for the three estates' coming together as one Assembly where he was one of the most vocal proponents of the abolition of privileges. Founding member of the Société des Amis des Noirs, he remained a committed abolitionist long after the society disappeared.

Grouchy, Sophie de Marquise de Condorcet (1764–1822): A highly educated aristocratic woman who became an atheist and a republican in her youth. She wrote a commentary and response to Adam Smith's *Theory of Moral Sentiments*, the *Letters on Sympathy (1798)*, in which she argued that understanding sympathy was the clue not only to morality but also to institutional reform after the Revolution. She also wrote republican essays for the journal she created with her husband, Condorcet, *Le Républicain*.

Guillotin, Joseph-Ignace (1738–1814): Medical doctor and revolutionary who proposed to aid the abolition of penal privileges and the barbarity of punishment by introducing a machine that would decapitate swiftly and painlessly. That machine was later named after him.

Guillotine, la: Proposed in 1789 by Guillotin, the design of the machine was directed by surgeon Antoine Louis and realized by harpsichord maker Jean-Tobie Schmidt. It was tested on live sheep and human corpses in April 1792. The first live execution was that of the thief Nicolas Pelletier on 25 April of the same year. It served for the last time in September 1977 to execute Hamida Djandoubi, a man convicted of rape and murder.

Jacobin, le club des: Originally known as Club Breton, this revolutionary society took its name from the convent of the Jacobins, on the Rue St Honoré, on the Right Bank of the River Seine. It was first dominated by Mirabeau, then the constitutional monarchists Barnave, Dupont and Lameth. When these left the Jacobin to form their own club, the Feuillants, the club came under the influence of Brissot, Robespierre, Desmoulins, Pétion and Buzot and a few others. In 1793, with the Girondin faction no longer welcome, the Jacobin was led by Robespierre, Marat and Danton. These then seceded into the Hebertistes and the Dantonistes. After the death of Robespierre, the Jacobin club lost its influence.

Keralio-Robert, Louise-Félicité (1757–1821): Historian, printer, republican journalist. Keralio published a history of Queen Elizabeth (1786), edited and printed the first few volumes of a planned fourteen of women's writings: *Collection des meilleurs ouvrages François, composés par des femmes*. During the Revolution she founded a journal – *Journal de l'Etat et du Citoyen*, then *Mercure National*. She married the politician Pierre-Francois-Joseph Robert. Together they left France during the reign of Louis XVIII.

Legislative Assembly (1 October 1791–20 September 1792): This replaced the Constituent Assembly once the constitution was drafted. Its members were elected through census suffrage. Its main task was to establish laws according to the principles of equality dictated by the constitution, and it was responsible for the reform of family law, in particular, legalization of divorce and laws regarding inheritance of illegitimate children. It was disbanded shortly after the 10 August attack on the king's army.

Louis XVI (reign 1774–92) (see Louis Capet): Successor to his grandfather, Louis XV, he was married to Marie-Antoinette of Austria in 1770 (while he was at the age of fifteen). He inherited debts that were worsened by France's involvement in the American Revolution. He employed Turgot and Necker in turns to help fill the deficit and called in the three estates to seek advice on this matter. In June 1791, he attempted to leave France but was recognized and captured in Varenne. He was arrested on 13 August 1792, tried in December and guillotined on 21 January 1793.

Louverture, Toussaint (1743–1803): Born into slavery in Saint Domingue (Haiti), Louverture was influenced by the French Revolution and became the military leader of the Haitian rebellion of 1791, turning it into a successful revolution. In 1797, he became the Governor General of Saint Domingue.

Macaulay, Catharine (later Graham) (1731–91): English historian, famous for her eight-volume *History of England*. An anti-monarchist and republican, Macaulay was influential in America and France, notably for Brissot and Manon Roland. In England, she also influenced Mary Wollstonecraft, who wanted to dedicate her *Vindication of the Rights of Woman* to her.

Marat, Jean-Paul (1743–93). Marat was born in Neuchatel, then part of Austria. He moved to Paris and then to England to study and practice medicine, eventually obtaining a degree from Saint-Andrews for his work on gonorrhoea. At the same time, he published works in political philosophy, physics and criminology. He became a journalist and a politician during the Revolution, known for his unpleasant ways. He was assassinated in his bathtub in July 1793 by Charlotte Corday, who held him responsible for the Terror.

Marie-Antoinette (1755–93), Queen of France (1774–92): Daughter of the empress Maria-Theresa of Austria, she was sent to France to marry Louis XVI in 1770 when she was fourteen. The couple had trouble conceiving, and their first daughter was born in 1778, followed by a son three years later and another in 1785. She reformed palace life by simplifying it, but she also acquired a reputation for debauchery and later encouraging her husband to treason via her foreign contacts.

Massiac, Club: Anti-abolitionist club established in 1789 to counter the efforts of the Société des Amis des Noirs. The club met at the hotel Massiac. It lasted until the Haitian Revolution of 1791.

Mercure National, le (1789–91): Revolutionary journal edited by Louise Keralio-Robert. Previously named 'Journal d'état et du citoyen' and later, combinations of both names.

Mirabeau, Honoré Gabriel Riqueti, Comte de (1749–91): Elected to represent Aix in the Third Estate despite his nobility, Mirabeau was instrumental in bringing the estates together (with Grégoire, Sieyès and Lafayette). As a compelling orator, he became a well-loved revolutionary figure, despite possible ties with royalty. He died of heart disease in April 1791, under the care of his friend and doctor, Cabanis.

Montagnards, les : A Jacobin faction led by Robespierre, Danton and Hébert, opposed to the Girondins. Leaders and architects of the Terror, they were so-called because they sat on the top row at the Jacobins (*montagnes* meaning 'mountains').

Napoléon, 1st, Napoléon Bonaparte (1769–1821): Born in Corsica, he distinguished himself in the Republican army, becoming a general in 1793. Through a coup d'état, he took over the government of France in 1799, establishing himself as First Consul in 1802 and Emperor in 1804. In 1802 he re-established slavery, and in 1804 he helped bring about a civil code, 'Code Napoléon', which restricted women's rights and made divorce nearly impossible. He died in exile on the island of St Helena.

National Convention (September 1792–October 1795): A single-chamber assembly created to replace the Legislative Assembly after the suspension of Louis XVI and the declaration of the French Republic. Members were elected by near-universal male suffrage. But it was one of the Assembly's organs, the Committee of Public Safety, which made the decisions that led the nation.

Necker, Jacques (1732–1804): Swiss banker who replaced Turgot as Finance Minister in 1777. He lost the position in 1781 after publishing a frank account of the king's spending – 'Compte rendu au Roi'. He was recalled in 1788 to help deal with the increasing financial crisis but dismissed again in July 1789, prompting the first popular action of the Revolution: the fall of the Bastille. Necker's daughter was Germaine de Staël.

Ogé, Vincent (1755–91): Mulatto from a well-off Haitian family who came to Paris to work with the Société des Amis des Noirs to argue for active citizenship for free men of colour in the French colonies. When this wasn't successful, he travelled back to Saint Domingue and organized a rebellion in October 1790. The rebellion was violently quashed, and Ogé died on the Catherine wheel, also known as the breaking wheel.

Paine, Thomas (1737–1809): English-born American citizen whose *Common Sense* inspired the American Revolution. Back in London, he published the *Rights of Man*, in which he defended the French Revolution in 1791. He became an honorary French citizen but was arrested in December 1793 and spent several months in the Luxembourg palace prison, where he wrote *The Age of Reason*. He remained in Paris until 1802 when he returned to America.

Patriote François, le (June 1789–July 1793): Revolutionary newspaper founded by Brissot.

Pétion (de Villeneuve), Jérome, (1756–94): Deputy of the Third Estate, Mayor of Paris and elected member of the Convention, Pétion was a Girondin sympathizer. When the order was issued to arrest all Girondins, he escaped and eventually committed suicide with Buzot in the countryside near Bordeaux. After he left Paris, his mother-in-law was guillotined for defending him publicly. His wife, Louise-Anne, was imprisoned with Manon Roland but was eventually freed.

Raimond, Julien (1744–1800): A free man of colour from Saint Domingue, educated in France and owner of property in Aquin, Raimond fought against colour prejudice and argued for free men of colour to be granted active citizenship, whatever their degree of whiteness. Raimond took part in debates at the Assembly alongside Brissot and Ogé. Later he worked with Louverture on drafting the first Haitian Constitution.

Refractory priests: In 1790, the Constituent Assembly issued a decree demanding that all members of the clergy should swear allegiance to the civil constitution. Those who refused were repressed, imprisoned or continued to follow Catholic practices in secret. The first victims of the September Massacres in 1792 were a group of refractory priests being transported from one prison to another. They were killed in the street.

Republic, French (September 1792–May 1804): France was declared a republic by the National Convention in September 1792, after the abolition of the constitutional monarchy in August 1792. Before it morphed into the First Empire, the French Republic saw three types of governments: the National Convention (1792–5), the Directory (1795–9) and the Consulate (1799–1804).

Républicain, le: Edited by Condorcet, Brissot, Paine, Duchatelet, Dumont and Sophie de Grouchy, this journal intended to show the French public that republicanism was a viable political option for France. It lasted for four issues in the spring/summer of 1791.

Robespierre, Maximilien de (1758–94): Lawyer from the north of France, educated in Paris, his political career began when he campaigned to be elected to represent the Third Estate. Known for his devotion to the Revolution, his virtuous ways and strong rhetoric, he made a name for himself at the Jacobin club and the Assembly. He rose to power during the Convention and was commonly held responsible for the Terror. In July 1794, after having most of his friends and enemies put to death, he was himself arrested. He was possibly dead from a gunshot by the time he was guillotined. His death marked the end of the Terror.

Roland, Marie-Jeanne (née Phlipon, known as 'Manon Roland' or 'Madame Roland') (1754–93): Daughter of a Parisian artisan, she was well educated and wrote political philosophy from a young age and developed her allegiance to Roman republicanism then. She married Jean-Marie Roland de la Platière in 1780, and their daughter Eudora was born a year later. For the first years of their marriage, the couple travelled (to England and Switzerland) and worked together in an attempt to forge an academic career for Jean-Marie. In 1791 the couple moved to Paris to participate in the Revolution. Although she did not believe women could participate in politics openly, her enthusiasm for the Revolution is visible in the letters she wrote then and the memoirs she wrote in prison at the end of her life. She died at the guillotine in November 1793.

Roland, Jean-Marie, de la Platière (1734–93): Before the Revolution, Roland worked as an inspector of manufactures. Shortly after he married, he used his wife's superior thinking and writing skills to attempt to start an academic career. One of his projects was an encyclopedia of manufacture. When the couple moved to Paris, his wife's efforts turned to his political career. In 1792 he was appointed minister of the interior. He committed suicide upon hearing of his wife's death in November 1793.

Saint-Just, Louis Antoine de (1767–94): Legal clerk from the north of France, he corresponded with Robespierre before joining him in Paris. Elected to the Convention as its youngest member, he joined the 'Montagnards' and died with Robespierre in July 1794.

Sieyès, Emmanuel-Joseph, Abbé (1748–1836). Elected member of the Third Estate, he was instrumental in the three estates' joining into the Assembly both through his speeches and his influential pamphlet, 'What Is the Third Estate?'. Sieyès helped draft the constitution and was, in turn, a member of the Convention, the Directory and a Senator in Napoleon's Consulate.

Staël, Anne-Louise-Germaine Necker, Baroness de (1766–1817): Philosopher, novelist, political and travel writer, defender of the Revolution and constitutional monarchy, a vocal opponent of Napoleon, she had to go into exile several times and spent part of her life in her father's Swiss home, Coppet, where she kept an influential salon.

Swiss guards: Swiss soldiers who were employed to protect European royalty between the fifteenth and nineteenth century. The soldiers protecting Louis XVI were attacked at the Tuileries Palace on 10 August 1792. Those who were not killed then were taken to Paris prisons and murdered a few weeks later during the September Massacres.

Terror (Reign of): Typically refers to the years 1793–4, but was brought on by the events of 1792, that is, the attack on the Tuileries Palace in August 1792 and the massacres of prisoners the next month. It was marked by the trial of Louis XVI, the arrest and death of the Girondins, and the rise to power of the Montagnards, led by Robespierre, Marat and Danton. During the Terror, there was an increase in 'surveillance' with more power granted to committees such as the Committee of Public Safety. The Terror ended in the summer of 1794 with the death of Robespierre.

Turgot, Anne-Robert-Jacques (1727–1781): French economist, close to the physiocrats in that he believed in freeing the market from restrictive royal controls. Appointed financial minister in 1774, Turgot attempted to reform agricultural commerce by freeing the trade of grain, but a poor harvest in 1774 led to the flour wars (or bread riots) and his eventual dismissal in 1776. He was replaced by Necker in 1777.

Wollstonecraft, Mary (1759–97): English feminist republican philosopher and supporter of the French Revolution, which she defended in her *Vindication of the Rights of Men* (1790) and *Vindication of the Rights of Woman* (1792), translated into French the year of its publication. She travelled to Paris in 1792 to write about the Revolution. The resulting (unfinished) *An Historical and Moral View of the French Revolution* condemned the Terror but still praised the Revolution.

Women's march to Versailles: On 5 October 1789, Parisian market women led by Reine Audu walked to Versailles and brought the king and his family to the Assembly and persuaded them to relocate to Paris. Reine Audu was later offered a post at the Paris Commune in recognition of her role on that day.

Women in the Revolution

On a rainy afternoon in November 1793, Olympe de Gouges stood alone in the two-wheeled cart that brought her from the prison to the guillotine. She faced backwards, as instructed by her executioner, Charles-Henri Sanson, who felt that prisoners should not have to watch the approach of the guillotine. And as the tumbril clattered on the cobblestones, presumably sending pain searing through her recently injured leg, she would have scowled at the Parisian crowd hurling insults at her. On the scaffold, before she laid down on the plank, she looked one last time at the people she had wanted to save from tyranny and shouted: 'Children of the nation, you will avenge my death!'[1]

Five days later, Marie-Jeanne Roland had one companion in the tumbrel: one very scared civil servant, Simon-François Lamarche. Marie-Jeanne was supposed to go first: Fouquier-Tinville had scribbled 'Hurry!' on her death warrant. But she kindly offered Lamarche her place so he wouldn't have to watch as she was decapitated. When her turn came, Marie-Jeanne Roland stood proud and looked beyond the crowds to the monumental statue of liberty erected a few months earlier. 'Oh, Liberty!' she cried. 'What crimes are committed in thy name!'

That same month, the Jacobin newspaper *Le Moniteur* printed a ferocious attack on women who tried to be active in the Revolution.[2] The only way for a woman to support the republic, it said, was to stay home and teach her children the values of citizenship. Women who went into politics, who came out in the streets or wrote pamphlets, were unnatural monsters, a danger to the nation. Let the deaths of Gouges and Roland be a warning to them all.

Gouges and Roland were the third and fourth women to die at the guillotine in Paris that year. Charlotte Corday had been executed in July and Marie-Antoinette in October. Their deaths were unusual; far fewer women than men climbed the scaffold during the Terror. Out of a total of 18,613 victims of the guillotine between 1792 and 1796, only 2,567 were women, while in Paris, there were 370 women out of a total of 2,918.[3] Some of these were unfortunate aristocrats. Others, Gouges and Roland included, were philosophers and activists who articulated ideas that were central to the

Figure 1 Execution de Marie-Antoinette, engraving, BnF.

Revolution's cause – ideas whose influence would be lasting. But even by the more radical revolutionaries' standards, they had gone too far in neglecting the proper duty of women and focusing their brilliant minds on what was right, what should be done and what goals the new republic should embrace (Figure 1).

1 The French Revolution

The French Revolution began in May 1789, with the meeting of the Estates-General[4] in Versailles. Three hundred deputies composed the First Estate, the nobility, and 300 the Second Estate, the clergy. The Third Estate representing everyone else had 600 elected representatives, some of whom were middle-class men, passionate about the Revolution (like Robespierre), and some who decided to join the Third Estate despite belonging to one of the other two, like the Comte de Mirabeau and the Abbé Sieyès. The estates were called by the king in January as a last resort to try and save France's economy. Then came the campaigning and the elections. On 5 May, men representing the three estates met for the first time in a large room in Versailles normally used to store materials for the king's entertainment. The king sat at one end under a canopy, the three estates were positioned along the three other walls and the audience, men and women, stood above them in the tribunes. Olympe de Gouges was there, as were Sophie de Grouchy and her husband, Condorcet, who had failed to get himself elected as a representative. Germaine de Staël was also there, and there were several reports that she did not like to mix with the lower-class members of the audience. Marie-Jeanne Roland could not come. She was home in Lyon, nursing her husband, sick with pneumonia.

At the time the estates began to meet, the king and queen were concerned with the health of their eldest child, Joseph, who was convalescing in the countryside. Joseph died on 4 June and was buried on 13 June. On the day of his death, the three estates resolved to examine their role and see if they could work together. On 17 June, they dissolved the orders, and the Third Estate, led by Mirabeau, invited the other two to join them in forming the first French National Assembly. Still in the early days of mourning, the king responded by having the room where the estates met closed for renovations. On 20 June, finding themselves locked out, the new Assembly found another room, the Tennis Court, and there, together, swore an oath not to part until they had written a constitution for France.

The king's next move, on 11 July, was to fire his secretary of finance, the very popular Jacques Necker, father of Germaine de Staël. The fall of the Bastille on 14 July was almost directly a consequence of that decision. Camille Desmoulins, a radical pamphleteer who believed Necker could help France, stood on the table of a café in the Palais Royal quarter and harangued the crowds calling for them to take up arms and wear a green cockade so they could recognize each other. The crowds went first to the Invalides, a hospital for wounded soldiers, and helped themselves to the guns held there in storage. Next, they needed powder for the guns, and the Bastille was known to have stores of it. But the attack on the Bastille was also a symbolic gesture: this was the prison where people could be sent without a trial by anyone who could obtain a 'letter of cachet' signed by the king of France.

Meanwhile, the Assembly continued its work, and on 4 August, produced the first article of a constitution which abolished aristocratic privileges. The complete draft of the *Declaration of the Rights of Man* was finished three weeks later. In October, the market women of Paris led by the famous Reine Audu, a fruit seller from the Halles, walked to Versailles and brought the king and his family and most of the Assembly back to Paris where they could be among their people and at the centre of the Revolution. Although the rest of France soon caught up with the events of the capital, they had not yet done so, and the summer and fall of 1789 were marked by the 'Great Fear'. The provincial and rural French people worried that they would be attacked in their homes by armed peasants and escaped convicts, protestants or even the English. This led to a rural panic, with landowners retreating to their city homes to escape potential attacks.

Throughout the following year, the constitution slowly established itself, with the king looking on in increasing concern. After an attempted flight from the country with his family in June 1791, he was captured and brought back to Paris, and in September, forced to swear allegiance to the constitution. In August 1792, the three men who would eventually lead the Terror, Robespierre, Danton and Marat, took over the Paris Commune. A month later, in September 1792, the Convention, the new National Assembly, was elected, and its members declared France a republic. In December, the king was tried, and in January 1793, executed.

The period known as the Terror began in August 1792, with an attack on the Parisian Palace of the Tuileries which resulted in the death of a large number of Swiss guards, the king's personal army. This attack was closely followed by the September Massacres, during which many men and women, including priests, Swiss guards who had survived the Tuileries and aristocrats held in Parisian prisons, were savagely murdered. The Terror ended on 28 July 1794, with the death of Robespierre. During those months, many were executed, following summary trials ordered by the new government organ, the Committee of Public Safety. Many of the victims were politicians, many associated with the so-called Girondin faction, which included Jean-Marie Roland and Brissot, and, indirectly, Olympe de Gouges, Marie-Jeanne Roland and Sophie de Grouchy. After the Terror, the surviving men of the Gironde played a role in setting up a more peaceful government, the Directory. This lasted until Napoleon seized power in 1799.[5]

2 Revolution and philosophers

How did philosophers become so involved in what started as a popular movement that they became its victims? The Revolution was a time when philosophers came into the limelight, when books inspired acts and reforms and when the words of Rousseau, Voltaire, Adam Smith, Thomas Paine and the Marquis de Condorcet were (at least for some time) authoritative. These are the names history remembers.[6] But revolutionary France was full of philosophers whose writings were influential, and some of them were women who described themselves as philosophers. Among them were Olympe de Gouges, Marie-Jeanne Roland and Sophie de Grouchy.

These statements may give us pause. Were philosophers really that important for the Revolution or was it a myth that France, wishing to legitimize itself intellectually as well as politically, chose to disseminate after the fact? Are we reading the influence of Rousseau and Voltaire back into history by seeing too much of their thoughts into revolutionary discourses? Why would a mostly uneducated people – those who took the Bastille or marched to Versailles – know or care anything about the philosophers of the Enlightenment? And even if they did, would they also care about what women philosophers had to say?

If it is a myth that Rousseau and Voltaire had laid the foundations for the Revolution, it is not a recent one. In 1817, two years after the restoration of the Bourbon family on the French throne, the church issued a pastoral letter to be read at mass throughout the country and posted on church doors. This document denounced two new editions of the works of Voltaire and Rousseau and went on to argue at length that these philosophers were primarily responsible for the Revolution:

> Their writings have perverted public character and morals [. . .] it is to the principles of incredulity, immorality and rebellion they present so seductively that France owes the first attempts of those who provoked its Revolution, the prestige of so-called rights of the people, which led many crowned heads to the scaffold and threatened all nations with a universal upheaval, civil wars, and armed confusion, which, abandoned to its fluctuations will have been for humanity nothing short of a first hell, which would have continued, and grown more terrible each day, until the end of days.[7]

Although we might be tempted to dismiss this edict as an isolated eccentricity, it did not go unnoticed at the time. In March 1817, a popular satirical songwriter, P. J. de Beranger, composed a song with the title of the mandate: 'Mandement des vicaires géneraux de Paris to be sung to the tune of another song: Allez voir à St Cloud.' The song was reported and printed in *L'Esprit des journaux français et étrangers*, in April 1817 alongside a review of a volume of Voltaire's complete works.[8] The song, which was still being printed fifty years later, is composed of twenty verses of eight lines each, with the chorus (in the sixth and eighth line): C'est la faute de Voltaire, C'est la faute de Rousseau (It's Voltaire's fault, it's Rousseau's fault). The song remained popular, and when Victor Hugo wrote *Les Misérables* four decades later, he gave a version of the song to his young character, the street boy Gavroche.[9] The influence of philosophers on the French Revolution and its aftermath was not a myth. Voltaire and Rousseau were not unknown to the masses, and their influence on those who fought tyranny was still potent, half a century after the first French Revolution.

But what about the women? It's one thing to believe that a few high-profile men might have figured in the popular imagination and even that their books might have helped shape the Revolution. But Gouges, Roland and Grouchy were not celebrated philosophers, nor were they part of the previous generation that people called the 'Enlightenment' and which preceded the 'Enlightened' age of the Revolution. At the time of the Revolution, they were young or middle-aged, yet had to make a name for themselves and, as women, had little access to philosophical fame. But the effect of Voltaire and Rousseau's fame was that the French people of that time were receptive to dialogue and argument. Even the speeches pronounced in the Assembly had a philosophical quality that is now rarely heard. Robespierre and Brissot's heated exchanges about whether France should go to war, for instance, appealed to philosophically framed arguments on the relative worth of preserving life through not fighting (Robespierre) and spreading republicanism to the rest of the world (Brissot).

From 1789 to 1795, political philosophy was everywhere, in the streets and the clubs as well as in the Assembly or the Convention. Pamphlets, often anonymous, were pasted on the city's walls and distributed. Men and women read them and talked about them. Olympe de Gouges, who began her political career as an anonymous poster, soon signed her name and reclaimed her earlier work. She became a well-known figure at the clubs and in the Paris streets. Marie-Jeanne Roland was published anonymously by Brissot, but once her husband became minister, it was easy to guess who the 'lady from Lyon' was. And during her Paris years, it seemed that the more she tried to stay in the shadow of her husband's political work, the more she became renowned for doing that work for him. Sophie de Grouchy, as a member of the aristocracy, and the wife of a celebrated member of the prestigious Academy, was never going to remain in the shadow. But much like Roland, her influence, instead of being hidden or erased, was magnified by her enemies, who saw in her the force behind Condorcet's growing republicanism. Like Roland's, her revolutionary period writings were anonymous – but because she published some of them in a journal spearheaded by Paine and Condorcet, they were also influential.

Gouges, Grouchy and Roland were not the only women to participate in the French Revolution. But they did have that in common that their participation manifested itself in their philosophical writings as well as their actions.

Some women wrote about the Revolution from a distance, like Madame de Staël, exiled in Switzerland. Other women acted without writing, like

Reine Audu and the anonymous market women who walked to Versailles with her; or like Pauline Léon, the chocolatière and Claire Lacombe, a provincial actress, who together led protests against the legislation that caused the price of bread to rise and the Parisians to starve, and later founded a society for revolutionary women; or the Belgian swordswoman Théroigne de Mérincourt, who tried to found a woman's Republican army; or again the infamous 'tricoteuses' who sat through the executions and trials of the Terror knitting Phrygian caps.[10]

Olympe de Gouges, Marie-Jeanne Roland and Sophie de Grouchy began to think and write political philosophy before the Revolution.[11] All three were concerned with social justice and equality. All three felt the call of the Revolution and became engaged in its efforts, their writing becoming less theoretical and distributed in a format that was more likely to influence action. Before the Revolution, Gouges had been a playwright and a novelist, engaging with philosophical debates, particularly with Rousseau's ideas on the theatre, education and women. Roland had been a prolific letter writer but also wrote philosophical essays (on liberty and reason), travel diaries and encyclopedic articles with her husband. Grouchy, the youngest of the three, did not have a career as a writer before the Revolution – she did, however, translate political and economic texts from the Italian and the English and studied philosophical writings from Marcus Aurelius to Rousseau. After the Terror, she published a short philosophical treatise, the *Letters on Sympathy*, a commentary on Adam Smith's *Theory of Moral Sentiments*.

All three women's writing careers took a definite political turn during the Revolution: Gouges started printing posters that she pasted throughout Paris and pamphlets that she distributed widely. Roland's letters became political rather than literary and were published in revolutionary papers, and instead of helping her husband draft articles on the science of textile production, she wrote his political letters, including his resignation to the king. Grouchy translated Paine's republican exhortations and wrote political articles for a journal she edited with her husband.

Gouges, Roland and Grouchy wrote about social and political reforms as they were happening: the drafting of the *Declaration of the Rights of Man*, and the first constitution, the creation of a voluntary tax for poverty relief, the rewriting of the educational curriculum and various other attempts at institutionalizing the ideals of the Revolution, liberty and equality (fraternity came later). Their thought also tied them to movements and events in the rest of the world, from the American Revolution to the abolition of slavery and to the emancipation of women.

Yet, despite their influence at the time of the Revolution, most people outside of academia know very little about these women.[12] Why? First, because their influence was curtailed by a severe and violent backlash against women's participation, one that had been brewing since the beginning and came to its full manifestation after the murder of bloodthirsty Marat, the 'people's friend' and leader of the Paris Commune, by the Girondin sympathizer Charlotte Corday. A second, more important reason why we no longer remember them is that they did not always publish like men, writing books in their own names, but often had to find surreptitious ways of sharing their ideas.[13]

3 Becoming authors

'A woman has the right to stand onto the scaffold. She must also have the right to stand up in the Assembly.'

– Olympe de Gouges.[14]

Women of revolutionary France are often portrayed either as witty, decadent aristocrats or the rough and ugly fishwives whom Burke held responsible for the desecration of the royal family's chambers in Versailles. They are decorative or raucous but rarely useful or admirable.[15] Gouges, Roland and Grouchy were useful *and* admirable. All three were, in their own ways, exceptional writers and activists who fought to make the world a better place for all, where 'all' meant more than just those who were rich, white and male. All three were to some extent self-educated and made their ways to positions where they could be influential despite the fact that as women, they could neither vote nor talk at the Assembly.

Olympe de Gouges, born in 1748 in a butcher's shop in the south-east of France, was guillotined in Paris on 3 November 1793, aged forty-five. Marie-Jeanne (Marie-Jeanne) Roland, born to an engraver father in Paris in 1754, died aged thirty-nine, five days after Gouges, also guillotined. Sophie de Grouchy, Marquise de Condorcet, born at the ancestral family manor of Villette in 1764, survived the Terror – unlike her husband – and died in 1822, aged fifty-eight.

All three discovered their political nature early on, even though none of them came from a family or social milieu, which would predispose them to revolutionary ideas. Olympe de Gouges claimed to be the illegitimate daughter of a provincial poet and aristocrat, but on paper, she was the offspring of a low-middle-class family. She spoke Occitan rather than Parisian French and educated herself by going to the theatre, where she saw plays dealing with the injustices of the ancient regime by Beaumarchais and others. Gouges, who was married and widowed by the age of twenty and ran away to Paris to become first an actress, and later a playwright, made her own way into the political circles of the time. Roland, brought up in a more established middle-class Parisian family who owned books and hired tutors for their bright daughter, hid a copy of Plutarch's *Lives* in her catechism on her way to Sunday school and dreamt of being a Spartan or Roman soldier, dodging her parents' attempt at marrying her off. Grouchy was an aristocrat, brought up by an intelligent and well-educated mother as a good Catholic. But while at convent finishing school, she threw aside her Bible to read Rousseau and Voltaire instead. Grouchy and Roland both married older men, politicians who shared their republican ideals and moved with them into the world of the Revolution.

Olympe de Gouges was married off against her will as a teenager and widowed shortly after. She decided early on that she would not rely on the services of men to further her career (although she accepted financial help from her lover Jacques Biétrix de Rozières), so when she began to write, she took her pieces directly to the printer. In this way, she published pamphlets, to be pasted all over Paris, plays, to be presented to theatrical companies, or volumes of *Works*, to be sold or given to patrons. Gouges devoted all her effort and energy to putting out her works. Her plays were rarely performed: the Paris theatres, under the control of the actors and more successful playwrights who did not like to share the limelight with a woman turned against her. Because she spoke French with a strong southern accent, she acquired the reputation of being illiterate. Once as she was travelling to Paris from the suburbs, she sat next to a man who informed her that the famous Olympe de Gouges was only a front for her male writer friends. What a surprise he must have had when she told him her name![16] Despite this reputation, Gouges's political writings did meet with remarkable success. Her first piece, proposing a voluntary tax on the French people to relieve the national debt and alleviate poverty, resulted in several collection points being set up in Paris and many women from the artistic milieu donating their jewels. Her last piece, demanding that the form of the new government should be put to the vote throughout France, cost her her life.

Roland and Grouchy wrote early and often. But neither of them found it easy to publish their work. Until a few days before her death, Marie-Jeanne Roland was quite convinced that a woman ought not to publish in her own name.[17] Admittedly this did not stop her from publishing anonymously or in her husband's name. For a long time, she portrayed herself as his secretary, going over his writings to smooth over sentences or add detail. But in her *Memoirs*, she finally admits that she was more, that she either co-authored or single-authored his most significant political and scientific pieces.

Jacques-Pierre Brissot, one of the most vocal of the Girondins, published her republican musings in the form of letters to the editor anonymously.[18] Despite having to burn manuscripts while she was in prison, Roland left a copious number of pages of her own unpublished writings.

Grouchy also published anonymously, alone and with her husband when they worked together on the republican paper they co-edited with their friend Thomas Paine. Before he died, she helped her husband finish his final piece, the *Sketch of the Progress of the Human Mind*, an influential book that John Adams read and annotated twice. Sophie's name does not appear as co-author and even her editorial work was erased by a later editor. Only when she needed money, after her husband's death, did she publish her own work, a translation of Adam Smiths's *Theory of Moral Sentiments* and a critique of that work entitled the *Letters on Sympathy*.

4 Becoming revolutionaries

In eighteenth-century Paris, political ideas were formed and exchanged in circles or private gatherings, later called salons. Sophie de Grouchy had her own. Marie-Jeanne Roland, coming back to Paris from the countryside in 1791, did too, although hers did not admit women but only members of the government and their (male) associates. Gouges and Grouchy were regular guests at the home of Madame Helvetius in Auteuil just outside Paris, where intellectuals met to prepare for the Revolution and later to escape the Terror. This salon is where the idea of a republic was first broached, the abolition of slavery defended and women's citizenship proposed.[19]

All three of our heroines gravitated around the Girondin faction.[20] Both Roland's and Grouchy's husbands were regarded by the Gironde's enemies as influential members of the group. Olympe de Gouges integrated the group on the merits of her writings, particularly those against slavery, as the Girondins were also the founders of the first French anti-slavery society.[21] The Girondins now have a reputation for moderation. But this is only because they set themselves up against the Jacobins during the Terror, opposing the senseless massacres and executions deemed necessary by Robespierre. Far from being the half-hearted revolutionaries, they are now portrayed as having been, the Girondins were responsible for spreading the very idea of republicanism in revolutionary France. They were also pushing for France to declare war on its neighbours in the hope that this would help spread republicanism throughout Europe.

The sphere of influence of our three philosophers extended beyond France. Many of those associated with the Girondins admired America and held it up as both a model and a promised land. In the early years of the Revolution especially, America was cited as evidence for what could and could not be achieved in France. There was much exchange between the two republics, physical and intellectual. Grouchy and Condorcet had a working association with Thomas Paine, and the Rolands had planned, together with their Girondin friend Brissot (who had visited America and written about it), to move to America and found a republican commune there. All parties died before they could realize that dream.[22]

While America was a new model, England was an old and trusted one. Voltaire and Montesquieu, in particular, had held it up for their followers to see. Strange as it may seem to us, in the late eighteenth century, England still was a bedrock for republican thought, and France became the example that English revolutionaries looked to, crossing the channel at much personal risk to witness the miracle of the Revolution. Among the English republicans, two women stand out: Catharine Macaulay and Mary Wollstonecraft.[23] Macaulay was highly regarded by French and American revolutionaries alike, and her history of England was held as a model for republican political thought. Wollstonecraft, having written in defence of the French Revolution, travelled to Paris to witness it first hand and spent several of the Terror years there. Our protagonists felt the influence of Wollstonecraft or Macaulay, and in some cases, we know their paths came very close. Wollstonecraft is said to have collaborated with Condorcet on a rewriting of the national curriculum. And although she only knew Marie-Jeanne Roland for a short time, the two were friends, and Wollstonecraft visited Roland in prison. Macaulay was a popular author in republican circles, and Brissot counted her as a friend. Among Roland's last written words is a wish that had she lived, she should have become a 'French Macaulay'. Given these connections, it is natural for us to wonder whether any of them had met.

5 Dying for their ideas

In the summer of 1793, Brissot occupied the cell that Marie-Jeanne Roland had had in the Prison de l'Abbaye before she was moved to Sainte Pelagie. Olympe de Gouges was, briefly, in a neighbouring cell. On 24 October 1793, twenty-two Girondins were guillotined. (Mary Wollstonecraft is reported to have fainted when she heard the news.) Olympe de Gouges and Marie-Jeanne Roland were next to the scaffold. Condorcet, fearing for his life, went into hiding for several months, until in March 1794, he ran away, in order not to expose his friends to the ever-growing danger, and died a few dozen miles from Paris, in a small-town jail, ostensibly, of suicide by poison (Figure 2).

Figure 2 Brissot's execution, engraving, BnF.

Sophie de Grouchy was one of the few survivors from the Girondins's circle. She spent much of the Terror in Auteuil, travelling to Paris on foot, twice a week, disguised as a peasant, to visit her husband. She set up a studio in the Faubourg St Honoré, where she made a living by painting miniature portraits. On several occasions, she saved herself from the guillotine by painting the portrait of those who had come to arrest her. Throughout her husband's months of hiding, she helped and supported his work, encouraging him, bringing him the books he needed, and perhaps helping him write. At that time, she had little time for her own writing.

Grouchy lived to confront Napoleon, who told her in the autumn of 1800 that he did not like women who meddled in politics. Napoleon had become First Consul of the republic a year previously, after a coup. In October and November 1800, he was busy executing all those who had plotted against him, in speech or writing. This was a dangerous time to disagree with him. Nonetheless, when, perhaps in her salon, Napoleon expressed his opinion to Sophie, she replied:

> In a country where they might lose their heads, it is natural that women should want to know why.[24]

Four years after her husband's death, Sophie de Grouchy published her *Letters on Sympathy*, drafted in 1792. The *Letters* were a response to Adam

Smith's *Theory of Moral Sentiment*, but more than that, they presented a philosophical discussion of the physiological and social origins of morality and of what might be done to turn our moral impulses into republican social reforms. In his testament to his daughter, Condorcet refers to other writings by his wife – she must have been quite active during the period.[25]

Despite the fact that historians and philosophers have begun to look at Grouchy as an important actor of the Revolution, some aspects of her work still remain very much a mystery. Investigations reveal that, like Roland, she also produced political journalism, contributing with her husband and Paine to their short-lived journal *Le Républicain*. But if Condorcet is right – and why would he not be? – there may be other manuscripts by Grouchy. One wonders what these might be and whether someday, we will find, in some dusty family archive, a novel or a philosophical treatise by Sophie de Grouchy.

6 A note on sources and how to find them

Researching unknown women authors is never easy: their works have not been preserved with the same care as those of their male counterparts. Until recently, few scholars have found them interesting enough to write about them. This is changing, and some works have now been edited and translated and can even be found online. In some cases, the work is still to be done. At the end of the book, I have listed those texts that are available in print, online, in the original French and in translation. I have also listed the commentaries and biographies that I found most helpful, including philosophical commentaries. Most of these are quite recent, which reflects both the dearth of interest in female authors previously and the energy that scholars have put into their recovery in the last two decades. Revolutionary philosophers read some of the same books we read – but many are now unknown to us, and I have listed them together with a brief description in the Appendix titled 'A revolutionary bookshelf'.

Although many readers will be familiar with the main lines of the French Revolution, sometimes more details are needed to understand the context in which our three heroines evolved. Before the start of this chapter, I have included a timeline of the Revolution and a glossary of its principal actors, events and places.

Readers interested in the research I did for this book can follow it on my blog 'Liberty in thy Name'. There I give snippets that I couldn't include in this book and record the frequent shock and horror at my discovering the sexism that I kept encountering from historians.

The women and the prisons

A walk through eighteenth-century Paris

In the summer of 1793, Olympe de Gouges and Marie-Jeanne Roland were arrested. That fall, they were executed. Sophie de Grouchy narrowly escaped the same fate by bribing arresting officers with portraits she painted. While this is not perhaps the most interesting period of their lives, it is worth exploring these months, if only to highlight the political drama that surrounded them and which, to some extent, they helped create.

Let us then retrace the steps of Olympe de Gouges, Marie-Jeanne Roland and Sophie de Grouchy at the end of the year 1793. For Olympe and Marie-Jeanne, their last steps led them to the guillotine. In Sophie's case, there was no guillotine, but there was certainly death: her husband, the Marquis de Condorcet, was one of the few Girondins who escaped the blade; he died in prison a few months after his friends were executed. Sophie's steps in 1793 were the last that took her to her husband's side.

Retracing steps means looking at maps, street names and buildings that our eighteenth-century protagonists were familiar with. But the Parisian landscape of today is very different from the one in which the Revolution took place. In 1853, Napoleon III commissioned his prefect, George-Eugène Haussmann, to redesign Paris so that it would be beautiful, united and airy, and less easy to block with barricades. The old Paris was dirty and unhealthy – there were too many people living in confined spaces and a lot of sickness and death. It was also a place of deep unrest: there had been at least seven revolts and uprisings between 1830 and 1848. Between 1859 and 1867, the capital was transformed from a nest of narrow streets breeding disease and discontent to a network of large, airy boulevards connected by the remaining truncated streets. The first boulevard constructed was the Rue de Rivoli, lounging the Seine river on the Right Bank. This is by far the fastest way from the Conciergerie, on the Ile de la Cité, to the Place de la Concorde, previously Place de la Révolution. Had this road existed in 1793, Marie-Jeanne Roland and Olympe de Gouges would have had a much more comfortable journey from their prison to the guillotine. The Boulevard St Germain on the Left

Figure 3 Map of the Ile de la Cité, engraving by Michel Turgot, BnF.

Bank was one of the last of Haussman's projects to be realized. Many buildings were taken down to make space for this, including the prison where Marie-Jeanne Roland was first held, l'Abbaye. The space where the prison building once stood is now occupied by a restaurant from a chain specializing in Belgian mussels.

The narrow streets Gouges, Roland and Grouchy walked have been replaced by boulevards, changing many routes. Their small seventeenth-century houses have been replaced by elegant nineteenth-century ones. The bridges where they stopped to shop and chat are now roads where cars drive by fast or tourist promenades. Public transport means we don't have to walk. The one constant, though, is the traffic. Driving through Paris in a chair, or a hired carriage, was not, even then, a way of getting anywhere fast (Figure 3).

1 The Left Bank: Prison de l'Abbaye

We will start on the Left Bank, opposite the Saint-Sulpice church and walk up to the Boulevard St Germain where the prison of l'Abbaye once stood. This was where Marie-Jeanne and Olympe were first brought to, on 1 June and 20 July 1793, respectively. Just nine months earlier, that prison had witnessed

Figure 4 Massacre of the prisoners at l'Abbaye. Engraving, BnF.

one of the goriest scenes of the September 1792 massacres, counting 326 victims. Men and women were dragged out of their cells, summarily judged in the courtyard and massacred by soldiers cheered on by the people. It is likely that when first Marie-Jeanne, then Olympe, were shown to their cells, they saw traces of that day, dark stains on the stone (Figure 4).[1]

The Prison de l'Abbaye had, in fact, been where the massacres had started on 2 September 1792. That afternoon the city's bells were rung and a cannon shot. Word was out that the French army had lost against the Prussians at Verdun, and because someone had to be blamed, traitors to the republic were accused of having passed on intelligence to foreign powers. These so-called traitors or counter-revolutionaries were mostly of two kinds: the aristocrats and the priests who had refused to pledge allegiance to the new civic religion, known as the refractory priests. But in September 1792, most of those were already in prison.

Given that the fall of Verdun was still only a rumour and given the population of Paris was unstable, to say the least, whoever decided to ring the alarm was calling for blood. Jean-Marie Roland de la Platière, Marie-Jeanne's husband, was minister of the interior, and the management of prisons fell to him and his staff. In her memoirs, Marie-Jeanne Roland tells us what happened before the alarm was rung: one of Roland's deputies who had been on an inspection of the prisons came to alert the Paris Commune that he thought some of the prisoners were at risk. He found Danton, who replied testily:

I don't give a fuck about the prisoners or what happens to them![2]

The sound of the bells and the cannon together with the news that France was losing the war with foreign powers were indeed cause for worry: the last time the alarm had been rung and the cannon had been shot had been three weeks earlier, on 10 August. On that day, the Parisians had stormed the Palace of the Tuileries, where the king and his family were held after their attempted escape, and they had massacred the Swiss guards who were there for the king's protection. The king and queen were now imprisoned in a tower of the Temple fortress and relatively safe for the time being. But the Swiss guards that survived, and some of the nobles of their entourage, such as the princess of Lamballe, were in the Parisian prisons.[3]

By the evening of 5 September, most of them were dead.

Marie-Jeanne Roland, who knew this could have been prevented and who had tried, with her husband, to prevent it, was beyond outraged. She could no longer see herself as allied with the leaders of the Commune whom she held responsible for the massacres, or the Parisians, who had committed them:

> If you knew the horrible details of these expeditions! Women are brutally raped before these tigers tear them apart, entrails are worn as ribbons, human flesh eaten, still bleeding! You know my enthusiasm for the Revolution. Well, I am ashamed of it. It has been stained by scoundrels; it has become ugly![4]

More generally – but perhaps in part through Marie-Jeanne's influence – this episode marked a turn in the Revolution. Those who had been critical of the Commune, or Robespierre, Danton and Marat – 'My friend Danton leads all, Robespierre is his dummy, Marat holds his torch and his knife' – were now reluctant to have anything to do with them. Marie-Jeanne Roland blamed not only the Commune but also the people of Paris and felt they no longer deserved the freedom they had fought for.

> The whole of Paris allowed it to happen . . . the whole of Paris be damned as far as I'm concerned, and I no longer hope that liberty may take root among such cowards, insensible to the worst outrages inflicted on nature and humanity, cold spectators of attacks that could easily have been prevented by fifty armed men.

By January, Jean-Marie Roland had handed in his resignation from the ministry. Then, five months later, on 1 June, his wife was arrested, and on 2 June, a decree for the arrest of the Girondins, the political party they were part of, was issued. By mid-November, all were dead.

The prisons of Paris had not been built to hold quite as many people as were in them during the Revolution. Indeed, many of them had not been built as prisons. The Prison de l'Abbaye had been first an abbey, then, in the seventeenth century, a military prison. The cells held multiple prisoners, and even so, most of the time, that was not enough. When François Jourgniac de Saint-Méart, an officer accused of writing a royalist journal, was brought to l'Abbaye at the end of August 1792, he was put to sleep in a hall that had previously been a chapel, and in which nineteen others were sleeping. He was offered the bed of a man recently beheaded. But the September Massacres cleared some space, and when Marie-Jeanne Roland arrived at the beginning of June 1793, there were only five men left sleeping in that hall.

The building itself, a square structure with three floors and two turrets, no longer exists – it was demolished in the nineteenth century to make room for the Boulevard St Germain.

A few minutes walk from the site of l'Abbaye is the Rue de la Harpe, where Marie-Jeanne Roland lived when she was arrested. Her building no longer exists, and the street has been remodelled, but we can still see where number 51 would have stood, opposite what is now number 35. The street would have felt very different in 1793. It is narrow, but it would have been narrower and much longer. The Rolands rented rooms in the house at number 51 in 1792 when Roland's position at the ministry first became under threat. From the ministry hotel, where they lived in comparative luxury, Marie-Jeanne rented and furnished these tiny and very cheap rooms, ensuring a place to retreat to, should Roland lose his place. The rooms were so small that once they moved in, the Roland couple shared a bed most nights, despite their recent estrangement (Marie-Jeanne was in love with the Girondin François Buzot). They stayed close together also for safety: Marie-Jeanne slept with a pistol by her bed and knew how to use it. The Rue de la Harpe is no longer the cheap option it once was. Now its proximity to the Boulevards St Germain and St Michel make it the location of expensive boutiques and restaurants. Many of the buildings on the right side of the Rue de la Harpe date from the seventeenth and early eighteenth century so that we may get an idea of what the Roland Home would have looked like. Only a faint idea, though, as the facades were remodelled, and we no longer see the courtyards or through them the steps leading up to the apartments. But the courtyards are still there, such as the one Marie-Jeanne crossed to hide her husband in the caretaker's rooms from where he could escape as soon as she heard of his impending arrest. She did not count on being arrested herself. Marie-Jeanne had been preparing for their escape. She had ordered the necessary passports for herself and her daughter to go back to their country home. She thought that if there was any running to do, it would be best for Roland to run alone, as he would be less likely caught. For herself, she did not fear. She was, after all, innocent of any politicking, as she was a woman. And even if injustice were to fall upon her, she was courageous enough, she thought, to resist it.

At the beginning of June 1793, there were only eighty prisoners left in l'Abbaye. A few months earlier, before the September Massacres, it had contained over 400. That is not to say that the prison was deserted when Marie-Jeanne first arrived, as one of her first sights, when she was brought in, was of five men lying on camp beds next to one another. The prison wardress apologized, but she had not been expecting her and had no room for her. She was inclined to be kind to the wife of a minister and a woman reputed for her virtue and her enthusiasm for the Revolution, so she found her a sitting room and had a bed brought up. There Marie-Jeanne set up a writing table and asked her maid to bring her Plutarch's *Lives*, her favourite book since childhood, and Hume's *History*. She would have preferred, she writes, Catharine Macaulay's *History of England*, a republican text she had started reading the first few volumes of in English and that she greatly admired. But it was Brissot who had lent them to her, and the mandate had been issued for his arrest, along with twenty-one other Girondins, her husband and another minister, so Madame Roland surmised that he was probably not at home.

The prisons did not stay empty long. The Terror took care to replenish the cells that the massacres had bared. A week after Marie-Jeanne was incarcerated, more prisoners arrived, and she was moved to a smaller room – her sitting room could take more than one bed, and the wardress still wished to let her have a room of her own. Again, she set up a place to write, and in the tiny cell, which she kept as clean as she could, she recalled her childhood spent writing in her bedroom. Healthy and comfortable, and only worrying for the sake of others – she read, and she wrote. As well as letters to friends and letters to officials asking for her release, Marie-Jeanne wrote a set of historical notes, describing the two ministries her husband served on, making her own role extremely clear – she no longer wished to hide the fact that she was the author of her husband's most important political letters, but at the same time wanted to emphasize the extent to which she had stayed out of the way of the men's debates, not wanting political dinners to turn into what she saw as the gossip of the salons. As she wrote, she gave her manuscripts to friends who visited. Unfortunately, most of these notes were lost. The friend she had left most of her papers with, Luc-Antoine de Champagneux, was in turn arrested, and the person he gave Marie-Jeanne's papers destroyed them, for fear of being caught with them. Marie-Jeanne described her reaction by saying she had rather been thrown into the fire herself and had her writings preserved! But she recalled most of what she had written, and we now have a version of *Notices Historiques*, to which she added a portrait of Danton, and one of Brissot, and some anecdotes in which she describes her interactions with other famous members of the Revolution such as Condorcet and Robespierre.

Twenty-four days after her arrest, Marie-Jeanne was set free again. She was almost reluctant to leave her peaceful cell and contemplated – fleetingly – having her dinner before going home. But the room was needed – and only later did she learn that its next occupants were first, her friend Jacques-Pierre Brissot, and a bit later the famous Charlotte Corday. Marie-Jeanne's maid came, and together they packed her bag, and the waiting car took her home to the Rue de la Harpe. But as soon as she set foot on the stairs to her home, the guards arrested her again!

There had been, she found out later, some irregularities in her previous arrest so that her house, though under seals, could not be searched. The cruel solution was to set her free and arrest her again. She tried to fight it, calling on the police of her 'section' of the districts created by the Paris Commune. She was not successful – her husband was still missing, as was her lover, Buzot and those of the Girondins that had been caught were under arrest, awaiting trial. There was really very little she could have done.

2 Rue de la Huchette

The Rue de la Harpe, where Marie-Jeanne was twice arrested, is just a stone's throw from the Pont St Michel, where Olympe was arrested on 20 July 1793. Three weeks before that, she was moving her furniture from Paris to a small house she had bought in the countryside near Tours, La Closerie des Figuiers, where she was about to retire.

The house which still bears that name is a bit derelict and has been rebuilt in the late nineteenth century, but in 1793 it would have been a very pleasant house, surrounded by a fruit garden, especially fig trees, and a fence (*closerie*) to stop the animals eating the fruit. The novelist Balzac described another *closerie*, in the same region:

> Nowhere else would you meet with a house at once so modest, so large, so rich in fructations, perfumes, and views. It is in the heart of Touraine, a small Touraine where all the flowers, all the fruits, all the beauties of this country are all represented: grapes from each region, figs, peaches, pears of every kind, and melons in the fields [. . .]. ('La Grenadière').

Such a retreat would have seemed appealing indeed to a woman brought up in the south and the countryside. She had just signed the contract for the new house and was back in Paris to see to the removal of her things. She was no doubt aware that by being in Paris and publishing more political tracts, she was putting herself at risk. But the decree against the Gironde had just been issued. Olympe felt she had to react: she wrote to the Convention, accusing them of giving up and handing in the best of the elected representatives to monsters thirsting for blood (the Commune). In full knowledge that she had just endangered herself, she then wrote a pamphlet, her 'Political Testament':

> If in a final effort, I can still save the Republic, I desire that even while they immolate me to their fury, my murderers should still envy my fate. And if one day, posterity notices women, perhaps the memory of my name will be of value. I have planned everything. I know that my death is unavoidable, but how beautiful and glorious it is, for a well-born soul, when ignominious death threatens all good citizens, still to give one's life for our dying country!

Her next tract, the 'Three Urns', was an attack on the Paris Commune. Like the Girondins, Olympe not only disliked the violence and bloodthirstiness of the members of the Commune but also was appalled by the fact that they had usurped the Convention, with its deputies from all over France, and that it was now, in fact, Paris, not France, that governed. She demanded that the French people be asked what they wanted, be it a republic, a federation or a constitutional monarchy. She suggested that the Commune itself, rather than helping France become a republic, was ruling as a tyrant. Louis XVI may be dead, she wrote, but he still reigned among them.

The tract was printed by her usual printer, Longuet, on 15 July. He drew 1,000 copies. Olympe dutifully sent a copy to the Committee of Public Safety and one to Herault de Seychelle, responsible for the censorship of printed material. Then she waited a few days – no reply, which she took to mean that she could go ahead and paste her pamphlet all over Paris. Her distributor, or *afficheur*, a Citizen Meunier, lived and worked Rue de la Huchette.

On 20 July, Olympe left her apartment on the Ile de la Cité, crossed the St Michel bridge and turned left into the Rue de la Huchette. The St Michel bridge and the Rue de la Huchette are still there. The current bridge dates from the mid-nineteenth century. Earlier photographs show a similar looking bridge, but with four arches, rather than two, and somewhat less flat. In the eighteenth century, it would still have had the more traditional aspect of the Medieval bridge; it would have been covered in wooden shops and houses.

The Rue de la Huchette is also still here, and it retains some of its original houses. It used to be a place where one could buy roasted meat. It is now a place where one can buy 'Greek Sandwiches' or 'doner kebabs', that is, thin slices of roasted lamb served in flatbread. It is also where one of Paris' legendary jazz clubs is based. Le Caveau de la Huchette claims on its website that it was called Le Caveau de la Terreur during the Revolution, and that Jacobins and Cordeliers drank there.[5]

Assuming that some Jacobins did meet Rue de la Huchette, then the proximity to members of the Commune may have been a reason why Meunier decided not to post Olympe's 'Three Urns'. What he actually told her, on the morning of her arrest, is that he was worried that it would rain. One imagines Olympe looking up at the clear sky, puzzled and then annoyed, before she set out to find another distributor on the Pont St Michel. Meunier had her followed by his daughter and three members of the police. As soon as Olympe knocked at the door, Meunier's daughter pointed her out to three policemen and members of the national guard who arrested her and dragged her to the Depot prison of the City Hall. She was kept there in an isolated cell, '*au secret*' for several days, in order, presumably, to prevent her from getting the word out to her friend Michel de Cubière, who was a secretary of the Commune and powerful enough to get her out, provided he heard about her arrest. Olympe wrote to him, but her letters were not delivered. On 28 July, she was taken to the Prison de l'Abbaye, which Marie-Jeanne had left a month earlier, and where Brissot was still awaiting his trial.

3   Ile de la Cité: La Conciergerie

When Marie-Jeanne was freed and arrested again at the end of June 1793, she was taken back not to l'Abbaye but to the much less pleasant Sainte Pélagie prison. This prison housed chiefly prostitutes, and many priests had been butchered there in September of the previous year (Figure 5). The warders were not as eager to make her comfortable as they had been in l'Abbaye. She was asked to pay a lot of money to be alone in a tiny cell. There were two beds in the cell, and she wanted one out to make space for a table, but this was refused, and she was asked to pay for the extra bed. The food, also expensive, made her sick. There were no facilities in her cell, and she had to buy even a chamber pot – she, who had decorated her previous cell with books and flowers! But eventually, she managed to set things up so that she could work again. And as in l'Abbaye, Marie-Jeanne fell into a routine, practising her English in the morning (she was now reading Shaftesbury) and in the afternoon writing her *Memoirs*.

The *Memoirs*, which were published, shortly after her death, alongside her *Historical Notices on the Revolution*, are where we find details of her

Figure 5 Conciergerie and Pont au Change, ink and watercolour, BnF.

childhood, her marriage, her role in the Revolution, and, finally, her imprisonment and trial. There are also historical sections discussing the progress of the Revolution. These, far from being a repetition of the *Historical Notices*, add a personal touch to the stories and portraits of its key players, many of whom Marie-Jeanne knew intimately. She tells us how during the August attack on the Tuileries, Robespierre feared for his life and hid in her apartment and how the Keralio-Roberts did the same and were later ungrateful. During her two years in Paris, she socialized with Robespierre, the Brissots, the Condorcets, the Pétions – the mayor of Paris and his wife – and many others. Marie-Jeanne was not a gossip, but she was observant and a sometimes harsh judge of character (Condorcet, she said, was a coward, brave only through his ideas). In prison, too, Marie-Jeanne socialized, as unfortunately, Madame Pétion, wife of the mayor of Paris, was also at Ste Pélagie.[6] This was a welcome relief from her other neighbours, the prostitutes, whose only thoughts were to party, entertain visitors and pretty themselves up. Marie-Jeanne had few visitors, as most of her friends were in prison now, and her husband Roland, as well as her lover, Buzot, were both in hiding. When she did not visit with Madame Pétion, write her *Memoirs* or work on her English, she wrote letters. She stayed at Ste Pélagie for more than four months.

Olympe did not do as well as Marie-Jeanne had at l'Abbaye. She was famous and controversial but not beloved as Marie-Jeanne had been. Her reputation was not for virtue and certainly not as a good wife. Her son was grown up, so she did not get the pity reserved for mothers. Moreover, she was injured and suffering. A day or so before her arrest, she had tripped from a car and cut her leg. The cut had become infected during her incarceration at the Depot, and she needed treatment. At the end of August, four weeks after her arrest, Olympe was transferred to the infamous prison of La Petite Force, where the Princesse de Lamballe had been massacred in September 1792. Again a prison for prostitutes, it had been converted into a hospital for prisoners of the Revolution who needed treatment to survive until their trial. Olympe was an important prisoner, her fame and her constant provocation of the leaders of the Terror meant that she had to be tried and could not just disappear. La Petite Force was not, however, good enough as far as Olympe was concerned. In October, she pawned what she had left to pay for a private hostel for prisoners in the Chemin Vert, a long street on the Eastern edge of Paris, so named because of the vegetable gardens surrounding it. Men and women who had health troubles and who could pay went to spend their prison term there.

Early in November 1793, both Marie-Jeanne and Olympe were brought to the Conciergerie, a medieval fortified prison on the Ile de la Cité, adjoining the Palais de la Justice and the Chapelle St Louis, and very near to the Paris Cathedral and to where Marie-Jeanne was born. This was – for most – the last stop before the guillotine.

Olympe arrived first. Just as had happened when she was first arrested, she was again put 'au secret' in an isolated cell where she could not communicate with others who might pass on messages to her friend Cubière. Her cell was the same one Marie-Antoinette had been taken to after her alleged attempted escape. It was isolated but probably quite loud, as it was positioned right next to the infirmary where sick prisoners were taken. The cell can still be visited, but it has been turned into a chapel to the memory of Marie-Antoinette, and all that is left of the infirmary itself is a sort of anti-chamber to the chapel, and one of two narrow windows, visible from the women's courtyard. When Robespierre was imprisoned in the Conciergerie, and he too had to be 'au secret', he was allegedly taken to the same cell. In fact, he probably spent no time in that cell as he was dying of a gunshot and would have remained in the infirmary.

The prison hospital was not a pleasant place to be. One survivor reports the following:

Seven by thirty metres, closed on both sides by iron fences, two narrow windows, a vaulted roof, like some sort of gothic hell set at the opera. Forty or fifty dirty straw beds on either side, with two or three patients each, sharing unwashed blankets. The privies were in the middle of the infirmary, and sick patients who had collapsed on the way there lay in their waste. The corpses, three or four each day, were removed at a specific hour of the day, and until that time, the dead remained in bed with the sick.[7]

Although she was no longer suffering from her injured leg, Olympe also had cause to spend time there during her very short stay. After Fouquier-Tinville found her guilty of having produced a text in which she attacked the 'choice of the people', which was punishable by death, she announced that she was pregnant:

> My enemies will not have the glory of seeing my blood flow. I am pregnant and will bear a *citoyen* or *citoyenne* for the Republic.

The law stated that she had to be examined by a medical team. Three health inspectors and a midwife took her to the infirmary but could not draw any conclusions: Olympe said she had been pregnant for five weeks only.

Fouquier-Tinville chose to ignore their doubt and declared that her claim was false:

> The Public Prosecutor notes that the accused was incarcerated for the past five months and that according to regulations, no contact was allowed between men and women in prisons. Therefore she made it up to avoid the death penalty.

There was, in fact, some romantic commerce between prisoners, as they were kept in adjoining wards and often not very efficiently. In any case, Olympe had been staying in a private pension for mixed prisoners, a fact that Fouquier-Tinville, although he was aware of it, kept quiet.

When Marie-Jeanne arrived at the Conciergerie, she noted that, unlike her two previous prisons, there was nothing to be done in terms of arranging one's surroundings. The stay at the Conciergerie was never a long one. Marie-Jeanne slept on a cot with no bedding given to her by another prisoner. While she was there, she dressed with care, presenting a cheerful and peaceful exterior to her jailors and the other inmates. She even had her portrait painted. There is a miniature of her entitled 'Marie-Jeanne Roland at the Concièrgerie'. While the picture is not signed, it bears some resemblance to Sophie de Grouchy's style: it is drawn in pastels, Sophie's favourite medium, while the curve of the lips as well as the outlining of the eyes recalls Sophie's own self-portrait with a hat and feather (Figures 6 and 7).

Figure 6 Madame Roland at the Conciergerie. Pastels by Anon. BnF.

4 The Right Bank: Place de la Revolution

On 2 November 1793, two days after the Girondins were executed (all twenty-two of the accused guillotined in half an hour – Sanson, the executioner, and his sons must have had sore arms the next day), Olympe was tried. The next day, after her failed attempts at saving herself by appealing to her pregnancy, she climbed the stairs up to the Rue de Mai, stepped into the tumbrel and was driven to her execution. Her last words: 'Children of the nation, you will avenge my death!'

A few days before Olympe's death, Marie-Jeanne's trial began. She pleaded innocent – she was, after all, only a woman, a virtuous wife and mother, and what could such a woman achieve politically? But her enemies, because they were once her friends, knew that she was responsible for much of the Girondins's policies and that she had even written some of the decrees and letters her husband signed while he was a minister. Indeed, Danton had once objected to Roland's re-appointment as minister of the interior on the grounds that they might as well appoint his wife, as she was the one doing all the work. It was hoped that she would denounce others or betray the whereabouts of her husband. The trial lasted a week. On 8 November, she was taken to the room on the ground floor of the Conciergerie where Sanson cut his victims' hair and split their shirts at the back – all to facilitate the work

Figure 7 Self-portrait in pastels with hat and feather, Sophie de Grouchy. This is a reproduction of a medallion belonging to Marie-Liesse d'Aboville; the photograph was taken by Jérome d'Aboville, and it is owned by Madeleine Arnold-Tétard.

of the blade. Then up the stairs to the street, the Rue de Mai, where the Seine once run, and into the tumbril.

It was afternoon, half-past four, when her tumbril crossed the Pont au Change. The weather was probably not very warm, and Marie-Jeanne did not wear a coat. On the other hand, it was probably not so dark as it would be now, at the same hour of the same day, as the winter-time clock change had not yet been imposed on the world.

Anyone travelling from the Conciergerie to the place where the guillotine stood would not take the same route Marie-Jeanne did. Her cart took a turn on the Place des Trois Maries which no longer exists, continued Rue du Roule, which does, but instead of turning into Rivoli, which did not yet exist, went up to the Rue St Honoré, and then back to the Place de la Révolution, now Place de la Concorde. The journey would have taken at least an hour, with the cart being interrupted by the people yelling insults or words of encouragement.

Several people in the audience testified that Marie-Jeanne Roland displayed great courage on the scaffold. The fact that she lost a lot of blood after she was decapitated suggested to some that she had been calm and her heart beating normally, whereas those who were very scared lost hardly any blood. As a witness noted:

When the knife cut off the head, two enormous blood sprays erupted from the mutilated trunk, which wasn't usually the case: most often, the head fell, colourless, and the blood, which the emotion of this terrible moment had sent back towards the heart came out weakly, drop by drop.[8]

5 Rue St Honoré

Now that we have crossed from the Ile de la Cité to the Right Bank, we can take a look at Robespierre's last home and the rooms that Sophie de Grouchy rented when she visited her husband, Condorcet, while he was in hiding.

But first, this necessitates another detour to the Left Bank and the home of Madame Vernet, a widow in whose house Condorcet lived in hiding between October 1793, when the warrant for his arrest was issued, and March 1794 when he escaped on foot to the town of Bourg-la-Reine, where he was arrested and died. Madame Vernet's house was situated at 21 Rue des Fossoyeurs, now 15 Rue Servandoni, a short and narrow street close to the Odeon, and the Palais du Luxembourg, where Thomas Paine and other foreigners were held prisoners during the Terror. A few doors down from number 15, at number 18, there is a plaque commemorating Olympe de Gouges. This is perhaps it was where her sister lived when Olympe first came to Paris. Or perhaps it was one of the many rooms she took when she was trying to have her plays performed at the French Theatre (now the Odeon). Olympe evidently liked to move, and there are many addresses associated with her name.

Number 15 is not the actual building Condorcet lived in but was built in 1840 over the foundations of the seventeenth-century house that had belonged to the Vernets. By the time Condorcet was declared an outlaw, Madame Vernet was a widow with rooms to rent that she decided to offer to citizens running away from the Commune. Condorcet was brought to her with no luggage – his arrest could be imminent. Having established he was an honest man, she decided to take him in, answering his protests that she could be at risk because he was an outlaw: 'The Convention can make you an outlaw. But it cannot put you out of humanity. You will stay.' When Condorcet wrote to his daughter, he encouraged her to see in Madame Vernet a second mother.

Condorcet was safely set up in the Rue des Fossoyeurs. But he had nothing with him to work on. Without his books, his notes and no doubt feeling rather sorry for himself, he began to write an 'Apology', explaining his role in the Revolution and describing how badly he had been treated. Meanwhile, Sophie herself had to stay out of Paris as much as possible and lived in the *faubourg*, or suburb, of Auteuil, with her friend the famous salonière Madame Helvetius as her neighbour.

Several times a week, Sophie walked into Paris to visit her husband.

As she did not want to be recognized or to attract anybody's attention to Condorcet's hiding place, she came dressed as a peasant woman, pretending to be part of the groups of farmers who come to sell their goods to the starving capital. Once through the gates, she would lose herself in the crowds and come to see that day's executions at the Place de la Revolution. She would then cross the river to reach the Left Bank and walked towards the church of St Sulpice and beyond that to the street where her husband was hiding. The walk would have taken between two and three hours, depending on how thick the crowds were. Much of that would have been spent in the detours to the Place de la Révolution, as the walk from Auteuil itself did not take more than an hour.

Often Sophie would bring her husband books or notes that he needed for his work – at least as much as she could carry discreetly. She would also stay and encourage him and work with him. She could see that writing the 'Apology' did no good either to Condorcet or to posterity. Sophie encouraged him to quit. On the manuscript of the fragment of his Apology, we can read in Sophie's hand – 'Ceased at my request'. Instead, she suggested that he start working again on the introduction to an encyclopedic project he had begun decades earlier, a history of the progress of the human mind. He took her advice. There is some evidence that he and Sophie worked together on his last work, the *Sketch of Human Progress*.[9]

After seeing her husband, Sophie would walk back across the Seine towards the Rue St Honoré, where she rented a lingerie shop and the half-floor above it. Putting Auguste Cardot, younger brother of her husband's secretary, in charge of the shop, she set up a studio in the alcove and worked on painting her miniatures from there. Thus she ensured that she had sufficient income to meet the needs of her husband, her family and herself until she could claim back some of what the government had seized.

The Rue St Honoré starts from Rue Royale, which gave on the Place de la Révolution. At its end, the street becomes the Rue du Faubourg St Honoré, marking the entrance of the old suburb of that name. Just before that, at number 398, is Robespierre's last address, between 1791 and his death in 1794. His windows would be visible from the street, but the nineteenth-century facade and the twenty-first-century locking system mean that only those who live there can see them. They are on the first floor, to the left in the courtyard. In July 1794, before Robespierre was arrested, the walls of his house were splashed with blood – the blood of a pig, perhaps? Not, one hopes the blood of his victims, although that would have been fitting. Robespierre fled his home to take refuge in the Hotel de Ville with other members of the Commune. He was arrested there and either shot himself or was shot, shattering his jaw and part of his skull.

Number 352, a little further down, probably a bit too close for her comfort, as she was hiding from the Commune, is where Sophie had her studio, above her lingerie shop. The building is nineteenth century. But next to it is a much older one, which houses a shop selling very expensive looking luggage on the ground floor and may give an idea of what the original building would have looked like. Inside number 352, there is a courtyard, a staircase and a few locked doors. Nothing indicates where the shop or the studio would have been in the original building. Sophie's biographer tells us that twice she was nearly arrested at that address. Both times, she bribed the men who'd come to arrest her by painting their portraits in miniature. Sophie used this studio as a base for her business, but some of her work was done in the Parisian prisons, as many of her customers were prisoners who wanted their loved ones to have one last memento. Perhaps it was she who painted Marie-Jeanne Roland at the Conciergerie (Figure 4). Although we lack evidence as the portrait is not signed, the style is not unlike the one we see in her self-portraits.

Awakening to injustice

The formative years of Gouges, Roland and Grouchy

1 Introduction

Like most women of the time, Roland, Gouges and Grouchy had their lives planned for them before they were born. They were to be married to men who would enrich the family, financially or by reputation; they were to take up a certain place in a certain class of society, and to that effect, they were to receive a certain kind of education. This was clearly and rigidly determined in ancient regime France. But all three somehow managed to subvert their family's plans for them before even the Revolution interfered. Grouchy was an aristocrat, brought up by a saintly mother as a good Catholic. But while at convent school, she threw aside her Bible and read Rousseau and Voltaire instead. Roland, the daughter of a Parisian artisan, preferred Roman history to her catechism and turned down all the suitors presented her, until she found one after her own taste. Olympe de Gouges, the illegitimate daughter of a provincial poet and aristocrat, did everything she could to be noticed by her birth father, including running away to Paris to become a playwright. Widowed in her late teens, she remained more or less single until her death.

Gouges, Roland and Grouchy all, to some extent, influenced the course of the Revolution through their writings, and yet, none of them is remembered for having done so. Indeed, even among their contemporaries, some found it hard to take them seriously as writers, questioning their authorship and refusing to work with them. Gouges and Roland, for instance, both sought the patronage of famous men, and both were turned down because those established authors could not conceive that mere women could have produced the texts they had presented them with. So instead, we remember that Marie-Jeanne was brave, that she inspired the men of the Gironde and that she wrote her memoirs in prison. Sophie is mostly known to those who have read about the Salonières of the Revolution – but not as well known as Madame de Staël, Madame Helvetius or Julie de Lespinasse. Olympe's name is well known, and many have heard of her *Declaration of the Rights of Women*, though this is one of her writings that did not, in fact, influence the course of the Revolution: French women did not get the vote until 1944!

Part of the reason we know so little about these women's works is that we know very little about the women who wrote them. In order to understand the role they played in history, intellectual and political, we need to know what they did and how they fitted into that history. But we do not. This biographical chapter is meant to remedy this gap before we move on to discuss their work.

2 The mirror of history

Why do we know so little about Gouges, Roland and Grouchy? Why did history forget them or confine them to chapters on women? A large part of the answer lies in the question of representation: how we see women philosophers of the past and how they saw themselves is often centred on their appearance and their relationships, things that tend to be more ephemeral than the written word. Historians who were closer to their lifetime described their beauty or lack of it, and more recent historians have very little else to go on, and unless they specialize in women's history, this is often their cue to leave them out altogether. Part of the work of bringing back these women to intellectual history means looking at the way historians have dealt with them. Can we look at them differently enough so that we can see their true worth? This is our challenge.

2.1 Historians and women

For the bicentenary of 14 July, the prestigious Pleiade publishing house came up with a small illustrated volume about the writers of the Revolution. The editor of the volume, the essayist Pierre Gascar (1916–97), managed a very respectable selection of male writers and wrote about them with the reverence at least some of them deserved. But one gets the feeling that even the most psychopathic among them had to be treated fairly – after all, they played a role in the Revolution that shaped the French Republic.

What Gascar did not do, however, was waste much time on the women writers of the period – with the exception of Olympe de Gouges, who is mentioned on nine (four of which are pictures) occasions, with one fairly long section in which her name recurs, and some passing comments.

In two passing comments, Gascar uses the adjective '*ardante*' to describe her. That is, Olympe de Gouges was 'fervent' or 'passionate'. She was also driven to a near 'delirium' by her attempts to assert herself in the political scene. She was, Gascar tells us, led in all things by the desire to succeed and the need for glory. But because she was a woman, he concludes, she presented a 'disarming' picture of the thirst for fame. Her writings, then, did not reflect her judgements but rather her sentiments. Her objection to putting the king to death was based not on any belief that this could harm the Revolution or that it would be morally wrong but on disgust.[1]

The reliance on feelings rather than reason in writing is a failing often attributed to women. Writing in 1915 in *Modern Philology* (13:7), G. A. Underwood claims that in her reading of Rousseau, Madame de Staël saw only the sentimentalist of the *New Heloise* and not the rationalist of the *On Social Contract*, and that her *Notice sur le Caractere et les Ecrits de J.J. Rousseau* demonstrates 'little beyond an enthusiasm for Rousseau's ideas' (adding that 'the enthusiasm itself was significant'). Underwood concludes the introduction to his paper on Staël's interpretation of Rousseau by announcing: 'The thesis will be that Rousseau leads Madame de Staël to become absorbed in her feelings.'

The conclusion of the paper reads as follows:

> Such is the somewhat undeveloped Rousseauism of Madame de Staël when she began writing. It is an emphasis on temperamental inclination rather than a ripened criticism. A continuation of this study would show how in her mature and original work, Madame de Staël gradually thought out to definite literary and philosophical tenets those ideas of Rousseau to which she was so strongly attracted.[2]

Then in 1927, Jean Martin, writing about a member of the Girondins, Achille Duchatellet, describes Sophie de Grouchy as a 'fiery head'. He derives this description from one by her friend Dumont, who wrote about Sophie that she had

> A serious character, a mind that flourished on philosophical meditations, republican readings, and a passion for Rousseau's works had inflamed her head.

Describing a letter Sophie wrote to Dumont about the state of French politics after the massacre of the Champs de Mars, Martin alerts the reader to the overflowing feminity of the letter and the instances of 'coquetry' that fill in the spaces between the writer's attempt to engage with the political thought of her time. But, Martin notes generously, she does make a sensible point in passing about governments presenting an obstacle to Enlightenment. The rest of her descriptions, however, only serves to 'stir her nerves' because she dreams of a moving persecution of which she would be the heroine.[3]

Historians are not kind to women. Even under the guise of admiration and respect, they are often damning. Take, for instance, Jules Michelet's *Women of the Revolution* (1855). This volume is comprised of portraits that Michelet had sketched in his *History of the French Revolution* (1847–53, nine volumes). All three of our heroines are discussed. Marie-Jeanne Roland, a *'femme de coeur'*, is an example of womanly republican virtue. She is just as Rousseau wanted women to be – domestic, ruled by their heart and entirely given to nurturing the virtues of the republic in their family. But Roland, Michelet adds, is rather more muscular and less ethereal than Rousseau's Julie, for instance. And when she sees that being nurturing and domestic is no longer enough, she acts. Perhaps, Michelet surmises, this is due to her more plebeian background (Rousseau's Julie was, of course, an aristocrat).[4]

Sophie is described as a Salonière, a beautiful woman who was skilled at entertaining republicans and who, moreover, was the dutiful wife of one of the Revolution's greatest intellectuals, Condorcet. One senses that Michelet thinks we should be grateful that she looked after this national genius and enabled him to shape the republic's future. She was more than that, of course.[5]

Michelet's Olympe is notable for her ignorance: 'She was quite illiterate.' He wrote. 'It was even said that she could neither read nor write at all.'[6] However noble he may have thought of her, this is what stands out. Olympe, the writer, could not read or write.

Michelet's book is not uninteresting. But the message of the first part of the book is that, no matter how admirable, his subjects were only women, and as such, even for the most compassionate, fair historians, their value was only anecdotal.

Yet even this is a charitable reading of Michelet, and a most telling chapter in his book is not on individual salons or famous women but the moral downfall of the Girondins. In 1793, Michelet said, the Girondins were giving in either to suicide or depravity, gambling and participating in orgies. Many women, whether professional prostitutes or milliners, were involved in these orgies.

Michelet goes on to elaborate on the way women can cause the downfall of men.

> women, especially, and even the best, in such a case, exert a dangerous
> influence to which there is no resistance. They influence by their graces,
> but still more often by the touching interest they inspire, by their frights

which they wish calmed, and from the happiness, they truly feel at receiving support from you. [. . .]

These ladies were very skilful, being careful not to show the after-thought. One day, good, moderate, and mild republicans would be seen in their salons. The next day, Feuillants and Fayettists would be presented to you.[7]

And before you knew it, he continues, the charming salonist had turned you into a royalist.

Even 'true love', Michelet continues, when it involved a male Girondin and a woman, contributed to the downfall of the Gironde:

The love of Mademoiselle Candeille was conducive to the destruction of Vergniaud. This pre-occupation of the heart increased his indecision and his natural indolence. It was said that his mind seemed to be wandering elsewhere, and they were right. This mind, at a time when the country should have claimed it entirely, inhabited another soul.[8]

Note that Julie Candeille, far from being an insignificant side character, a love interest for a hero of the Revolution, was a successful composer and a famous actress. She had, for instance, taken on the role of Mirza in Olympe de Gouges's abolitionist play. She was also the author of a musical comedy that ran for forty-seven years – the longest-running opera by a woman.[9] Her lover, Pierre Victurnien Vergniaud, was a speaker for the Gironde. He was the last of the twenty-two Girondins to be executed on 31 October 1793. His oratory skills may have been a match for Candeille's acting skills, but there seems little reason why he should be represented as a major actor of the period and not her.

Michelet wrote his book sixty-seven years after Gouges and Roland's death. Until the end of the book, his sexism is latent, as he emphasizes the good but women-specific virtues of his subjects. Nearly half a century later, a man who was not a historian and whose work did not shape posterity in the same way Michelet's did, wrote an account that did not even attempt to offer praise. His study on Olympe de Gouges, if not influential, was a precursor of the ways in which women who shaped history through their writings and actions were to be perceived.

In 1907, Alfred Guillois, a 24-year-old Parisian studying medicine in Lyon, presented his doctoral thesis on Olympe de Gouges and women's psychology during the French Revolution. A strange topic for a doctor! But Guillois was interested in the diseases of the mind and wanted to study the effect that the Revolution had on the fragile minds of women, and especially how crowd psychology led them to become less womanly. Unfortunately, he tells us in his preface, he ran out of time. This is why he decided to focus on the mind of one particularly flamboyant woman, Olympe de Gouges. In his conclusion, he tells us that his findings, as a matter of fact, do apply to other women who participated in the Revolution – though there is no time to provide an actual argument for it.

Guillois's interest in the women of the Revolution is perhaps less surprising if we know that his father, Antoine Guillois, a civil servant and part-time historian, had published a biography of Sophie de Grouchy a few years previously. But whereas Antoine's biography was a eulogy, Alfred's view of Olympe is not in the slightest flattering:

> Olympe de Gouges suffered from a delirium with systematizing tendencies which has been described by some authors as paranoid delirium (paranoia reformatoria). [. . .] She was predisposed to this, and the Revolution working on these prepared grounds found it easy to divert her from a normal mentality.

Guillois junior adds that her case is not isolated: 'we can say of numerous women who were active in the revolution and played a sanguinary role that they were unbalanced.'[10]

At the time Alfred Guillois defended his thesis on Gouges in Lyon, Antoine Guillois, his father, was living in Auxerre with his wife, where he was conducting archaeological research (which he'd taken up full time when he retired from the civil service). Guillois's own biography of Grouchy, carefully researched by going through the letters and newspaper clippings his patron, a descendant of Grouchy's daughter, Eliza, had given him, was full of romantic detail about the recent past, which he saw as an era of bravery and progress.[11] His son's research methods are very different, as he focuses more on gossipy accounts of Gouges's enemies than he does on those of friends. His view of the revolutionary period is also dissimilar– the word 'sanguinary' comes up a lot in Alfred's dissertation. Perhaps that is a natural attitude for a medically trained author. And it is also true that the Gouges's life was more 'sanguinary' than Grouchy's. Grouchy's life, though tragic enough, did not end under the guillotine.

One would hope that the sexist attitude that permeated the writings of Michelet and André Guillois would have been shed by the beginning of the twenty-first century. With a few exceptions – mostly confined to historians who write specifically about women, such as Olympe's biographer, Olivier Blanc or the author of the Roland couple's biography, Sian Reynolds – women are still relegated to the amusing anecdotes of history. This is true of Max Gallo (1932–2017), a French historian and Academician who published a history of the French Revolution in three volumes between 2008 and 2010.

The first volume, focusing on the events that took place between 1788 and 1793, is where we would expect to find a discussion of the women of the Revolution. There is no mention of Olympe de Gouges. This is particularly surprising as much of that volume deals with the people of France's unwillingness to do anything substantial to reduce poverty. Gouges, as we will see in the following chapters, was influential in bringing about a temporary solution to extreme poverty by encouraging women artists to give their jewels to a patriotic fund. The final part of Gallo's first volume, which deals with the king's trial, could also have mentioned Gouges's various writings on the topic, including her offer to serve as the king's advocate.[12]

Sophie de Grouchy is mentioned in passing as hosting a salon (as Madame de Condorcet).[13] But it is the treatment of Marie-Jeanne Roland which is most astounding.

Gallo writes that Danton is wary of his enemies, the Girondins, especially:

This Madame Roland, hounding him with her hatred, perhaps simply because he was not affected by her charms, and she is an imperious seductress, who imposes her ideas on her husband, on Barbaroux, Brissot, the leaders of the Girondist party.[14]

How Gallo managed to create such a portrait of Roland from the available evidence is a mystery. We should not assume in any case that Gallo had not read Marie-Jeanne Roland's works. He cites from one of her letters, written after the September Massacres:

My friend Danton leads all; Robespierre is his puppet; Marat holds his torch and dagger.[15]

But in citing the letter, Gallo omits to attribute it to its author, putting it down instead as a popular rumour.

Written but a few years later, and more popular among academics, perhaps, than Gallo, Israel's *Revolutionary Ideas* (2014) uses the French Revolution to argue for his greater intellectual agenda, which is to show the historical importance of the Enlightenment. Putting the radical ideals of the Enlightenment into practise, he argues, is what the French Revolution was mostly about.

Israel's previous books on the Enlightenment were not models of inclusion and, in particular, offered less discussion than one might have reasonably hoped, for instance, of Mary Wollstonecraft or Catharine Macaulay. *Revolutionary Ideas* follows a similar trend: out of 167 names listed as the 'Cast of Main Characters', only 8 are women.[16] Some omissions are surprising: Pierre-Francois Robert is listed but not Louise Keralio-Robert. In the book, she is referred to as his collaborator on the *Mercure National*.[17] It would be more accurate to say that he had been her collaborator, as it was Louise who started the journal (previously, *Le Journal d'Etat et du Citoyen*), and she was its editor-in-chief. Robert joined the journal later, and they eventually married.

While there are several references to Grouchy and Gouges, they are not particularly enlightening or accurate. Grouchy is referred to as a 'leading exponent of women's rights', but we have no real evidence that she was even interested in women's rights.[18] She did not write about it under her name – that we know – nor is she reported to have discussed it with anyone. She did, however, contribute in writing and in editing Le *Républicain* to the leading ideas and arguments of the Revolution. Israel adds her names to various others, including other women's names (women are referred to as clusters, rather than individuals), but also, oddly, to Desmoulins's – they never met! – and to a list of people released from prison after the Terror – she never went![19] Olympe de Gouges is referred to as an ex-prostitute ('high class courtesan'), which she certainly was not.[20] She did, as far as we know, have several lovers over the course of her lifetime, but by that criterion, it's likely that most of the characters listed by Israel were also prostitutes! She also gets the usual treatment of being described as an emotional creature – she is in turns 'angry', 'fiery' and 'disgusted'.[21] Gouges is also referred to, several times, as a leading feminist, which she was; but although her other political writings and activities are noted, it seems that Israel only considers her notable for her feminism, which means that, like Grouchy, the greatest part of her contributions to the ideas that shaped the Revolution are forgotten.

Gallo and Israel, when they do mention the women of the Revolution, focus on their relationships and their emotional attributes. Guillois father and son also spend time discussing their physical attributes. For Guillois senior, Grouchy is always beautiful and known for her beauty. For Guillois junior, Gouges may have been good looking once, but by the time she begins her writing career, he says, she has lost her looks, and she has lost them because of her promiscuous behaviour. Their concern with the physical appearance, and in particular, beauty or absence of it, of their heroines, is far from uncommon in female biography. The reason for this focus is quite straightforward: historians always want their subjects remarkable, and women must be remarkable through their looks before their intellects or achievements. And when they fall from grace, they must also be ugly.

2.2 What the mirror reflected

Given that talking about their appearance has historically distracted them from their work, why should we be so concerned with historical women's looks? It is partly because they are women and their looks were their first commodity, the first and sometimes the last thing others noticed about them, their ticket to the world in which they wished to belong, and as such, we supposed they must have mattered to them. As John Berger once put it,

> A woman is always accompanied, except when quite alone, and perhaps even then, by her own image of herself. [. . .] She has to survey everything she is and everything she does because how she appears to others – and particularly how she appears to men – is of crucial importance for what is normally thought of as the success of her life.[22]

Certainly, women were expected to spend time on their appearance, and this led to some amount of reflection. Olympe admitted that this was quite a big concern for her:

> Often I have been called pretty – I do not know whether I am – and I did not believe it then since I spent so much of my days at my mirror trying to make myself beautiful.[23]

Marie-Jeanne tried to minimize it:

> Moreover, it is not surprising that women who spend their time in useless visiting and think they are badly dressed if they have not spent a great deal of time at their mirror, find their days too long through boredom and too short for their duties.[24]

But she too cared for her appearance, and for her final days, she had prepared a 'death outfit': 'an English style dress of white muslin, decorated with pale yellow, and tied with a black velvet belt. She wore a bonnet style of hat, of elegant simplicity, and her hair was loose on her shoulders.'[25]

For her part, Sophie de Grouchy was very much the fashionable young lady she was supposed to be, and while at the convent school of Neuville, she would write to her aunt, Madame Dupaty, to ask her for the latest fashionable items she would need for attending parties: velvet ribbons, buckles, gloves lined with fur and pearl earrings – all this, she added, to be hidden from her mother.[26]

When we read their biographies, all the women of the Revolution are described as handsome, beautiful, or at least striking, pretty or attractive. This could be a romantic notion, of course. But looking at their portraits, we find that there were no female Dantons or Robespierre in the Revolution – or any other time in history – hardly any women who were influential despite their looks. If there was a woman determined to make a difference, but her face was pockmarked, either she did not make it to the historical records, or, as was the case for Princess Elizabeth of Bohemia, Descartes's correspondent, the scars were erased from all representations, and a perfect complexion was all posterity got.

Of course, to some, all republican women were ugly: Edmund Burke decrying the crimes of the people of France against their king and queen described the women who marched to Versailles in the most unflattering terms, 'the abused shapes of the vilest of women'. Marie-Antoinette, on the other hand, whom he'd glimpsed from a distance when she'd just arrived in France: 'And surely never lighted on this orb, which she hardly seemed to touch, a more delightful vision. I saw her just above the horizon decorating and cheering the elevated sphere she just began to move in – glittering like the morning star, full of life and splendour and joy.'[27] But to the republican painter David, who sketched her as she was on her way to the guillotine, there was little beauty left in the queen. Women could be beautiful only while they were valued.

Let us look at one example.

Charlotte Corday died at the guillotine in July 1793, a few weeks after Marie-Jeanne Roland's arrest and a few days after Gouges's. Corday had come down from her home in northern France to murder Jean-Paul Marat, the 'the people's friend' and leader, with Robespierre, of the Terror. She was an aristocrat, who left to her own devices, and had 'read everything' in her parents' library. She was a republican, a friend of exiled Girondists, who had suffered at Marat's hand. Determined to help, she came to Paris, rang Marat's doorbell and was turned down. She wrote him a note and the next day tried again, this time successfully. She was admitted upstairs where he was writing in his bathtub, and she stabbed him. She was arrested immediately and tried very publicly. A few days later, she died at the guillotine. When she was arrested, a letter was found in her clothes, explaining her actions. She had wanted to save the republic by ridding it of Marat.[28]

Tellingly, descriptions and portraits of Corday after she was caught are very different from earlier portraits and descriptions, or portraits by the English who thought her, wrongly, a royalist. Before the murder, Corday was described as pretty, beautiful even, by all who saw her. Even Chabot, the 'Montagnard' – ally of Marat – who thought her a horrifying accident of nature, and fancied he could detect plainly her criminal propensities painted on her face, still described her as having 'spirit, grace, superb height and bearing'.[29]

But the death of Marat did change the way she was perceived. Fabre d'Eglantine, actor and Danton's private secretary, captured this reversal in his

Figure 8 Charlotte Corday, engraving from a life portrait, BnF.

'Moral and physical portrait' of Corday for the daily newspaper *Le Moniteur Universel*.

> This woman who has been called very beautiful was not beautiful. [. . .] she was a virago, fleshy and not fresh, without grace, dirty, as are nearly all female philosophers and blue stockings. Her face was covered in red patches and featureless. Height and Youth are proof indeed! That is all it takes to be beautiful while on trial. Moreover, this observation would not be needed if it were not for the general truth that any woman who is beautiful and knows it cares for life and fears death.[30]

This special issue of *Le Moniteur* was widely distributed throughout France: those in charge wanted all women to know what happened to those who fought back and to realize that they could either be beautiful and silent or ugly and dead (Figure 8).

Charlotte Corday was not the only target of the campaign to dish out physical criticism in lieu of political disagreement. Monsieur Suleau, in his royalist journal, praises aristocratic ladies for their anti-revolutionary attitude but in a long note lists exceptions:

> There are, of course, exceptions amongst the old, the ugly, the infirm, whatever class they belong to. I have carefully checked that of all the women who harnessed themselves to the cart (or more correctly, the

tipcart) of the Revolution, there is not a single one that does not belong to this disgusting category.

A few toothless and disgusting dowagers (starting with the duchess of Anville) allowed their folly to persuade them that it was a talisman of youth, that to throw themselves in the torrent of novelty, thinking in their folly that that famous system of equality, which first wishes to bring all humans back to the infancy of beautiful nature, would necessarily have the virtue to wipe away their wrinkles and to freshen up their fusty attractions.

The ugly, starting with the rotund Staël, thought that by painting themselves with the colours of the nation, they would themselves take on a human appearance and that by wrapping themselves in tricolour fripperies, they would succeed in hiding their deformities.

In the lepers' infirmary, I would place (starting with the Condorcet woman) these pieces of fresh meat who, with a varnish of health and engaging figures, still threw themselves in the rights of men's cooking pot. We must not be mistaken: even with their fresh face and eager demeanour, these poor creatures are infertile and covered in ulcers. Mange, gripe, ringworm, clap, sores, yaws, farcy, bleb on their necks, suction cups on their chests, poultices on their thighs, and plasters everywhere – we find these pleasant accoutrements behind all the pretty faces who gave themselves to the cult of demagogy. These unfortunates, to make things worse, are periodically subject to epileptic fits. I am not worried that any of these interesting dolls will dare to contradict me, for I will call to witness a legion of sans-culottes who have been in a position to verify this by eye and hand.[31]

And of course, then as now, women were the butt of political caricatures, often sexist, such as the one depicting Grouchy, Staël, Genlis and a few others showing their behind to the royalist soldiers, and Théroigne de Méricourt, showing off her 'republic', causing the soldiers to disperse and lose their erections (a play on the word 'débandement' which means both) (Figure 9).

But as well as the potential for abuse and for minimizing the intellectual productions of women authors, there is some value in knowing what the writers of the past look like. All canonical philosophers have images associated with them, portraits that turn up everywhere from book covers to students' presentations. But this is only true of male philosophers. Women's portraits are hard to come by, as a simple Google image search for 'philosophers' will show. The work of creating a cultural database of images that we can refer to for women philosophers has begun, for instance, with the Project Vox,

Figure 9 Grand Débandement, engraving, BnF.

an internet database that offers well-sourced images as well as original texts, translations and commentaries. Unfortunately, the period Project Vox is concerned with stops short of the French Revolution (for now).

We can at least begin to bridge the gap here with portraits and descriptions of Gouges, Roland and Grouchy. So let us go back to our heroines and attempt to reconstruct what they might have looked like, so we can picture them when we think of their works.

Olympe, of medium height and slim, had been described as a 'femme superbe', beautiful to look at. But also, according to Guillois junior, she had aged before time, 'lost her looks' early on, he says, ruined by her immoral lifestyle. According to a laissez-passer she was given in Auteuil, her nose was aquiline.[32] In company, she wore her black curls powdered, swept-back high over her forehead and rolled on either side of her neck. We can see it worn that way on the famous pastel by the polish portraitist Kucharski, an early portrait attributed to Ingres (Figure 12), and the engraving on her 1788 brochure, 'Remarques Patriotiques' (Figure 10). In those representations, she wears her dress tied at the waist closely, which makes her look quite tall. Her shoulders are covered by a shawl crossed over her chest, as was the fashion in the late eighteenth century (Figure 10).[33]

Marie-Jeanne Roland liked to wear simple clothes, such as a sensible dress, blue or white, covered with a plain white scarf, neatly tied at the front, sometimes with a rose. Her brown hair was worn either up or down, with a revolutionary fringe, and covered by a simple Girondin bonnet, a white scarf tied in a bow on her forehead. A little short, and perhaps stocky, she was not particularly striking, but her face was mobile and engaging, which explains why so many found her attractive. In her memoirs, she described herself as a young woman (Figure 11):

Figure 10 Olympe de Gouges remettant sa Déclaration des droits de la femme et de la citoyenne à Marie-Antoinette, BnF.

The mouth is rather large; one may see hundreds prettier but none with a sweeter or more winning smile. The eyes, on the other hand, are smallish and prominent. The irises are tinged with chestnut and grey. The impression they convey is of openness, vivacity and sympathy, reflecting the various changes of mood of an affectionate nature. Well-moulded eyebrows of auburn, the same colour as the hair, complete the picture. It is, on the whole, a proud and serious face that sometimes causes surprise but more often inspires confidence and interest. I was always a bit worried about my nose; it seemed to me too big at the tip. On the other hand, seen in its setting, and especially in profile, it did not damage the general effect. The broad forehead, issuing from a high brow and covered by a fringe, was unusually expressive of the most fleeting emotions and the firm, rounded chin suggested a natural sensuality. No one so obviously made for voluptuous pleasure has enjoyed so little of it.[34]

Sophie de Grouchy was very tall, unusually so for a woman of her century. She had a small, heart-shaped face with a short and pretty nose. She wore her hair tied, sometimes under a hat, her face framed with artfully loose curls. Her dresses were cut aristocratically low. Her scarves were light and fuzzy, expensive and fragile. But when, during the Terror, she visited her husband in hiding, she wore a simpler dress, with a high neck and a coarse shawl

Figure 11 Madame Roland, portrait, engraving Johann Lips, BnF.

wrapped tightly around her shoulders and chest, revolutionary style. She wore her hair with a fringe then and loose around her shoulders, much as Marie-Jeanne Roland did around the same time.

There was nothing remarkable about these women's appearances. They varied in height and weight, could easily be told apart and were probably no more nor less attractive than many of their male counterparts. There is no reason to think that their looks brought about their achievements. Yet, there is a strong reluctance, still, to look beyond their appearance as women and the effect they had on men, to see their achievements as their own, or to see them for their true worth. Guillois junior did not think, like many before and after him, that Olympe was the author of any of her works, but claimed instead that she was an attention seeker, using others' work to put herself in the limelight:

> My subject was undoubtedly a shining mind. She could invent and imagine. But mostly, she was vain and ambitious. She wanted to be talked about in the Paris salons.[35]

3 Beginnings

Just as it helps to know what women of the past looked like, so that we can represent them to ourselves when we think about them, knowing something of their lives is also useful. Not too much, perhaps – we don't want to reduce a woman's work to how many children or siblings she had. And there is a tendency, when we look at women, to think of them as family members – daughters, sisters, wives and mothers – rather than persons in their own right. We don't know very much about Thérèse Levasseur, and we don't write about her when we discuss her lover, Rousseau's works. But she is there in the background, as are Descartes's Jesuit teachers and Aristotle's physician father. We don't talk about their backgrounds because they are somehow already established in our common cultural consciousness, just as Descartes's moustache and long black hair, or Rousseau's boyish good looks and Aristotle's stocky build are. So while we should avoid turning scholarly papers on women philosophers into biographical reports, it's useful to have this background somewhere, and where better than in an intellectual biography?[36] Among the questions we need to ask in order to build up a similar background of reference for women philosophers are questions about their education, their introduction to intellectual and political circles, and their early struggles to become writers. Who were these women before they became revolutionary writers, what were they at the beginning and what led them to become what they did become?

3.1 Olympe

Born Marie Gouze[37] in Montauban, near Toulouse, she was registered as the daughter of Anne-Olympe Mouisset and daughter of Pierre Gouzes. Gouzes was not, however, her biological father, as she was the illegitimate daughter of the local poet, playwright and aristocrat Jean-Jacques Lefranc de Pompignan.

We know very little about Anne-Olympe Gouzes. In an autobiographical novel, Gouges wrote about her adventures with her birth father's family – *Mémoire de Madame de Valmont*, she describes her mother, declining in health, alone and in abject poverty in Montauban, while she is trying to make a life for herself in Paris as a Salonière. Her birth father, she tells the reader, did not offer the financial support he'd promised, and his family refused to help. The dutiful daughter in the novel is torn. Should she spend what little money she had to visit, she wondered, or should she instead send the money to buy food and pay for the doctor? The fictional Anne-Olympe loves her daughter dearly and wants her by her side. But she also seems quite adept at making her feel guilty and conflicted.

Young Marie barely knew her adoptive father, the butcher Gouzes: he drowned in the Tarn when she was still a toddler. And although she took his name, she did not recognize him as her father. She knew early on that Pompignan was her father. Her mother took her to visit him regularly until they argued about who would be in charge of her education. Had Pompignan won, she would have been educated by a private tutor, a learned father and have had access to a large library.[38] Instead, Marie was brought up speaking mostly Occitan, the oral language of the south. In the north, Occitan was often mocked, and it was implied that those who spoke it were illiterate. But although they spoke Occitan among themselves, and although few girls received any sort of an education, the natives of Montauban who were at all educated were taught to read and write French.

It seems likely that the education Olympe received from her mother was minimal. Until 1753 when she married again (to a policeman, Dominique-Raymond Cassaignaux), Anne-Olympe was a single mother, trying to keep up the family business by herself. Her biographer, Olivier Blanc, surmises that Marie may have gone to a local day school, run by Ursuline nuns, where she would have been taught the basics of reading, writing and needlework, but not much more. But her mother was no mere seduced peasant girl. Her family had been linked to the Pompignan's for several generations, and she came from minor nobility or at least upper-middle class. That meant that she could at least teach her daughter how to dress and to behave in polite society, a skill that probably came in handy when she moved to Paris.

When Marie turned sixteen, her mother and stepfather married her off to Louis-Yves Aubry, a cook. She protested, as he was unattractive and had unpleasant manners.[39] Guillois, in his doctoral thesis, scolds her for complaining. She lies, he says, referring to herself as a fifteen-year-old when in fact, she was nearly seventeen, and surely, he adds, Aubry was good enough for her, and she must have had ideas above her stations if she thought otherwise.[40] He is chiding a sixteen-year-old forced to leave her mother and share the bed of an older man with whom she had little in common.

Olympe obeyed her parents and gave birth within a year. Shortly afterwards, Aubry disappeared. There were rumours that he drowned in the Tarn, like her father – there is no official record of his death or departure.[41]

One year into her widowhood, Marie met Jacques Biétrix de Rozières. Although they remained a couple throughout her life, they never married: perhaps she had already decided then that marriage was the death of love.[42] A year later, the 21-year-old widow and her infant son moved to Paris. First, she lived with her sister, Jeanne. Then she set up a home and a salon of her own. In Paris, she shook off the last of her unfortunate marriage by taking back her maiden name, Gouzes, spelling it with a g, as some family members did, and adding 'de', as many young women from the south did.[43] She added her mother's name, Olympe, to her own, calling herself Marie-Olympe, and then simply Olympe. Rozières was a wealthy man who could help support her and her son and helped smooth her introduction into Paris society, where she was welcome as a member of the Pompignan family. The next five years were spent frequenting salons, reading and going to the theatre. Olympe was building herself an education, becoming more familiar with the French language and culture, and slowly shedding her southern accent. By 1778, eight years after she came to Paris, Olympe was ready to write.

History does not, of course, see things that way. Why did Olympe only start writing at thirty? Because she craved attention, and she could no longer get it through her physical charms. Why did she not write earlier? Because she was illiterate, writing had to be a desperate last-ditch attempt to satisfy her devouring ambition.[44] Some of her contemporaries even went so far as to claim she did not write her own plays. Beaumarchais, whom she approached for support for her play *The Unexpected Marriage of Cherubino*, inspired by his *Marriage of Figaro*, ignored her at first and then blocked the production of her play in Paris, claiming – without having read it – that it plagiarized his own.

Beaumarchais was not alone in thinking she could not write. Olympe herself tells how she found herself sitting in a carriage by a man who claimed to know her (without realizing it was she he was talking to) and that she paid others to write her plays, having them taught to her by heart so she could then pretend to dictate them to her secretary.[45]

Her relationship with the actors of Paris made difficult by Beaumarchais's intervention was not improved by her constant arguments with them, and the fact that there were factions among the actors, with a powerful one, led by the royalist Fleury, set against her. She decided then that if she could not be played in Paris, she would go to the provinces and present her work to the Parisians in print.

'*Let me be printed . . . Let me be printed then! . . . Here is a pleasure at least that will not be taken from me.*'[46]

3.2 Marie-Jeanne

Around the time Olympe's father (or adoptive father) drowned in the Tarn, another middle-class child was born in Paris to parents who knew she was theirs and no one else's. Marie-Jeanne Phlipon, daughter of Gatien and Marguerite, was born on the Ile de la Cité, a stone's throw from the Concièrgerie, the prison where she spent her last days. As most Parisian children of the times were, Marie-Jeanne was sent to spend her first two years in the home of a wet nurse in the countryside. Paris was not a healthy environment for a baby, and Marie-Jeanne's parents had already lost several children, so they were bound to be more careful. Fresh air, a healthy nurse: this would keep her alive and make her strong. And by the time she came back to Paris, Manon, as her mother called her, was both healthy and strong and would no doubt have lived well beyond the age of thirty-eight had she not been guillotined.

Young Manon had the run of her father's library – not a large one – and on certain days, when she was sent out to run errands, she had the run of the town. She had tutors – no expense was to be spared for this clever child's education.[47] She knew her catechism by heart but was not convinced by what she learned. On Sundays, she hid a favourite book in the cover of her Bible: Plutarch's *Parallel Lives*, translated into elegant French by Anne and André Dacier. Marie-Jeanne Roland was not the first to treat Plutarch's book as a substitute for a religious text: Montaigne had written of an earlier translation into French by Jacques Amyot: 'It is our breviary!'[48] She embraced republicanism, admiring the values and virtues of the Roman leaders she read about. She began to wish she had been born Roman, or above all a man, so she could act on her convictions. But soon, even Plutarch was no longer enough. She wanted to learn more, and her tutors – music, languages – could not teach her enough.

Around that time, she was assaulted by an apprentice of her father. The experience shocked her deeply, and despite her childhood scepticism, she sought refuge in religion. Marie-Jeanne begged her parents to be allowed to continue her studies in a convent school. She was sent to the nearby convent of the Augustines, but Marie-Jeanne, a precocious child, was difficult to teach and knew more already than the kindly nuns who'd agreed to take her on. She quickly lost her faith again, which must have made educating her rather difficult. She stayed a year and made lifelong friends, two of whom, the Cannet sisters, became her correspondents and later introduced her to her husband to be.

Back home, Marie-Jeanne wrote in her bedroom, which she had arranged much like a cell in a convent, free of distraction. Unlike Olympe, she was good with a pen: her hand is regular, rounded and pleasant to read. She wrote daily letters to her convent friends and tried her hand at philosophical essays. She read avidly, moving from the ancients to contemporary philosophers. Through a family friend, she discovered Rousseau and became confirmed in her republicanism. And she lost her religion again, quickly and painlessly.

This peaceful, satisfying existence as a reader and writer continued until she was twenty-one when her mother died, and Marie-Jeanne found herself alone with her father, deeply upset by her loss and with no guidance for what to do next. A family friend then gave her a copy of *La Nouvelle Héloise*, the only one of Rousseau's works she had not yet read. Not only did the story of Julie and St Preux, the passionate lovers turned virtuous friends, soothe her pain, but she also could now see a way she could be both a woman of her times and a republican. All she needed to do was marry a man who shared her ideals, and together they could raise a family, living a peaceful country life and nurturing republican values in their children.

Wanting to learn more, Marie-Jeanne decided then she would visit the great man whose books had taught her so much. She wrote a careful letter of introduction, using the excuse that she was to pick up some music a friend had commissioned from Rousseau (who, in his old age, made a living as a composer). But even such a legitimate commission was not enough to be admitted to his presence. At the door, she was turned away by Thérèse Levasseur, Rousseau's mistress. The philosopher, she said, did not wish to see her as he did not like liars. At Marie-Jeanne's very genuine surprise, she elaborated. Rousseau did not believe Marie-Jeanne had written the letter herself: both its content and style (even the hand) obviously belonged to a man! This adventure is strongly reminiscent of Olympe de Gouges's own, who, wanted to seek Beaumarchais's patronage for her play on Cherubino, inspired by his own Figaro, was rudely turned down at the door, and later accused of plagiarism![49]

And still, Marie-Jeanne was writing, collecting her essays in a volume. She did not think she should publish – she believed a republican woman should not seek to influence those beyond the immediate circle of her family. But she did let herself be tempted by a competition to which she could submit anonymously. The question set by the Academy of Besançon was: 'How could educating women help make men better?'. In her answer, she wrote about the place of women in society, praising the simple lives of the Spartan women, who nurtured the virtue of soldiers and leaders to be. She wrote about how nations that enslaved women were always decadent and never successful. She did not win but received an honourable mention, an honour she shared with Rousseau's protegé, Bernardin de Saint Pierre, a naturalist and critique of the slave trade who went on to write the bestselling *Pierre and Virginie*.

Marie-Jeanne was not discouraged, and she kept producing essays and writing daily letters. Writing became a habit, a form of sustenance. Her constant writing, she said, prepared her for the secretarial work she later did for her husband, as well as for the writing of her memoirs in prison.

After turning down several unsuitable suitors – she wanted to become a good wife, but if it was going to interfere with her writing, she would be picky about it! – Marie-Jeanne met Jean-Marie Roland. And after a three-year-long courtship, she married him at the age of twenty-six. Their daughter, Eudora, was born a year and a half later, in 1782, and both parents threw themselves entirely in her education, following Rousseau's precepts as closely as they could (sometimes conveniently forgetting that Eudora was a girl and that Rousseau's educational views were heavily gendered).

Early on in their marriage, it became clear to Marie-Jeanne that her husband's writing skills did not match his intellectual and academic ambitions. Roland was an inspector of industries. But he wanted to become a member of an academy and was working on an encyclopedia of the textile industry, with articles on every aspect of cloth production, starting from botany and ending with sewing. Marie-Jeanne, perceiving that her husband stood little chance of success if left to his own scholarly and literary devices, started to 'copy' and 'revise' his work, rewriting paragraphs, drafting others completely. She read everything there was to read on the various topics Roland wanted to write about, and more besides, as she was still an avid reader of political thought and history.

For several years, husband and wife worked side by side, and Marie-Jeanne was happy to be engaged in doing what she loved and be useful at the same time. Only later, when she was about to die, did she reflect that her skills and her intellect were somewhat wasted in this secretarial work. But she kept on writing for her own benefit: travel journals on England and Switzerland, letters, political, literary, philosophical; and it is in those writings that we see the development of her own political thought.

3.3 Sophie

Around the time a young Marie-Jeanne was smuggling her Plutarch to Sunday school, Sophie de Grouchy was born in the castle of Villette, near Meulan. The land had been in the family since Louis XV. The family was old, of Norman extraction. We find some Grouchys with William the Conqueror, some in St Louis' crusades. The military fame died with Sophie's brother, Emmanuel, who has been held responsible for Napoleon's defeat at Waterloo – legend states that he did not react to an emergency attack because he was at lunch and wanted a second dish of strawberries.[50] Thankfully the family was not only distinguished for its military exploits: one ancestor, Nicolas de Grouchy, was a teacher in the school Montaigne attended as a child.[51] And indeed, Sophie's family was a literary one: when they did not walk the countryside, hunting, fishing or distributing alms to the poor, they sat at home and read. In the winter, they gathered in Paris, in a private hotel rue Gaillon, and there they hosted the intellectual elite of the day: Turgot, d'Alembert, Beaumarchais, Condorcet.

Sophie was quick to show that she belonged in such circles. Her bedtime reading of choice was Marcus Aurelius. She joined in with her brothers' studies, picking up English, some Latin and German.[52] She was such a good student that when the tutor was ill, she took over. But her mother ensured that her education was not merely intellectual. Sophie and her sister, Charlotte, were taken on charity rounds to visit the poor and the sick and taught by their mother how to help and comfort and how to value the well-being of others.[53]

As soon as her family could spare her, Sophie was sent to the Chanoinesse school of Neuville, an ostensibly religious establishment but mostly a finishing school for the very rich and very well-connected aristocrats.

The school was exclusive: the parents of applicants had to demonstrate long-standing nobility and pay large sums in fees and expenses. The admission ceremony was a cross between a knighting ceremony and entering a convent, starting in a church and finishing at a ball in a private home.[54] There was, in general, more partying than praying at Neuville. Sophie enjoyed it to the full, staying up late going to balls and getting up early the next day to study. She worked and played so hard she became ill, nearly losing her eyesight.[55] When she worked, Sophie practised her languages by translating works from the English and the Italian, such as the poems of Edward Young and Tasso's *Jerusalem*. This was good practice for later when she would translate Adam Smith's *The Theory of Moral Sentiments*. And of course, she read, going far beyond the ancients to her contemporaries, discovering Voltaire, Diderot and especially Rousseau. And just as it had happened with Marie-Jeanne, she lost her religion – what would Rousseau, sometimes devout Catholic, sometimes stern protestant, have made of that?

Her early training in Christian charity, with her mother showing her how good it felt to relieve others' trouble, blended with her new readings and turned her towards social justice. Like Marie-Jeanne, she too became a republican, one concerned particularly with eradicating the psychological distance between the rich and the poor, with no one so rich or powerful that they could dominate others.

Coming home to Villette, Sophie announced to her horrified mother that she had become an atheist. Madame de Grouchy responded by burning all her Rousseau, Voltaire and Diderot and bringing out Marcus Aurelius again. Every night Sophie would pray that God may give her back her faith – until it became obvious that he would not oblige, and she gave up. Fortunately for her, she was still much loved and valued, not just by her immediate family but by her uncle and aunt Dupaty, who put her in charge of their son's education. Through her uncle, she developed further her passion for social justice – he was a magistrate and fought to reform the French criminal system, which punished the poor heavily and unfairly while letting the rich get away. Uncle and niece saw eye to eye on this and greatly admired each other.

By the time Sophie met Nicolas de Condorcet, a friend of her uncle Dupaty whose son she was tutoring, Sophie was a confirmed atheist and republican. She was also highly educated and could hold her own in political debates with her uncle. This in itself would have pleased Condorcet, but he also found out that she was brave and devoted. One day her tutee was attacked by a rabid dog: Sophie threw herself between the child and the beast. Condorcet, not himself very daring – Madame Roland in her wisdom called him a coward – admired her from a safe distance, and soon the two were engaged and, in 1786, married in the chapel at Villette, with the Marquis de Lafayette as their witness.

The newlyweds moved to Condorcet's apartments in the Hotel des Monnaies where Condorcet worked as the inspector general of the Monnaie – he had worked with Robert-Anne Turgot and Jacques Necker, during their terms as minister of finances. Condorcet's home bore traces of a slightly odd childhood, a portrait of him aged nine, dressed as a girl.[56] Sophie quickly set things to order, and soon they had a salon – or as it was then called, a 'circle'. Her English was excellent by then, so theirs became the house of choice for foreign visitors: Jefferson, Paine, Cloots, Dumont and others. Their devoted friend, the doctor Cabanis who later married Sophie's sister, Charlotte, was also a frequent visitor.

Sophie did not stop studying after she married. Shortly after she moved into the Hotel de la Monnaie, Condorcet, together with another Academician, La Harpe founded the Lycée, a school on the Rue St Honoré, where famous scholars and Academicians lectured and where the cream of society learned. Sophie attended assiduously, learning mathematics, history and botany. She became known as the Venus of the Lyceum. She also took lessons in painting in the studio of Elizabeth Vigée le Brun, developing skills that later saved her life. By her own account, Vigée le Brun didn't enjoy taking pupils and didn't think much of their talents. Sophie painted well, though, as we know from the several miniatures she left behind, including several self-portraits. And she was good enough that during the Terror, with all her wealth confiscated, she could make a living out of it.[57]

4 Olympe, Marie-Jeanne and Sophie at the eve of the Revolution

Our three heroines, each from a background very different from that of the others, each educated in their own, somewhat idiosyncratic ways, were, at the eve of the Revolution, ready to grow as political thinkers and writers.

In 1789, Olympe was dividing her time between Paris, where she was active in theatre and where she hosted a salon, and Auteuil, where she was attending the salon of Madame Helvetius and refining her views on social justice. She was beginning to think about how she might put her experiences and ideas to good use. Marie-Jeanne was in the countryside, near Lyon, working with her husband on an encyclopedia of textile industry, harvesting grapes, befriending her neighbours, developing an epistolary friendship with Brissot and writing still. Sophie was in her salon, at the Monnaie de Paris, entertaining Parisians and foreigners, taking painting lessons and attending scientific lectures at the Lyceum.

Sophie and Marie-Jeanne both had youthful writings. Marie-Jeanne's were published after her death by Champagneux, a family friend. We don't know what Sophie wrote: aristocrats guard their secrets well. Olympe's work was published since 1787.

Making her own way

Olympe de Gouges

Olympe de Gouges, lacking the advantages of sex and education that would have paved the way to publishing, decided to take her writing career into her own hands. In 1784, after she had lived in Paris for eight years, she hired a secretary and began to dictate plays, political tracts and works of philosophy. Rather than wait for success to come to her, she took her pieces directly to the printer's, whether pamphlets to be pasted all over Paris, plays to be presented to theatrical companies or volumes of *Works*. Despite the many obstacles thrown her way, most of them reactions to the fact that she was a woman from an uncertain background, she produced work that was both philosophical and engaged with the pressing issues of her time. Her interests ranged from equality – of gender and race – poverty relief, republicanism and democracy. Her texts were read and acted upon. She became notorious, if not always loved. And at the end, it was a piece of writing – *The Three Urns* – which cost her her life. So how did she become such a prolific and influential writer? (Figure 12).

1 Education, literacy and a famous playwright as a father

In the 1750s, when Marie, as she was then known, was of the age to learn how to read, the education of French children was under the control of the Catholic Church. There were few options: you could be educated at home, privately, by a parent or a tutor, or you could be sent to school. Boys who were not particularly rich might have done better at school than at home. Maximilien Robespierre, for instance, won a scholarship to leave his native Arras and study at the Lycée Louis-le-Grand in Paris. But there were no equivalent schools for girls, so unless they could be educated at home, working perhaps with their father, as Anne Dacier, the classical translator,

Figure 12 Olympe de Gouges, portrait, attributed to Ingres 1793, BnF.

had done, or with their brothers' tutors, as Sophie de Grouchy did, girls were sent to convents, or the Ursulines' day schools.

The Ursulines school at Montauban had been started in 1682 by six Ursuline sisters from Toulouse. The school was run by women who had taken religious vows and offered free classes to local girls in basic reading and writing, religious education and sewing. The point of such an education was to prepare girls for the life of good Catholic homemakers – this did not require perfect literacy, as Catholics, unlike Protestants, were not required to read the Bible.[1] The Ursulines school of Montauban is still running – it has been expanded to cover all ages from kindergarten to high school, and they have a very modern-looking building.

Olympe did therefore learn to read and write. But when she first became known as an author, she somehow developed a reputation as an illiterate. That she spoke Occitan better than French did not help nor did, presumably, her thick southern accent. The literacy level in southern France was then much lower than in the north, and the Parisians were, then as now, quick to mock. And although there were at least thirty different dialects spoken in France in the late eighteenth century, the revolutionary government would do its best to ensure that French was spoken throughout the country, sending school teachers to remote villages to teach children to speak French rather than their local dialect.[2]

It probably did nothing to aid her reputation as an illiterate that Olympe herself made a virtue out of her lack of formal education. She valued her image as a child of nature, a genius whose intellect had not been damaged by too much learning, whose language was less elegant, perhaps, but closer to the truth itself.

> Perhaps one day, I will receive, without any effort on my part, the respect that is granted to works arising from the hands of Nature. I can call myself one of its rare creations – everything I have comes from her; I have had no other tutor: and all my philosophical reflections cannot undo the strongly rooted imperfections that came with such an education.
>
> [. . .]
>
> I know no other constraint than the weaknesses of nature that humanity can only vanquish through effort. And she whose pride can tame her passions can properly call herself a Strong Woman (*Femme Forte*).[3]

It is clear that she did not feel comfortable holding a quill: this was a skill that could not be mastered with a few hours of practice at a day school, and one that required the purchase of good ink and paper and a set of quills – all tools that may not have been immediately accessible in the family home of a butcher. Olympe could write – there are documents in her hand preserved at the National Archives of Paris – but with difficulty: her letters are cramped and badly shaped, and the ink clogs. Once her career took a writerly turn, it made sense for her to hire the services of a secretary. But it is clear that the secretary's work was no more than that of a typist, that she herself composed the text, dictating it to him and revised the final document at the printer's. In a postscript to her *Declaration of the Rights of Woman*, in which she describes how a coach driver bullied her into paying more than she owed him by threatening to have her imprisoned, she tells us that she customarily reviewed her proofs while waiting at the printers:

> I live in the countryside. I left Auteuil this morning at eight and winded my way to the road from Paris to Versailles, where one can often find those famous roadside cafés that inexpensively gather passersby. No doubt an unlucky star was pursuing me that morning. I reached the gate, and I could not even find the sad, privileged hackney coach. I rested on the steps of that insolent edifice that secreted clerks. Nine o'clock chimed,

and I continued on my way; I spotted a coach, took my place, and arrived at a quarter past nine, according to two different watches, at the Pont-Royal. I took the hackney-coach and flew to my printer, rue Christine, for I could only go so early in the morning: when I am proofreading, there is always something to do, if the pages are not too tight or too full.[4]

2 Learning the theatre and becoming a writer

Olympe lacked a refined education; she was not good with a pen – but she definitely could write. However, she did not become a writer immediately after she left Montauban to pursue a career in Paris. Her first works date from eight to ten years after she arrived in the capital so she would have been in her late twenties or early thirties. Why did Olympe only start writing then? Her medical biographer, Guillois, interpreted this late start in the most uncharitable way possible as a desperate last-ditch attempt at satisfying her devouring ambition for fame and recognition.

> Her contemporaries were unanimous in saying that she faded early and that her charms diminished more quickly because she had abused them. So, tired of no longer finding in gallantry success sufficient to satisfy her too strong ambition, she decided to try literature. [. . .] She wants to be the centre of attention, therefore she will become a writer.[5]

A more plausible and less offensive explanation of the eight years between Olympe's arrival in Paris and her becoming a writer is that she was in the process of educating herself. Her schooling had not prepared her to produce plays good enough to present to the Comédies Française or Italienne – the two official Paris theatres. However, she did have a theatrical background in that her natural father, Jean-Jacques le Franc de Pompignan, whose work she read and admired, was himself a fairly successful playwright, his *Dido* having been performed at the Comédie Française in 1734. Pompignan was also a close friend of Jean Racine, the great tragedian's son, and Gouges, who was closely interested in her father's literary career, might have read their published correspondence in which they debated the aesthetics of drama. Moreover, Montauban had an Academy and a theatre where Olympe saw *Dido* performed at least once: the night she was introduced to her husband, Louis Aubry. We know she had read and admired her father's works and that she used his name to enter the Paris theatrical scene. Her big break was an introduction, through her friends Louis Sébastien Mercier and Michel de Cubière, to the salons of Fanny de Beauharnais and Madame de Montesson.

Cubière was a poet, a socialite and a flirt, whose mistress was Fanny de Beauharnais. During the Revolution, he managed to remain influential in the ever-changing government, and it is to him that Olympe attempted to write when she was first taken prisoner. Cubière survived the Revolution. Mercier, poet, novelist, playwright and philosopher, also survived, despite being put under arrest in 1794 for having protested the sentencing of the Girondins, including that of his friend, Olympe.

Madame de Montesson was a talented widow who became a patron of playwrights, welcoming, in particular, those like Olympe, who experienced difficulties having their work performed by Parisian theatres. She set up a private theatre in her Paris home in the Chaussée d'Antin, close to Mirabeau's home and several other famous literary salons of the eighteenth century, such as that of Juliette Récamier and Louise d'Epinay. Her theatrical manager was the Chevalier de Saint-Georges, a composer and soldier from Guadeloupe – his father was a planter and his mother, Nanon, an enslaved worker in his father's house. Saint-Georges became one of Madame Montesson's protégés after his first opera, *Ernestine* with a libretto by Choderlos de Laclos, failed miserably at the Comédie Italienne.[6]

Participating in Madame de Montesson's home theatre, together with experienced actors and writers, proved invaluable for Olympe. Between 1780 and 1784, Olympe set up her own theatrical company and put on plays. Her son Pierre – who in 1780 was fourteen – was one of her principal actors. Then in 1784, she began to write. Her first play was *Zamore and Mirza, or the Happy Shipwreck*, a play designed to raise the French public's sympathies for the condition of enslaved Africans. Although she does not mention it anywhere, it is likely no coincidence that she had spent the preceding years learning the theatrical trade with Montesson's friend Saint-Georges, from whom she may well have learned a few relevant facts about slavery. Nonetheless, her play demonstrates a surprising amount of geographical and racial confusion – are the enslaved people in the story native Americans, Indians, or Africans? All that Olympe seems to be confident about is that their skin ought to be dark – and when the Comédie Française eventually agreed to put the play on in the winter of 1789 and wanted them to be white-skinned, she argued with them – unsuccessfully.

It took five years for Olympe's first play to be performed in Paris. The Comédie Française had accepted it in 1785 – that is, it had been read, and the actors had voted unanimously in its favour. The play belonged to them from then on, and Olympe was not allowed to have it performed elsewhere in Paris – except, of course, in private theatres. The Comédie Française sat on her play for four years, during which time Olympe petitioned the actors again and again, but to no avail.[7]

3 Resistance: 'Le Bon Sens Français', Beaumarchais and the actors

Olympe de Gouges wrote two plays in 1784. As well as *Zamore and Mirza*, she wrote *The Unexpected Marriage of Cherubino*. A play both inspired by and written in homage to Beaumarchais's *Marriage of Figaro*, Cherubino told the story of the eponymous lovelorn page, now wealthy and powerful but still in love with the same Fanchette, previously a maid of the Count, but now his daughter. Olympe was hoping to attract the great author's interest or patronage. Unfortunately, all she attracted was his ire. Without having read it, Beaumarchais decided that her play plagiarized his own work.

Beaumarchais might have recognized the praise and accepted the homage – his Marriage of Figaro was, after all, a defence of the liberty of expression: 'Without the freedom to attack, flattering praise is worthless. And only small men fear small pamphlets.'[8] But Beaumarchais, a strong intellectual influence in favour of the Revolution and a cultural hero for many, was not always a fair-minded or generous individual. He spent most of his life pursuing fame for the sake of wealth, twice marrying rich widows and even breaking up an engagement upon finding that his fiancée was not as wealthy as he had thought. This seems to indicate a predisposition on his part to regard women mostly as financial assets so that offering his patronage to a woman without name or fortune would not have been one of his priorities.

Beaumarchais had himself been engaged in disputes over his *Marriage of Figaro*. Though written in 1781, the play had been censored by the king himself for its very critical attitude to aristocratic privilege and could not be performed until 1784. Recovering from this long dispute, Beaumarchais may not have felt particularly generous towards a newcomer trying to benefit from the long-awaited success of his own play.

Another factor that played against Olympe in her quest for patronage was perhaps that Beaumarchais was in the process of arguing for intellectual copyrights.[9] At the end of the eighteenth century, the rights to a play were passed on to the theatrical company as soon as they'd accepted it so that even when the company subsequently refused to perform a play, as they did with *Zamore and Mirza*, the author does not have the option to have it performed elsewhere. Beaumarchais created an Office of Dramatic Law, and under his influence, authors' moral and legal rights were officially recognized in 1791.

All this goes some way towards explaining Beaumarchais's negative reaction towards the young author who came to him in 1785, asking for his help – but not entirely. His reaction, unfortunately, points to a lack of generosity. All that Beaumarchais saw in Olympe's *Marriage of Cherubino* was an attempt on his authorial rights. He immediately contacted the French theatre actors, with whom he then had great influence – due to the financial and critical success of his Figaro – not to take it.

Undeterred, Olympe decided that she would make the best of things and seek actual feedback from Beaumarchais on her work. If he hated it so much that he would have it censored, the least he could do was tell her what was wrong with it. She wrote him a note that she hand-delivered, hoping for an immediate interview.

The note she handed at the door said:

I had the honour, Sir, of writing to you, as to all the men of Letters; but I come to you as the oppressed ran to Voltaire; I am at your door, and I flatter myself that you will do me the respectful honour of receiving me.[10]

Beaumarchais's servant took the note to his master and came back with the response that Beaumarchais was busy and could not see her right now, upon which Olympe asked for his at-home day so that she could come back when he was not busy. But the servant replied that his master could not be certain when he would be free next. Olympe left in a huff. A few months later, she published her play, and she gave her account of the incident in the preface, with a half-hearted attempt to hide Beaumarchais's identity through the use of initials.

I leave it to the Public to decide if M. C. de B . . . did well to punish my enthusiasm that compared him to the famous man [Voltaire], the defender of the oppressed, the support of widows and orphans. Moreover, I have lifted the weight off my heart that smothered it for four months; I tell him all this without artifice or witticisms. Perhaps he will reply; I could learn from him, better than anyone, the art of writing a Preface: I admit my ignorance; natural instinct is the sum of my science. Neither knowledge nor sex holds sway, for Writers express themselves through the weapon of their pens. Still, if all used them with this frankness, there would be fewer wicked people in Society: a cowardly calumniator's cleverness is applauded. If he lies wittily, everything is considered charming. Such are men and their dreadful principles.[11]

The Unexpected Marriage of Cherubino remained unperformed until Gouges decided to take it and others (her reputation with the Theatre Français never quite recovered from Beaumarchais's assault) to the provincial theatres.

Olympe's reputation was tarnished by Beaumarchais's petition to the theatre. Among the actors, some, such as François-René Molé, were definitely on her side and would have gladly performed her work. Others, such as Fleury, hated her with all the passion of sexism and misogyny. Fleury later argued that women who wrote were hardly women at all. They were 'reverse chrysalis', who'd lost their feminine charms without the hope of ever acquiring masculine strength and power. Olympe de Gouges, he said, had no talent of her own and 'felt faint' whenever she was not surrounded by those who did, authors and academicians, not because she wished to learn from them, he said, but to steal their light.[12]

Unfortunately, the theatres were not the only sources of calumnious gossip against Gouges. By the beginning of the Revolution, she had become more widely known through her political tracts, which were published in newspapers and posted as placards. People knew her name, and they were eager to belittle her and claim that they knew her. Part of her reputation was, we know from her biographer Guillois, that she was a courtesan and that her success, such as it was, came from relationships she had had with powerful men. She was linked, in particular, to the Duc d'Orléans, future Philippe Egalité, because she dedicated a work to him and asked his help to find a post for her son (which she paid a large sum for). There was, however, no particular evidence that she was romantically linked to him or that they were indeed at all close.[13]

Gouges seemed less troubled by such gossip than her inability to win over the theatres. In a 1791 text entitled 'Le Bon Sens François', she relates an incident where she overheard two men in a coach talking about her – without knowing she was sitting next to them.

Gouges interrupted the conversation:

'So you know her quite well?'
'Certainly. Her husband was a cook: she refuses to bear his name! No one knows who her father is. As to her works, not one word comes from her. She cannot read; they were written for her, affecting carelessness and ignorance in the style to make it seem that they are hers.'
'But I have seen her draft a piece in front of several witnesses, and she even won a bet by doing so.' Replied Olympe.
'Ah! Madam! The play was written for her in advance, and she was made to learn by heart.'
'Are you quite sure?'
'So sure that I am prepared to bet she could not do the same again in front of me. Besides, I know what I am talking about – I am one of her fortunate admirers.'

Despite the double insult – that she was a fake and this man's lover – Gouges kept her cool. As she left the car, she replied:

> 'Sir, I have listened to your idiotic claims with the calm of a philosopher, the courage of a man and the eye of an observer. I am this same Olympe de Gouges that you never did know and never could. Take advantage of the lesson I am giving you: men like you are common enough, but women like me are the work of several centuries.'[14]

4 Impact: 'Zamore and Mirza' and le Club des Amis des Noirs

Despite her troubles with the Parisian actors, Olympe's theatrical work was not without success. At any rate, it was influential. If she could not get them performed by the Paris companies, she could get them to read and perform them privately and in the provinces with her troupe. Olivier Blanc suggests that we have some reason to believe that sometime between the spring of 1786 and the autumn of 1787, Gouges left Paris to tour the provinces with her theatrical troupe.[15]

At the end of 1789, her play *Zamore and Mirza* was finally performed. Jacques-Pierre Brissot, who had just founded, together with the future Girondin minister Etienne Clavière, the abolitionist Société des Amis des Noirs, thought it would be good to have it performed and used his energy and influence with the actors. The actors gave in to Brissot but with bad grace. The play was put on at the end of December, the day before New Year's Eve, when Parisians would celebrate and then go home to their country homes. The theatre could give up a play if it did not make a certain sum over the first three days – so by deliberately choosing an opening date when Parisians would be otherwise engaged, the theatre doomed the play. The first night was extremely well attended, which gave Olympe some hope that the sum needed would be made. But the public was divided between those sympathetic to the cause defended by the play – and widely publicized by Brissot – and those against. Critiques could not judge whether the play was any good as there was too much noise to hear any of it. Fortunately, the play had been in print for several years, and the critics had read it. Unfortunately, good reviews did nothing to upturn the theatre's decision to give up the play after three nights of insufficient takings.

Olympe's luck turned afterwards – the position she had bought for her son from the Duc D'Orleans was rescinded, and she received very bad press for her play which she blamed on the anti-abolitionist sentiment which was rising in response to Brissot's club. In January, she published a response to this bad press, a letter addressed to the unnamed (or perhaps fictional) 'An American Champion', a plantation owner whose wealth depended on the continued existence of slavery. In that letter, Gouges defends herself against claims that she is encouraging violence against planters, saying that although she defends the Revolution as the fall of tyranny, she remains a patriot and a royalist. But also, she distances herself from Brissot's society:

> It is not the philosophers' cause, of the friends of negroes that I am defending here; it is my own. [. . .] You claim, Sir, that the friends of negroes have used a woman to provoke the colonists.

Perhaps she did feel used by Brissot, who had derived a great amount of publicity for his club and was then happy to let her play fall out of favour. Yet Olympe de Gouges is listed as a member of Brissot's society, and she carried on, through pamphlets, and a revision of *Zamore and Mirza* in 1792, to defend abolitionism.[16]

5 Impact: The Patriotic tax and early political writings

If Olympe's theatrical work put her name on the list of authors to watch, it is her political pamphleting that made her widely known. On 6 November 1788, her first political pamphlet was published on the front page of *Le Journal General de France*. The text of 'A letter to the people, or project for a patriotic purse, by a Citoyenne' is long – thirty-nine pages when it was printed as a pamphlet. But the pages of a newspaper were significantly bigger, and the print smaller, so the text could well have fitted on part of the front page. But the text is long indeed, and one wonders at readers' patience, especially as the proposal itself does not come till the end of the argument.

In the fall and winter of 1788, the weather was especially severe, the frost meant no wheat to be had for bread, and the people were dying of cold and hunger. The king was scrambling to find money in the light of a large debt he had inherited from his predecessors and made worse by his support of the American Revolution. Jacques Necker had been finance minister between 1777 and 1781, replacing Turgot after the disastrous flour wars, which witnessed violent riots over the price of bread. In 1781, the king dismissed Necker, blaming him for the American debt. In 1788, faced with impending financial disaster, the king called him back to his side, earning himself goodwill from the people who regarded Necker as fundamentally honest.

In the article's opening paragraphs, Olympe complains that human beings are often very unkind and unfair to each other and notes that the people of France have been unfair, in particular, to their king. Louis XVI, she says, is doing his best to deal with a deficit created by his great-grandfather and perpetuated by his father. He is doing his best because he has asked Necker to help. And the queen is also doing her part because she asked the king to call him back.

There follows a long paragraph on her own character, her virtue and abnegation, and the fact that were it not for her love of her country, she would be ending her days in quiet retirement (she was barely forty at the time and intent on growing her career as a writer).

To help the king relieve the terrible poverty and famine of so many, she says, we must first stop fighting him. The riots that she has witnessed in Paris and which the king forbade are counterproductive. A worker who spends his night rioting will not work the next day and not earn the little money he absolutely relies on to feed his family. But this, she goes on, will not be enough, and the king will be forced to demand more taxes, indiscriminately harming those who are already too poor to survive and turning them against him. So instead, Gouges proposes a voluntary tax, one to which all those who can should contribute.

> The King, to ease the financial crisis and to honour his commitments, asks for extra taxes. Parliament, sensing that the populace is facing ruin, refuses. These alternatives of demand and refusal aggravate the situation and do nothing to restore confidence, a voluntary tax . . . a voluntary tax in the name of the Nation would allow it to distinguish itself. The generous relief offered to those affected by the frost that devastated the fields at harvest time is proof positive that my system would work.

She calls for contributions from the produce merchants who have a few coins to spare every week if they do not spend it on drink and who will be pleased to have their names inscribed next to that of princes on the list of the country's benefactors. Then she calls the actors and other entertainers, who strike her as having far more than they need, and the wealthy women, who can save by buying two hats instead of eight per season. Those small sacrifices from all who can make them, proportionate to their means, she concludes, will help the country recover and avoid a dreaded civil war.

In June of the next year, when the meeting of the Estates-Generals was put on hold due to the death of the king and queen's eldest son, Olympe drafted a new pamphlet which she dedicated to the Third Estate, reminding them of her earlier project for a patriotic fund:

> No doubt, Gentlemen, the First Session of the Third-Order will be marked by a memorable action; you will reveal yourselves and manifest your union by the most august of all good intentions.
>
> You will open a patriotic Purse across the whole of France; the Sovereigns of fortune will make it their duty to contribute; following this example, all wealthy Citizens will bring offerings; even the avaricious will lighten their pockets, and the pennies that accumulate from this tax will be used to pay the extraordinary expenditure necessitated by the famine in the Kingdom's Villages.
>
> The countryside is deserted: the unhappy Peasant cannot survive in his humble shelter; today, pigswill is his only nourishment; what was once lavished on swine is now shared between man and beast.
>
> The People ask only for bread; they are even willing to pay for it with the sweat of their brows: at least let them eat it without watering it with tears.
>
> This patriotic tax, as I named it in my *Letter to the People,* now imposed by the Nation for its benefit, will engage all Citizens and procure immense sums sufficient to make bread available at six *liards* and two sols per pound.[17]

The three estates became one and swore to produce a constitution for France, so Olympe's project might have skipped their minds. A few months later, in September 1789, she writes: 'I became the butt of all satire last year after I presented my project for a Patriotic Tax to my fellow Citizens. My recommendations were far from being approved; rather, I received only insults or perfidious praise.'[18]

But in fact, her appeal did work, and on 7 September, a group of eleven women, all from artistic circles, went to the National Assembly and offered up their jewellery. These women, led by the artist, Madame Moitte, acknowledged that Olympe de Gouges's pamphlets had brought them here. Other women followed their example. Soon afterwards, two offices for collecting gifts to the nation from women were opened, one by the wife of a goldsmith, Madame Rigal, and the other by the daughter of a sculptor, Madame Pajou. Olympe responded with another pamphlet, 'Heroic action by a French woman or France saved by women'. She likened these women's actions to Roman matrons saving their city by donating their clothes and jewels (Figure 13).

> Virtuous women, female citizens who are enflamed by the saintly zeal of patriotism, it is to you that I address the feeble fruits of my talent. [. . .]

Figure 13 Patriotic gift, engraving, BnF.

There is one noble and efficacious method that I dare ask you to bring to mind: I can find none so apt to restore plenty and the national credit as the one the Roman Matrons used in a similar moment of distress. Rome, the seat of glory and virtue, if indeed they had such a place on earth, Rome, I say, weakened by costly wars was reaching its end. Public funds had run out; no resource or method was left to repulse the enemy about to swoop down upon her. It was women, then, who saved this City that men despaired of defending much longer. Generously ridding themselves of all vain and luxurious ornaments, they carried their jewellery to the public treasury; soon, thanks to this unexpected assistance, there was no shortage of arms or Soldiers. From that moment on, victory was determined, and the free Romans only thought to thank the Gods for having given them such virtuous mothers and wives.[19]

Her influence was recognized not just by the women who donated their excess wealth but by Mirabeau, who wrote, on 12 September, five days after the first donations, to thank her for the way she had advanced the Revolution.[20]

6 Impact: Louis's trial and the real threat to the republic

Before she herself became a victim of the guillotine, Olympe de Gouges played a role – albeit an unofficial one – in the trial and execution of the ex-king of France. While her interventions were at the time portrayed as royalist, what she was, in fact, arguing was that having Louis executed would be harmful to the republic.

The guillotine's first victim, Nicolas Jacques Pelletier, was a highway robber whose main distinction was to be condemned to death when the machine was ready to be tested on a live human being. A few months later, on 21 August 1792, Louis David Collonot d'Angremont, a royalist, was executed on the Place du Carousel (in front of the Palais of the Louvre, so inaccessible to the masses). This was the first political execution. Collonot d'Angremont was accused of trying to prevent the attack on the Tuileries on 10 August. After their attempted flight, the royal family had been brought back to the Parisian royal residence, where they could be more closely watched than at Versailles. Their security was ensured by their private army, the Swiss guards. On 10 August 1792, the people of Paris, led by the Commune de Paris and its leaders, Pétion, Danton, Robespierre, and the others elected to represent the twenty-eight participating 'sections' (the ancestors of the Parisian 'arrondissements'), stormed the Tuileries.[21] The royal family managed to escape, looking for safety in the rooms of the Assembly, but the Swiss guards were massacred.

The king, the queen and their children were removed to a tower in the Templars prison. The Trial of Louis Capet, previously Louis XVI, king of France, began on 10 December 1792, less than two months after the Assembly abolished the monarchy and four weeks after discovering a secret compartment in the Tuileries's rooms where the king had apparently stashed away riches.

Mary Wollstonecraft, who in December 1792 had only just arrived in Paris, claimed she saw Louis's carriage drive past on his way from the Temple to the Palais de Justice, where he was tried.

> I can scarcely tell you why, but an association of ideas made the tears flow insensibly from my eyes, when I saw Louis sitting, with more dignity than I expected from his character, in a hackney-coach, going to meet death, where so many of his race have triumphed. My fancy instantly brought Louis XIV before me, entering the capital with all his pomp, after one of the victories most flattering to his pride, only to see the sunshine of prosperity overshadowed by the sublime gloom of misery. (Wollstonecraft and Wardle 1979, 227)

On 15 January, the king was found guilty by an overwhelming majority of the 749 deputies. Two days later, the deputies were asked to vote for a penalty. Three hundred forty-six voted for the death penalty. Others, including Thomas Paine, honorary French citizen, voted for exile or imprisonment. But one citizen, who had not voted because she was not allowed to, argued against the death penalty. Olympe de Gouges started by offering herself as Louis's unofficial advocate on 16 December, arguing that while as a king, he had harmed the people of France by his very existence, once the monarchy had been abolished, he was no longer guilty.

> As King, I believe Louis to be in the wrong, but take away this proscribed title, and he ceases to be guilty in the eyes of the republic.
> Does Louis the Last threaten the republic more than his brothers or his son? His brothers are still united with the foreign powers and only work on their own behalf. Louis Capet's son is innocent and will survive his father.
> Louis Capet's greatest crime, it must be conceded, was to be born a king at a time when philosophy was silently laying the foundations of the republic.[22]

This proposal, written as a letter to the Convention, was then printed as a placard and distributed throughout Paris. The Convention disregarded the letter. Raymond de Sèze was given the job of defending Louis, and the argument that Gouges put forward was not considered. Louis Capet, stripped of his title, was still tried for high treason, that is, for actions he had performed while still king of France.

Gouges did not stop at this. On 18 January, after the king had been found guilty, but before his death had been voted, she put up another placard addressed to the Convention and to the people of Paris, entitled 'Decree of Death against Louis Capet, presented by Olympe de Gouges.'

> Louis dead will still enslave the Universe. Louis alive will break the chains of the Universe by smashing the sceptres of his equals. If they resist? Well! Let a noble despair immortalize us. It has been said, with reason, that our situation is neither like that of the English nor the Romans. I have a great example to offer posterity; here it is: Louis' son is innocent, but he could be a pretender to the crown, and I would like to deny him all pretension. Therefore I would like Louis, his wife, his children and all his family to be chained in a carriage and driven into the heart of our armies, between the enemy fire and our own artillery.[23]

Here Gouges is appealing to a fact about the workings of royalism: a king cannot die. The title-holder may die, but the title passes automatically to the next contender, without, even, the necessity of sacrament. The king's immortality was such an important precept that a Chancelier, when a monarch died, could not wear mourning. Bossuet captured the phenomenon thus in a famous sermon:

You die as men. Nevermind, you are gods, and even though you do die, your authority does not [. . .] The man dies, it is true; but the king, we say, does not: the image of God is immortal.[24]

However, the sentiment among those who voted for Louis's death was that he who had been the king of France ought to be tried as a man, not as a king. As Sèze, his official advocate said: 'In the current state of our ideas on equality, we want to see in a king nothing more than an ordinary man.' Gouges, however, noted the inconsistency of such a position, and it worried her. If Louis was an ordinary man, then he had no business being punished for crimes committed in his capacity as king. But if he was tried as a king, he could not be killed – the man may die but not the title. The inconsistency could be resolved – by saying that the execution of Louis was symbolic and that his real death was the abolition of monarchy a month earlier. But Gouges worried about the effect such an act would have at the time the republic was being created, a creation that itself requires its own carefully thought out symbolism if it is to succeed. In her last published work, in July 1793, so six months after the king's death, she raised the problem again, this time appealing to elements in the history of the Roman Republic to make her point that Louis the man ought not to have been put to death:

Oh French, what has caused your dissension? The death of the tyrant? Well, he is dead! All factions must fall with his head and, despite myself, your extravagant criminality recalls to my mind the panoply of great revolutions: I place it before your eyes; dare to observe it.

The Syracusans, having dethroned their tyrant told him to flee far from their shores or stay and become their equal; they allowed him to be master of his fate, the chap obeyed his sovereign and became a schoolteacher. The Roman republic chased out the Tarquins. In vain did they attempt to arm their tyrannical friends against a people who wanted freedom; they died itinerant vagabonds. The English, whom you try so hard to *mimic*, sent Charles I to the scaffold. This historic act of justice could not free them from tyranny, for the dying Charles perpetuated Royalty in England. Alas, oh French, such is our actual state: Louis Capet is dead, yet Louis Capet still reigns among us. Stop pretending it is not so. It is time for the mask to fall and for each of you to freely pronounce, openly, if you do or do not want a republic. It is time to put a stop to this cruel war that has only swallowed up your treasure and harvested the most brilliant of your young. Blood, alas, has flowed far too freely!

Spouting republicanism with hearts full of royalism, you arm region against region, little caring about the outcome of this bloody drama.

Despite seeing the thoughtlessness and imprudence of your horrible dissimulation, I still want to serve you and save you.[25]

Letting Louis Capet live would have made it clearer, she says, that he was no longer a king, no longer a threat to the republic – as no one individual can be. Having him executed shows a certain amount of doubt about whether his kingship is truly gone – a doubt which perpetuates itself since the title of king is transferable to the next king.

It is perhaps not surprising that this text led to Gouges's arrest and eventually to her execution. She calls the Paris Commune (Robespierre, Danton, Marat, etc) royalists at heart. She, who is known for her lack of learning, gives them a history lesson and suggests that they do not truly want a republic because they do not understand what it means. The strength of her conclusion and the confidence with which she makes it is symptomatic of what the women philosophers of the Revolution could be: confident players in the creation of the new order. It's also, unfortunately, symptomatic of the limitations of their roles, in that if they got too close to criticizing the leaders of the Revolution, they were simply cut down. Gouges was listened to as long as she proposed social reforms. When she became too obviously political, she was killed. Roland, although political from the start, sought to hide her role behind her position of a housewife. Grouchy's writings were published either anonymously or after the Terror, and – perhaps to protect her husband whose fate she did not come to know until 1795, several months after his death – she kept her criticisms of the Commune to herself – or at least out of print. She is, of course, the only one of the three to survive the Terror.

Speaking for herself

Marie-Jeanne Roland

Although her name comes up a lot in accounts of the French Revolution, very little is known about Marie-Jeanne Roland as a political philosopher. Yet she was an important political writer and actor of that period, acting behind the scenes of her husband's ministry and writing official documents under his name. She also left a copious number of pages of her unpublished writings that were unknown until after her death.

1 To write or not to write

1.1 A woman of action

In 1839 and 1840, Mary Wollstonecraft Shelley, the daughter of philosopher Mary Wollstonecraft, published her two-volume *Lives of the Most Eminent Literary and Scientific Men of France*. This was part of ten volumes of biographies published in the 133 volumes series of Dionysius Lardner: *Cabinet Cyclopaedia* (1829–46), a series designed to educate the English middle classes. In Shelley's *Famous French Men*, out of fifteen lives, three were on women: Madame de Sevigné, Madame de Stael and Madame Roland. Shelley's mother had known Roland in the final months of her life and, according to her husband Godwin, visited her in prison. They had much in common – both were writers, republicans and had a predilection for simple English manners over decadent French ones.

Shelley's take on Roland is disappointing. She focuses on her virtues as a wife and mother and suggests that these were perhaps not real virtues because they developed from a position of subservience:

> She was her husband's friend, companion, amanuensis; fearful of the temptations of the world, she gave herself up to labour; she soon became absolutely necessary to him at every moment, and in all the incidents of

his life; her servitude was thus sealed; now and then it caused a sigh; but the holy sense of duty reconciled her to every inconvenience.

Shelley was probably not aware – because it was not revealed until the early twentieth century – that Roland had all but left her husband before she went to prison. She was in love with their friend and colleague François Buzot, a young Girondin who was six years younger than her, while her husband was twenty years her senior. François was also married, and neither he nor Marie-Jeanne had any intention of breaking up their marriages. Nonetheless, Marie-Jeanne told Jean-Marie that she no longer loved him and that she loved François instead. The letters she wrote her lover while she was in prison and he in hiding in the south of France are both full of romance and political enthusiasm – she encourages him to stay free so that he may still have a chance of saving the republic. This did not happen as Jean-Marie Roland and François Buzot both committed suicide shortly after Marie-Jeanne's death. Roland impaled himself with a cane-sword he carried with him. Buzot shot himself and his friend Pétion. Their bodies were found in the woods near St Emilion, eaten by wolves.

Another way in which Shelley misrepresents Roland is by portraying her as an activist, rather than a writer or a philosopher:

> Her fame rests even on higher and noble grounds than that of those who toil with brain for the instruction of their fellow creatures. She acted. What she wrote is more the emanation of the active principle, which, pent in a prison, betook itself to the only implement, the pen, left to wield, than an exertion of the reflective portion of the mind.[1]

In 1840, only one of the collections of Roland's works had been published: Champagneux's three volumes. This had not been translated, and Shelley perhaps may be excused for thinking that Roland had only written her *Memoirs*. She might also be forgiven (or maybe not) for not paying attention to Marie-Jeanne's own description of her lifelong writing activities. It is likely that only part of the *Memoirs* was translated at that time and that Shelley was better acquainted with Roland's reputation as a ringleader, or *Egeria* of the Girondists than she was with her autobiography as a writer, and a philosopher, preoccupied with questions about the meaning of liberty and equality, and the role women in building and maintaining a flourishing republic.

Whatever Shelley's reasons, the picture she drew of Marie-Jeanne Roland was not accurate. Marie-Jeanne Roland was a writer – producing hundreds of skillfully crafted letters in which she presents philosophical and political reflections as well as essays and travel journals.

1.2 Silence and the women

One reason why Marie-Jeanne Roland did not become known as a writer until her *Memoirs* were published after her death is that she did not like to write in her own name. Her reasons had very little to do with whether she felt it was appropriate for women to be authors and everything to do with the harm to her reputation she knew to expect if she did become known to the public as an author:

> Never have I had the slightest temptation of becoming an author; very early, I saw that any woman who would earn this title lost much more than she gained. Men do not like her, and her own sex criticizes her: if her works are bad, she is mocked, and quite rightly. If they are good, they are taken from her. If one is forced to recognize that she did produce the best part of it, her character, her morals, her behaviour, and her talents are dissected to the extent that her wit's reputation can be balanced against the weight given to her weaknesses.[2]

At the same time as she was protecting her reputation, Roland took care to make it clear to others – whether she meant it or not, it is not always easy to tell – that she knew her place and that she recognized how inappropriate it would be for her to seek fame by publishing work in her name:

> I know full well, Sir, that *silence is woman's ornament*; the Greeks thought so, and Mrs Dacier wrote it, and despite our century's general opposition to this sort of morality, three-quarters of sensible men, husbands especially, still live by it.[3]

The anecdote Roland alludes to is reported as follows: Anne Dacier, when asked to autograph the album of a learned German traveller, seeing the names of some very famous writers and scientists above hers, chose, out of modesty, or perhaps because she could not think what to say, to copy this infamous verse from Sophocles (*Encyclopedia*, Paris: Panckoucke, 1741). This was the same verse that had been cited by Aristotle in his *Ethics* when distinguishing male and female virtues, and that later found its way to the Catholic Church via Aristotle's translator Thomas Aquinas. Anne Dacier, a classical scholar of note, showed the depth of her knowledge by citing the original Sophocles. Dacier (1651–1720) had collaborated first with her father and then with her husband on several translations of Greek and Roman texts at the beginning of the eighteenth century – some of her work was collaborative. Still, she was the sole author of translations of Sappho, Marcus Aurelius and the Iliad. She became famous for her translation of Homer and her preface to it, which was translated into English.[4] Roland was well aware of Dacier's success as an author. When, as a child, she'd read Plutarch's *Parallel Lives*, she used the nine-volume integral translation produced by Anne and André Dacier in 1721. So surely there must have been a part of irony in Roland's retelling of that story?

2 Philosophical writings – Essays and competition

Between the ages of twenty-two and twenty-four, Marie-Jeanne Roland was keeping home for her widowed father. She spent as much time as she could in her bedroom, writing to the friends she had made while at convent school, Sophie and Henriette Cannet, and trying her hand at writing essays in philosophy.

Her working habits are outlined in a letter she wrote to Sophie Cannet in December 1776. The letter is dated 25 December, one in the morning:

> You might find it strange that I should write always at the first hour. Let me tell you something about my daily life, which will give you insight into how I spend my time. I never get up, this time of year, before nine. I spend my morning with the housework. In the afternoon, I do needlework, and I dream, building everything I fancy in my mind, poems, arguments, projects, etc. In the evening, I usually read till dinnertime, which is uncertain because it depends on when the master [her father] comes home. He is out at all times except meal times, without telling me or caring for any of his affairs, and too often leaves me to deal with those who come to do business with him. He usually gets home at half-past nine, but sometimes ten or later. Supper is soon over since when there are few dishes, one eats fast, and where there is no conversation, not even a feast will last long. In between dishes, I try to start conversations, but my attempts are foiled by his offhand replies. I struggle to hold a thread, but though I do my best, it is always in vain. Eventually, time passes, and it is eleven. My father collapses on his bed, and I go to my room, where I write for two or three hours.[5]

After a day spent reading and thinking alone, two or three hours writing time is far from negligible. During these two years, she wrote hundreds of letters and several essays, several of which were published a few years after her death by her close friend Louis Champagneux, including at least two on political philosophy: 'Rêverie Politique' (1776), and 'De la liberté' (1778).[6] She sent these out for comments to friends and friends of friends who were writers, and she was pleased with some of the comments she got. At that stage in her life, her failure to publish was more of a function of her not knowing how to go about it than the matter of principle in became for her later. She wanted to be read and discussed.

She did, in fact, prepare a text specifically for publication. In 1777, the Académie of Besançon proposed an essay competition with the following question: 'How can educating women contribute to the improvement of men?' Such competitions were common at the time, a way both for the provincial academies to make themselves known throughout the country and for fledging writers to get published. The Paris competitions were of course more prestigious, but all were advertised in national publications as well as in their local papers, and writers could find out what questions were posed in *Le Mercure galant/Mercure de France*, *La France littéraire*, *Les Nouvelles de la République des lettres et des arts*, the *Journal de Paris*, *L'Avant-coureur*, Linguet's *Annales politiques, civiles et littéraires*, les *Mémoires secrets*.

Competitions were especially rife during the decades preceding the Revolution, with 357 between 1770 and 1779, that is, more than thirty-five per year.[7] As well as Jean-Jacques Rousseau, whose career as a writer took off when he won the Academy of Dijon competition with his *Discourse on the Arts and Sciences* in 1749, many famous names of that time entered and won academic competitions such as Jean-Francois Marmontel, novelist and friend of Olympe de Gouge, Jacques-Pierre Brissot, the Abbé Gregoire and Jean-Paul Marat. The motivation for entering was often financial – the winner would take home a tidy sum and professional advancement. The winner was announced in national newspapers and then published, and this was a way of getting one's name known in the Republic of Letters and at court or in politics.

But what could have been Marie-Jeanne Roland's motivation, given that she submitted her piece anonymously? It could have been the money that appealed to her, as she was not yet married, and the absence of a decent dowry, together with her increasingly untrustworthy and unsavoury father, proved to be an obstacle. However, her letters on the topic denote a fevered anticipation and hope that has to be about more than money. Roland had always read philosophy, always written and whenever she could, she would correspond with real philosophers, people who had once met Rousseau, people who had published obscure books. But most of the time, her only correspondents were the Cannet sisters, whose philosophical pretensions were only as high as their friend Marie-Jeanne chose to pretend they were. Marie-Jeanne was desperate to become part of a world where her ideas would be heard, debated and praised by real philosophers. But she was not born or yet married into a world that would allow her to host a salon or have her work published or performed. She was the unmarried daughter of a widowed artisan who spent his spare time at the tavern.

Marie-Jeanne's first mention of her academic project to her friend Sophie Cannet is very brief and almost blustery – look at all the crazy things I'm trying to do, she seems to say – none of them will come to anything!

14 January 1777
I have never found myself with so many ongoing projects and so little disposition to work at them. I am a bit like those project makers who never perform and always plan. I have begun an academic discourse: ahem! That is no small affair; I have sketched out a metaphysical dissertation, I am mapping out in my head a little philosophical novel. My mind is wandering from one to the others, caressing them in turns and then forgetting them, and does not move forward in anything.[8]

The metaphysical dissertation may have become one of the essays that Champagneux published posthumously, and the novel seems to have stayed in her head. There is no further mention of it. But the discourse, which she worked on for three months and kept a secret for five, was finished. In April, she sent it to the Academy, and in June, still waiting for an answer, she told her friend about it:

21 June 1777
Would you be surprised if, as a reply to your jokes, I were to send you the academic laurels that I had picked behind your back? No such thing happened, and I jest. I would have to wait too long to let it be a surprise; I would not have the courage to keep quiet about my efforts for six months, for instance. We will know in October, through a public announcement, what happened on 1 May at the Academy of Besancon. Do you think that if I had sent a discourse at that time that I would be able to stop myself telling you then? It is hard not to say to one's friend, the custodian of one's follies. So I will tell you that a certain paper fell into my hands by chance a few months ago, and I saw the advertisement of the said Academy, offering this question: 'How could educating women contribute to the improvement of men?' I was struck, I dreamt, I wrote, amidst all the worries that my mind is perpetually subject to. I made a little discourse, and without showing it, without discussing it with anyone at all, I sent it off in April, under, by the way, the anonymity that suits me and that I want to keep whatever happens. I am ignorant of the decision that was made, and I do not hope for much. The Republic of Letters would have to be poor in clever skilful members for there not

to better answers than mine on such an important question. If I get the chance, I will send you this little scribbling.[9]

So what was in the essay?[10] And what does it tell us about Marie-Jeanne as a young philosopher? The argument Marie-Jeanne presented in her academic piece was at the same time conservative and innovative. First, she points out that in the best constitutions, women must remain in the home. Women's position in the home, she says, is crucial to the good development of society, as witnessed by republican societies, because domestic life is the best environment not only for happiness but also for learning. But more than simply holding up the moral backbone of the republic, women, she says, make it possible for society to come into existence:

> Women are, therefore, by their natural destination, appointed to make men better; only they can give birth to the affections that bring them closer to one another [. . .] We saw in the impressions they produce the origins of society and of all the goods that make it desirable, and in the contempt for their power or forgetting of their rights, a source of the horrors that tear it apart and disfigure it.[11]

The picture of domesticity she presents is one in which women, though confined to the home, are nonetheless central to the functioning of the nation and the source of republican virtue. A woman, she wrote, should be sweet and compassionate so as to inspire love and virtue; patient and hardworking so as to keep the household running smoothly.[12] This picture of domesticity is presented in a republican context: she makes it clear early on in the text that the ideal society is the Roman or Spartan republics. Women in such societies, she tells us, were confined to their home, and their virtuous presence there helped maintain the general happiness of the republic.

> More sedentary, more enclosed ordinarily in republican governments, left to domestic tasks, nourished by this patriotism which elevates the soul and sentiments, they laboured towards the citizen's happiness and that of the state, through the peace and order reigning inside their homes, and the care they take to cultivate in their children the germs of courage and virtues that must be perpetuated as well as liberty. Focused on their families, they could not set any other ends for themselves than that of being cherished for the qualities that are needed in the home and that they would be recommended for. The love of little things, seeking vain distinctions, is a feature only of superficial societies, where each brings pretensions devoid of real merit to sustain them.[13]

The very idea of a family modelled on the classical republican one, separate from the state, but at the same time nurturing the virtues that are required for it to carry on is precisely what Rousseau proposes in *The New Heloise* and *Emile*. And in both these texts, women are at the same time essential to domestic success and willingly subservient to male authority. Marie-Jeanne's concern that the family must take care not to fall victim to the temptations of 'superficial societies' is what Rousseau advises in the *New Heloise*, concerning the rural families who are Julie's neighbours:

> On this principle, they make a point here, and even more at Étange, of contributing as much as they can to rendering the peasants' condition easy, without ever helping them to leave it. The best off and the poorest have equally the mania of sending their children into the cities, some to study and one day become Important, the others to enter domestic service and relieve their parents of their upkeep. [. . .] They show them all the error of these prejudices, the corruption of children, the abandonment of fathers, and the continual risks to life, fortune, and morals, where a hundred perish for one who succeeds.[14]

Another aspect of Rousseau's thought on the family that clearly resonates with Marie-Jeanne Roland's academic essay is the idea that gender roles are complementary. In the opening of the *Discourse on Political Economy*, Rousseau tells us that as far as domestic economy is concerned, fathers must be in charge of the family because 'the father is physically stronger than his children'.[15] In the *New Heloise*, this is expressed in terms of complementarity. St Preux, when he visits the Wolmars, describes himself as basking in the glow of 'living reason and sensible virtue'. Wolmar is the embodiment of reason, as is shown by his wise discourses on their domestic arrangements. Julie, 'who never had any rule but her heart and could not have a surer one' implements these arrangements, led by her instincts and her complete trust in her husband's wisdom.

Marie-Jeanne Roland was influenced by this picture of the family as preserving society and the thought that women's nature is such that they must be dependent on men if they are to be part of society. Yet, some of her pronouncements on women's nature are difficult to take seriously and suggest that she was either not serious about them herself or that she failed to reconcile certain central contradictions between what she regarded as the respectable position and her own observations. For instance, she tells us that 'weak in their constitution, the great operations and abstract ideas are equally strange to them; anything requiring a powerful effort or deep meditation is beyond them' at the same time as she is herself competing with the best minds in the country in a highly abstract enterprise.[16] Nor are her claims to physical weakness any more credible than those of inability to handle abstraction. Her requirements for a woman include physically demanding work – such as washing the family's linen (a back-breaking activity if ever there was any) – not to mention the one which, she tells us in her academic essay, gives rise to women's intimate understanding of physical suffering: pregnancy and birth, and which again, requires a non-negligible amount of physical exertion.

These contradictions, taken together with her later writings recording both her lived experience and her advice for other women, suggest that the picture she draws here is more than just a youthful interpretation of Rousseau. Instead, we see the seeds of a more mature and complex position. For one thing, although she takes from Rousseau the idea that women, by nature, are destined to make men love them, she does not think that this is due to weakness and bodily charms. On the contrary, she says, women inspire love because they are themselves compassionate, and this compassion comes to them because they are used to suffering – through giving birth – and therefore understand more intimately than men what it is to be in pain and to need support from others.[17] What we may choose to retain from Roland's youthful essay – as it reflects something we find in her later writings – is the thought that politics begin at home, in the sense not only that political society is not possible without homes, but also that the welfare of society depends on what happens in the home, and how those running the homes are treated and allowed to behave.

Though Marie-Jeanne Roland does agree that families provide the environment in which civic virtues are taught and preserved, her view is more substantial than that. She believes that those who seek to determine and bring about the common good need to study families before anything else:

> Our century's legislators try to create a general good from which particular happiness will follow; I strongly fear that they may have put the cart before the horse. It would be in better conformity with nature, and perhaps reason, to study carefully what domestic happiness consists in, and to ensure that every individual has it, so that common happiness is composed of the happiness of each, and so that all should be interested in maintaining the order that procured it for them.[18]

Roland's argument relies on the premise that domestic good is desirable for all – in that one can only find happiness within a home or family. More than contentment, what the home provides is the right environment for individuals to discover what their happiness consists in. It follows that not only do homes enable the growth of happiness but also that the state cannot determine what happiness is without studying individuals in their homes.

The essays in political philosophy Marie-Jeanne published between 1776 and 1778 reflect, to a large extent, the republican outlook she adopts in the Besançon piece. But as they are not primarily destined to be about women's education or their place in society, the arguments are more straightforward and less inclined to contradictions. In the 1778 piece, in which she attempts to define what she calls political, metaphysical and philosophical liberty – Roland wrote that 'The rule of the general will is the only one that can maintain public happiness: from the moment power grants independence to some parts of the state [but not others], corruption is introduced and will manifest itself by enslaving the oppressed.'[19] The rhetoric of slavery is also present in her academic essay, where it is used as a critique of any sort of despotism, even when that despotism is not actually active – the slightest deviation from the rule of the people, she says, could lead to slavery. Conversely, she writes in the Academy essay, no republic is perfect if it allows slavery, whether Helots in Sparta or anywhere in the world where women are in (metaphorical) chains, 'the rust of barbarity covers their proud masters and ruins them together. The poisoned breath of despotism destroys virtue in the bud.'[20]

In her 1776 piece, Roland addresses the idea that liberty is non-domination: 'And now domination through fear is established; it is the resort of despotic governments: does it ever produce anything good? Alas! It can only feed bitterness, lead to despair and bury all virtues.'[21] Roland believes that it is not possible to become virtuous when one is dominated – whether by a political despot or a private master. So much so that it comes as a surprise that in her 1778 essay, she does not conclude that women cannot be virtuous while they are dominated by men. Her thought on women's place in society was still evolving, and the contradictions are rife.

> True courage only belongs to free men. What can those who are nothing apart from their master's will be capable of? And to what obligations will he, who has to fancy himself of a superior nature to those they command, feel bound?[22]

It seems as though it would have taken very few steps for Roland to conclude both that as a woman, she could not be courageous if she was bound to obey men and that men who thought they were by nature superior to her were not likely to be virtuous either. Does this constitute a reason why we should take her pronouncements with a pinch of salt? Was she unsure of where she stood, as a woman and a philosopher, on the debate about women's roles in society? There are no real clues, one way or the other in her writings, but what is perhaps significant is the evolution of her own output, from early philosophical writings as a single woman to helping her husband as a newly married woman, to taking matters in her hands in her revolutionary writings. It may look, from that perspective, that Marie-Jeanne tried to abide by Rousseau's ideal of a virtuous wife but decided in the end that it was not viable.

3 Peace writings: The encyclopedia of textile and other writings

In her biography of Roland, Shelley emphasizes the extent to which Marie-Jeanne's intellect was put to the service of her husband's political career. This was true, but before Jean-Marie Roland had a political career, he had scholarly ambitions, and these were realized in great part through his wife's willingness to write and conduct research for him.

3.1 Textile, botany and tactful editing: Writing the academic career of Jean-Marie Roland

In August 1782, Marie-Jeanne was in Amiens, while her husband, travelling for business, was in Paris. Jean-Marie Roland de la Platière was inspector of Commerce and Manufactures, had his office in Amiens. The couple lived there for the first four years of their marriage (1780–84), and their daughter was born there in October 1781. When Jean-Marie was promoted to general inspector, the family moved to Lyon, and Marie-Jeanne lived in the family's nearby country home, Le Clos. The couple had gotten together as aspiring writers, and both intended to carry on writing once they were married. For Jean-Marie, this meant trying to get published, one way or another, and being voted in for his accomplishments in an Academy. For Marie-Jeanne, it mainly meant helping her husband write.

Between 1783 and 1789, the couple were much occupied working on an encyclopedia of textile manufacture for which Roland was the editor. This project, an *Encyclopedia of Methods*, was the last encyclopedic project of eighteenth-century France, completing the collection started by Diderot and continued by the Academy of Sciences. The collection, which was intended to go up to fifty-one volumes, counted over 200 by the time it was completed in 1832. Two series within the collection were dedicated to the arts and crafts. Roland had negotiated a contract with the publisher Pancoucke to write the series dedicated to the manufacture of arts and crafts. Three volumes on textiles were published between 1784 and 1790, covering all aspects of textile manufacture, botany, chemistry, history of technological innovations and so on.[23]

Marie-Jeanne's letters for the year 1783 show that she was busy gathering materials – books, encyclopedic articles – and experimenting with botany, growing plants in her garden and exchanging specimens with their friend the botanist Bosc d'Antic. Together with her husband, she was also drafting letters to the publisher, Pancoucke and writing and revising plans for the several volumes of the work they were contracted to do.

3.2 Productivity eighteenth-century style

Between 1780 and 1789, although she no longer wrote philosophy, Marie-Jeanne Roland wrote, gardened, but also set up several homes for herself and her family, doing much of the work of maintaining them herself. The Rolands were well off enough to have some servants, but not so many that the woman of the house could remain idle. Moreover, she also decided that she would keep her daughter with her when she was born, rather than send her out to a wet nurse as was then still common. Marie-Jeanne had gone to a wet nurse for the first two years of her life, but her mother had lived in Paris and lost several children before Marie-Jeanne's birth, so perhaps had thought it healthier that her daughter should spend her infant years in the countryside. Marie-Jeanne did not have that excuse as she lived far away from the city's pollution when Eudora was born.

Moreover, as a disciple of Rousseau, she wanted to be the one who fed her daughter. During a lot of that time, she was alone at home, as Jean-Marie Roland's position as inspector of manufactures meant he had to travel quite a lot. Marie-Jeanne herself travelled, spending several months between Versailles and Paris in 1784, trying to better her husband's position. Marie-Jeanne never complained that she was too busy – her letters show that she enjoyed running her home as much as the research and writing and that she was only depressed when she was ill and could not do either. Whenever I despair about not having enough time to work on some writing project or other, I think of Marie-Jeanne Roland and her rigorous productivity regime.

> Those who know how to organize their work always have leisure time. It is those that do nothing that lack the time to do anything. Moreover, it is not surprising that women who spend their time in useless visiting and who think they are poorly dressed if they have not spent a great deal of time at their mirror find their days too long through boredom and

too short for their duties. But I have seen those we call good housewives become unbearable to the world and even their husbands through tiresome attention to little things.

A wife and mother, she says, ought to be well enough organized that she can fulfil her housewifely duties and do something useful with her life, such as write philosophy. She has firm ideas as to what those housewifely duties consist of:

> I expect a woman to keep her family's linen and clothing in good order, to feed her children, order, or herself cook dinner, this without talking about it, keeping her mind free and ordering her time so that she can talk of something else, and to please, at last, through her mood, as well as the charms of her sex.

But all this, she tells the reader of her *Memoirs*, ought not to take up so much of one's time that it would stop us from being productive writers. Even at her busiest, she never spent more than two hours a day doing housework.

> Although I have found myself in a number of different situations, nothing was ever done in my home without my having ordered it. And when those cares occupied me the most, they never took up more than two hours in a day.[24]

Obviously, two hours a day is still quite a lot of time for a woman to spend on housework if she also works full time. And for a woman whose primary work is to care for her children, unless she is rich enough to contract out most of her childcare duties, she will still not have a lot of leisure. Roland's advice is very much dated – it applies to the eighteenth-century middle classes. It also comes from a place of high privilege – working or lower-middle-class women often had to work late in the evenings to make enough to feed their families. They needed to send their children to wet nurses and cleaned their house whenever they could, but having a schedule allowing for private study was certainly not on their agenda. But the general spirit of Marie-Jeanne's advice, that unless one lives in dire circumstances, a little bit of organization and awareness of how one spends one time goes a long way towards making time for activities more valuable and more interesting than housework.

4 Political writings – The letters, the memoirs, the ministry's business

Although she became a political thinker at a very early age – eight, if we believe her *Memoirs*, being the age she discovered Plutarch and decided she too was a republican – Marie-Jeanne did not become interested in politics until the Revolution. Part of the reason seems to be that she had lost all illusions that the world would ever be ruled in a just manner. In 1783, she wrote to her friend Champagneux:

> Virtue, liberty are only to be found in the hearts of a small number of decent people; to hell with the others and all the thrones in the world!
> [. . .] I stay away from politics [. . .], and all I can talk about are the dogs that wake me, the birds that console for not being asleep, the cherry trees that grow under my windows and the cows that chew the grass in the yard.[25]

But from the very start of the Revolution, when she was recovering from pneumonia and writing powerful letters to her friends in Paris, advising and admonishing as to what had to be done, Marie-Jeanne became fully involved. She wrote letters and newspapers articles and helped Jean-Marie find a position for himself that would allow them to participate more fully. As soon as it became possible, that is when the commune of Lyon asked him to petition the Assembly to add their debt to the Royal debt, the Rolands moved to Paris. In June 1791, she wrote to her friend Bancal explaining her transformation:

> While peace lasted, I kept myself to the tranquil role and the kind of influence that seems to me proper for my sex. But when the King's departure declared war, it struck me that we must all devote ourselves without reserve; I went and joined the Fraternal Societies, persuaded that zeal and right-thinking could sometimes be very useful in times of crisis. I cannot keep to my home and am visiting all my acquaintances to excite us for the greatest actions.[26]

4.1 Women and politics

Even though she decided to become involved in politics in the summer of 1789, Marie-Jeanne Roland was always ambivalent about women's political participation, in very much the same way as she was about women authors. But again, in the same way, her reluctance to approve of women's political participation was very much a fear of the consequences rather than the result of any principled objection to women doing politics. So, for instance, she feared that Madame de Stael's influence would turn the Revolution into a joke, or a story of gallantry:

We hear tales of Madame de Stael that she is always at the Assembly, where she has admirers to whom she sends notes from the gallery to encourage them to vote for patriotic motions. They say that the Spanish ambassador has reproached her for this at her father's [Necker] table. You cannot imagine how much weight the aristocrats give such nonsense – born from their own brains, perhaps. But they would show up the Assembly as led by a handful of scatterbrains, excited and fired up by a dozen women.[27]

Roland bore this critique of Stael in mind when she moved to Paris and set up a salon in their small apartment, and later at the palace they moved to when her husband was made minister. Her gatherings were very different to those of her aristocratic contemporaries such as Stael, who hosted the whole of revolutionary Paris in their rich salons, serving champagne and entertaining with music and literature, Marie-Jeanne Roland had the reputation of being a rather prim hostess. The only drink she served was sugared water, and she invited only her husband's colleagues, all men. She would sit apart from the men, sewing at her table, listening quietly.

Why were women not invited to Roland's circle? She did not think that other women were worthless nor that they should not participate in politics. She was friends with and visited other Girondin women, such as Madame Pétion, Madame Brissot and Louise Keralio-Robert. She had been to Madame Helvetius's in Auteuil. She even frequented the English salon of Helen Maria Williams, and through her, she met and befriended Mary Wollstonecraft.

Marie-Jeanne's objection to inviting women to her political salon was not that she wished them to stay out of political debates. She had two distinct reasons for not inviting women. The first was that she had witnessed salons turn disreputable because men such as Danton or Dumouriez would bring their mistresses along, or even sometimes prostitutes. She did not want her home to become the scene of debauchery when it could instead be a haven of philosophy in which the new republic was nurtured. Second, Marie-Jeanne believed that the public was not yet ready to accept politicized women. She worried that the Girondin's enemies would use women's presence in her salon as a way of ridiculing them as they had done with Madame de Stael in 1789. On 6 April 1791, she justified herself on this point to Bancal:

Our customs do not yet permit women to show themselves publically. They must inspire goodness, ignite all the sentiments that are useful to the nation, but not appear to participate in political work. They will only be able to act openly once every French man will have earned their freedom. Until then, our lightness, our poor morals would turn to ridicule everything they would seek to accomplish and thereby destroy all the advantage that was to result from it.[28]

Marie-Jeanne Roland's insistence on being the only woman in her salon, although it may have kept the debates more focused and sober than they might have been, gave her enemies plenty to gossip about. Camilles Desmoulins, who was never in the Roland's home, remarked that as she was neither young nor beautiful, she must have been very well versed in the art of seduction in order to influence all of the Girondins.[29] Nor did it prevent other politicians from worrying about women's influence in politics. Danton was scornful of what he saw as Marie-Jeanne's influence on her husband – rather than what they would have described as their joint agency. And when Roland was named minister of the interior for the second time, Danton warned the Convention:

> If you offer the Ministry back to Roland, be sure to offer it to his wife as well. Everyone knows he was not alone in his Ministry as I was in mine. The nation needs ministers who can act without being led by their wife.[30]

Given how Marie-Jeanne Roland herself described her participation, mostly as a listener, either in her salon or at the clubs, it is hard to see that Danto could be justified. And indeed, he is probably unfair to Jean-Marie Roland, portraying him as a puppet moved by his ambitious wife. Danton, it seems, like many of his contemporaries, finds it hard to picture a couple working together as equals towards jointly valued goals. And yet, even though Marie-Jeanne had to work in the background and Jean-Marie had to be the face of the partnership, this is precisely what the Rolands did.

4.2 Letters to Brissot and *Le Patriote François*

The Rolands spent the year following the fall of the Bastille between Le Clos and Lyon, continuing work on the *Encyclopedia*, participating in the Parisian debate through constant letters to their friends Bosc, Bancal, Lanthenas and especially Jacques-Pierre Brissot, who edited *Le Patriote François*. Their part in the debate was to observe how Lyon and the countryside had been affected by the Revolution. This lasted a year until the end of 1790 when Jean-Marie Roland was made a municipal officer for Lyon. The commune decided to send him to Paris to represent them at the Assembly and petition for the city's debt to be ascribed as the king's debt.

Marie-Jeanne Roland prided herself on fully taking part in the country life, picking grapes during the grapes harvest, and mixing with her peasant neighbours on equal and easy terms (or so she thought, anyway). The weeks following the onset of the Revolution were to test her attitude. In July 1789, within six days of the fall of the Bastille, the rumour spread through France that brigands, or perhaps the English, were sacking the country. People everywhere panicked, and soon, the peasants who'd armed themselves to fight this fictitious enemy were added to the list of those fear.

Rich people were advised to lock up their homes, leave the countryside and come to Paris, or any large city, where they would be safer. Marie-Jeanne, who'd spent the previous few months in bed in Lyon nursing her husband's pneumonia, rushed back to Le Clos to see if it was in danger. She saw that it was not and came back to Lyon to nurse her husband, who was taking longer than her to recover from the same illness. She reflected on this experience in a letter published anonymously by Brissot:

> Everyone tells me to move to the city – I will not. I have not hurt anybody in the country, I have neither land nor title, I have only done good to my neighbours. Were they to become ungrateful, so what? I will pay the interest of the advantages that my position gave me over them. But I will not do them the injury of believing it before the event, and even if I were to fall victim to a few bandits, I would not despair of the *res publica*, as do the cowards who call for a counter-revolution because a few houses were burnt down.[31]

Brissot published several of Marie-Jeanne Roland's letters, as clearly he saw her as a valuable reporter on what was happening in Lyon. In particular, she saw herself as a necessary corrective to the misconceptions passed on by the city officials. On 13 July 1790, she reacted to an article published by Brissot, authored by one of her husband's political colleagues in Lyon:

> I believe you, Sir, so entitled to the truth, through your principles and character that I regard it as a duty to make it known to you or to put you in a position to find it when it seems as though it has escaped you. [. . .]
>
> You depicted the people of Lyon as carried away by the most violent insurrection, setting gates on fire, intimidating the municipality, gathered in loud assemblies, and committing excesses that deserve to be repressed forcibly – and they really will be; [. . .]
>
> You appear to have forgotten that a people who complain against harms it still feels always behave in an inflammatory manner; [. . .] you have forgotten that exaggerating wrongs angers the guilty instead of

calming them; that as a matter of fact, a people only ever does wrong out of ignorance, its interest is always just because it is the interest of the greatest number, that therefore we much teach when the people stray, and never attribute blame lightly, especially where there is suffering.

[. . .] It is not yet certain the people of Lyon did set fire to anything. Some have told me it was not so, others that they did not, in fact, see anything. If, so close to the place, I could not make up my mind, how could you, one hundred *lieues* away?[32]

Marie-Jeanne Roland is not only providing a better journalistic service to Brissot here, but she also seems to regard herself as a protector of the *res publica*. She is worried, rightly, that the principles of the new republic will not be applied to the people outside of Paris, that these will not be regarded as worthy of rights and liberties, and that the Parisians will be quick to condemn the peasants as underserving brutes (very much as they were during the Great Fear in July 1789). This is the misconception Marie-Jeanne Roland wants to correct, and the message she wants to send to Paris is that the people of the provinces are those whose rights are being drafted and that they should not be forgotten.

The Rolands eventually did leave Lyon and come up to Paris in February 1791, not out of fear, but because they wanted to participate in the political events that were taking place in the Capital. Unfortunately, this did little to increase their safety, as they both died in 1793.

4.3 'They are going to ruin our constitution': On drafting the *Rights of Man*

What did Marie-Jeanne contribute specifically to the Revolution? Her *Memoirs* – particularly her historical notes and portraits – certainly contributed to the historical representation of the years between the fall of the Bastille and the Girondins. Her letters to Brissot in 1789 contributed to creating a picture of revolutionary France that was not entirely Parisian. The writing she did on behalf of her husband at the ministry, in particular, perhaps, drafting his letter of demission to the king in 1791, may well have contributed to the end of monarchy and the birth of the republic. But it is in the private letters she wrote about the drafting of the constitution and the *Rights of Man* that we can best understand how the philosophical ideas she had developed in her youth on liberty and equality could be applied to the new republic. She wrote these letters in 1789 and 1790.

During the summer of 1789, Marie-Jeanne Roland and her husband were suffering from pneumonia, and during the fall of the Bastille, she was in bed, able to read and write, but not much more. At the end of July, when she heard of the Great Fear, she was well enough to leave Lyon and rush to her family home of Le Clos. But reassured that nothing was happening, she came back to Lyon to nurse her husband and write to Brissot, denouncing the cowardice of those who are hiding from their peasant neighbours. This letter came out anonymously in *Le Patriote Francais* on 12 August, and Marie-Jeanne Roland is described as a highly enlightened and really energetic woman.

What did Brissot mean by energetic? This comes out most clearly in the letters she wrote from her sickbed in the two weeks following the fall of the Bastille. To her friend Bosc d'Antic, who was in Paris with two other close associates of the Rolands, Lanthenas and Brissot, she wrote the following:

> No, you are not free; no one is yet. The public trust has been betrayed. Letters are intercepted. You complain of my silence, and yet I write with every post. It is true that I no longer offer up news of our personal affairs: but who is the traitor, nowadays, who has any other than those of the nation? It is true that I have written you more vigorously than you've acted. But if you are not careful, you will have done nothing but raise your shields. [. . .]
>
> You are but children, and your enthusiasm is but a flash in the pan. And if the National Assembly does not hold a proper trial of two illustrious heads, or unless some generous Decius kills them, you are fucked.[33],[34]
>
> If this letter does not reach you, let the cowards reading it blush when they find out that it is by a woman, and let them tremble when they realize that she has the power to breed the enthusiasm of a hundred, and they in turn of millions.[35]

Bosc d'Antic was a thirty-year-old botanist who had just founded the first French Linnean society. As a close friend of the Rolands and a collaborator on the encyclopedia of textile manufacture, he was also a republican and keen for France to change. In 1791, he became secretary of the Jacobin's club. It is not clear what role he played in 1789. In another letter, Marie-Jeanne mentions 'his districts' – these were the old parishes, which under the Commune became 'sections'. This may lead us to suppose that he had been elected at the Assembly of 20 June 1789, sworn to give France a constitution. His name does not feature, however, among the 300 Parisian members. Certainly, however, he and Roland's two other correspondents at the time, Lanthenas and Brissot, were active and influential. And they listened to her, asking for her advice and opinion on what to do, in Brissot's case even going so far as publishing her letters in *Le Patriote Francois*.

Marie-Jeanne was worried that the Revolution would peter out because her friends did not act firmly enough. But her worries were also specific, namely that the members of the Assembly would make a mess of the constitution and the *Declaration of the Rights of Man*. Her principal fear was that the members would agree on a few paragraphs and leave it at that. The constitution, and the *Rights*, she said, could only be drafted by the Assembly, but it should then be circulated throughout France, read and approved by all, revised if necessary before it became final.

> In the name of God, do not declare that the National Assembly has the power to fix the Constitution irrevocably; the project, when it is drafted, must be sent to all the provinces to be adapted, modified, approved by the constituents.
>
> The Assembly is made up of constitutional members who do not have the right to settle our fate. This right belongs to the people who can neither give it up nor delegate it.[36]

When the drafting of the constitution fails to fulfil these conditions, she writes again to Bosc:

> They are going to ruin our Constitution just as they spoiled the *Declaration*, which is incomplete and erroneous. Will I not see a petition demanding a revision of the whole thing? [...] It's up to you, Parisians, to set the example. Let a wise and vigorous speech show the Assembly that you know your rights, that you want to keep them and are prepared to fight for them and that you demand that they be recognized![37]

One might wonder why she cared so much that these texts be put to the vote throughout the country, given that she herself would not be able to vote. Only men over twenty-five and inscribed on the tax list were allowed the vote. But what she was asking, which makes sense, was that the texts should be read and discussed by all. That everyone concerned should have a say – not in the sense of placing a paper in a ballot, but by being put in a position where they could state their views, their worries and hear those of others. Marie-Jeanne Roland was already a proponent of what turned out to be so important during the early years of the Revolution – the clubs where citizens, men or women, voters or not, met to debate events. The Republic of Letters, with a few cultured individuals exchanging ideas on the state of the world, was no longer enough. What Marie-Jeanne wanted was a republic of the people, that is, for the people to be consulted, but also for them to be informed and generally part of the decision processes that would eventually affect them. Perhaps she knew how the decision to abolish feudal privileges had been taken – not on 4 August at the Assembly, as history records, but the night before, in the salon of an aristocratic member, when he and his friends discussed what should be done about the Great Fear. Had the mood been different, had they had less wine, perhaps, the decision could well have been the repression of the peasants rather than a move towards equality. Marie-Jeanne was weary of the Revolution staying in the hands of a few privileged boys and men. She wants everyone, including herself, to be involved.

4.4 Ghost writing and coming out of anonymity

Marie-Jeanne Roland, we saw, was reluctant to publish in her own name. But she was not reluctant to be published, either anonymously (as she was in Brissot's paper), or under her husband's name, 'helping' him with his work:

> For twelve years of my life, I worked alongside my husband as I ate because one was as natural to me as the other. If some part of his work was cited because it was found to be more gracefully written; if some academic trifle such as he liked to send out was accepted by one of the learned societies he was a member of, I was happy for him, and I did not take particular notice whether the piece was one of mine. And often, he ended up persuading himself that he had been on a particularly good streak when he'd written this or that passage, which in fact came from my pen. [. . .][38]

When her husband was named minister of the interior, Marie-Jeanne kept on writing for him. She found it easy because 'she loved her country' and was 'enthusiastic for liberty'. Only once, she tells us, did she allow herself to be amused by her ghostwriting when she penned a letter from the minister to the Pope, demanding the release of a group of French artists imprisoned in Rome.

By the time Marie-Jeanne was in prison, writing her memoirs, private and political, she decided that anonymity was not for her after all:

> Had I been going to live, I would have had, I believe, only one temptation left:
> that of writing the annals of this century, and to be the Macaulay of my country.[39]

Before her arrest, Marie-Jeanne Roland had been reading the *History of England* in eight volumes by Catharine Macaulay. Brissot had lent her the books. He knew Macaulay from his travels to England and had corresponded with her. Macaulay was extremely popular among the Gironde. Mirabeau had translated an abbreviated *History*, and it was well known for its philosophical republican approach to history. Marie-Jeanne may also have been aware of Macaulay's other, more recent book, her *Letters on Education* (1790). Macaulay argued that girls and boys should receive the same education, a text that so greatly impressed Mary Wollstonecraft that, had Macaulay not died the following year, the *Vindication of the Rights of Woman* would have been dedicated to her. At l'Abbaye, Marie-Jeanne lamented that she did not have the next volume of Macaulay's *History*. She could not ask for it – the order for the arrest of the Girondins had just been issued, and Brissot was on his way to l'Abbaye himself. When Marie-Jeanne was briefly released from prison, it was Brissot who occupied her cell next. So short of reading Macaulay, Marie-Jeanne did the very next best thing she could think of: attempted to write a republican history of the Revolution. This meant that, like Macaulay, she would not only report the events of the (very recent) past but also order them in a way that reflected philosophical republican principles, highlighting how actions and policies helped free France from tyranny – or not. In fact, her *Historical Notices*, at least, the version we now have – one version was lost when the person she had entrusted to, Helen Maria Williams, burned them for fear of being caught with them – are a lot more anecdotal and a lot less philosophical than her *Personal Memoirs*. The latter corresponds to Rousseau's autobiographical writings more than they do to Macaulay, and they do outline Marie-Jeanne Roland's republican principles and how she felt the Revolution succeeded or failed in implementing them. Her letters, we saw, do the same on a case by case basis. Had Marie-Jeanne Roland come out of prison alive, and had she had the leisure to go over her various writings from that period, there is no doubt that she could have become the Macaulay of France.

Working together

Sophie de Grouchy

1 Translator

For a long time, Sophie de Grouchy was best known as the translator of Adam Smith. Her French translation of his *Theory of Moral Sentiments* was the first authoritative one and remained in print until the late twentieth century. Grouchy began translating early on in her career. At convent finishing school, she translated to improve her command of languages. When her aunt visited her, she reported to Madame de Grouchy that her niece was 'translating by herself Tasso and the sublime Young. Her eyes', she added, 'are tormenting her. The only remedy is rest. But how can we force idleness on a soul as passionate and active as my niece's?'[1]

The translation from Torquato Tasso would have been from the sixteenth-century Italian poem, *Jerusalem Delivered*. This had been translated into French in 1774, already, and was well known through various theatrical and musical adaptations, but Sophie, at that time, was probably translating to improve her skills and to read the text – which had some republican overtones and strong female heroines – more closely.

The 'sublime Young' must have been the poet Edward Young, whose complaints were enormously popular and had already been translated into French.[2] Young had influenced Burke, but also Goethe, who claimed that he learned English by reading Young.

When Grouchy married Condorcet two years after coming out of convent school, her proficiency in spoken as well as written English enabled her to set up a popular international salon at the Hotel des Monnaies where her husband's work took them. Jefferson, Paine and others who were less comfortable with the French language came there to discuss their works and other English writers.

Later, when she worked with him on the journal *Le Républicain*, Grouchy likely translated works by Thomas Paine. Did she translate anything else? Almost certainly – good translators were scarce, and she had a reputation as a republican sympathizer. We do not know for certain whether she did. Probably there were some tracts that she hastily translated before somebody else could comment on it. There is one text that one would very much like her to have translated – but for which, unfortunately, there is absolutely no evidence: Mary Wollstonecraft's *Vindication of the Rights of Woman*.

The translation came out in May 1792, before Mary Wollstonecraft set out for Paris, where she was to act as a war journalist for her London publisher Joseph Johnson.

Just as she set off on her journey, Wollstonecraft wrote to her sister: 'I shall be introduced to many people, my book has been translated and praised in some popular prints.'

The translation in question, *La Défense des Droits des Femmes*, was published anonymously. Recent scholarship suggests that it might have been translated by a Félicité Brissot, and annotated by her husband, Jacques-Pierre.[3] This is entirely plausible as we know that the Girondins did defend women's rights. Brissot was an ally to all three of the women in this book, and instrumental in having Macaulay's work recognized in France. But even if she did not translate it, Grouchy would have found an interest in it. Condorcet – perhaps with his wife's help – had published an article arguing that women should be given equal political rights to men in 1791. With its emphasis on educational reform, Wollstonecraft's book would have struck the couple as important and topical.[4]

2 Editor

On 21 June 1791, the king of France, his wife and children escaped from Paris dressed as a bourgeois family in the hope of reaching Austria. For some, this meant it might be time to let go of the monarchy and let France become a republic. At lunch at the Pétions' with Brissot and Robespierre, the Rolands discussed what the Assembly should do next. Someone brought up the idea of France becoming a republic, and, according to Marie-Jeanne Roland: 'Robespierre with his habitual grimace, and biting his nails asked "What *is* a Republic?"'

The idea that France could become a republic was far from widely spread then. Most of the revolutionaries still believed that France should remain a monarchy of some sort – a constitutional monarchy, perhaps, if Louis could be persuaded to behave, or one with Louis's cousin, Louis-Philippe d'Orléans, in charge. When Sieyès had written his provocative and widely distributed pamphlet, 'What Is the Third Estate?' he had suggested a republic. But like Montesquieu before him, he only meant by this the rule of law or a government that was aimed at the good of all, rather than at the interest of the ruling class. For Sieyès or Montesquieu, this did not mean that France should necessarily become a democracy. The king could be persuaded to rule according to the law and pursue the public interest rather than his own.

In this context, Robespierre's snide comment is perhaps less puzzling: the idea of what a republic in France would look like was not yet clear. As well as Sieyès's Montesquian proposal, there were conflicting models to look to. The small European Republics, based to some extent on the Roman model, were not deemed suitable for a large country such as France. Nor was it clear that the people of the Dutch or Genoese Republics were significantly better off than those of monarchic France. The Dutch rulers were wealthy merchants and the Genoese aristocrats. Their model – the Roman Republic, was not a democracy but a mixed constitutional system of government that relied on slavery to free citizens to participate in politics. Eighteenth-century republics, if they did not enslave people in their own lands, relied on slavery abroad and a poor local population to produce food and other necessities. These were just as excluded from the political decision process as the French poor were.

The same lunch at the Pétions, Marie-Jeanne claimed, was also when the project of a republican society and the journal *Le Républicain* was first imagined. Given that Brissot was present, he was likely the person who brought it up. Brissot was already editing a journal, *Le Patriote François*, and was very active in publishing. But it is less clear that this was when the idea was first formulated, given that none of the editors of the journal was in fact present – Brissot merely arranged for printing and advertising. Perhaps Brissot mentioned that he had discussed it with others and the Pétions and their friends run away with the ideas? Or perhaps Marie-Jeanne simply wanted to take credit from Condorcet – as she did not like him much resenting the ease he drew from his aristocratic position and scorning what she perceived as his cowardice.

Notwithstanding the general confusion surrounding the concept – a confusion that the paper intended to clear – it was still dangerous to talk about republics. It is not, then, surprising that the authors and editors of *Le Républicain* did not advertise their participation. The names most clearly associated with the paper were Condorcet, Brissot, Thomas Paine (whose contributions were translated by Sophie), Achille Duchatelet, Etienne Dumont and Sophie de Grouchy.[5]

Thomas Paine was already celebrated in France for his 1776 pamphlet arguing that America should become independent and set up an egalitarian government, *Common Sense*. His *Rights of Man*, published the same year he came to Paris, also put him in favour of the Girondins, who were the most extreme of the revolutionary factions at the time because they were the only ones to consider republicanism to be a real possibility for France. Paine had received American citizenship for his support of the American Revolution. In the summer of 1792, he was granted French citizenship along with Jeremy Bentham, Anarchasis Cloots, Thomas Clarkson, George Washington and a few others – all men. Five months later, Paine used his citizenship to vote at the trial of Louis XVI. He voted that the ex-king should be detained and banished from France when peace came. Paine was not an extremist, and although he wanted to see the monarchy abolished, he did not support the Terror. His opposition to the king's death helped cement his fate as a friend of the Girondist, and at the end of 1793, he was taken to the Luxemburg prison, where he stayed until November 1794. Even in prison, he continued to dissent, arguing in a new book, *The Age of Reason* that the atheism of his friends the Girondins was unreasonable and rather extreme, proposing that they adopt instead his Quaker-inspired brand of Deism.

Despite his involvement in the French Revolution, Paine did not speak the language, or perhaps, he understood French but did not like to speak it and preferred to have an interpreter with him at all times. This was not a problem when he visited the Condorcets as both Nicolas and Sophie spoke English, as did several of their friends, including Brissot and Etienne Dumont.

Another of the contributors to the journal *Le Républicain*, Etienne Dumont, like Sophie, was a translator. Swiss-born, he divided his time between Geneva, Paris and London, where he wrote speeches and translated for famous politicians and philosophers. Dumont worked in London with Jeremy Bentham, translating his works into French. From his correspondence with Grouchy, we know that Dumont was close to the Dissenters in London and Birmingham, associating with Joseph Priestley. Dumont had a reputation as an honest man and a good man. He was also fairly conservative, morally speaking, and, as we will see, Sophie suffered from his silent censure as much as she admired his character.

In Paris, Dumont was especially close to Mirabeau, and by his own account, he either wrote or revised a number of the speeches Mirabeau was famous for. Through Mirabeau, he met the young Achille Duchatelet, who had fought for the American Revolution at seventeen, and during the French Revolution, served under Dumouriez. Duchatelet was arrested in October 1793, at the same time as the twenty-two Girondists, but he was not executed together with them. Instead, he poisoned himself in prison in April 1794. Dumont describes him as a 'young fool of an aristocrat' but seems to have shared Mirabeau's fondness of him. It was Duchatelet who introduced Dumont to the Condorcets.

The creation of the journal was preceded by the formation of a republican club or society. Marie-Jeanne Roland, writing to Bancal in July 1791, reported that the opening of the society in question had caused quite a scandal at the Assembly:

> You know that a new republican society was formed, and they are to bring out a paper, the title of which advertises its goals and principles. Payne is at the head of it. He wrote the content of the pamphlet that is pasted everywhere this morning as a sort of notice. Malouet denounces this pamphlet as deserving of the harshest punishment. The worst thunder was at the Assembly, and it is only by flattering its love for the monarchy and hatred of republicanism that we succeeded in convincing it that whatever the opinion, it should be let to run free.

The pamphlet in question was also the very first text published by *Le Républicain*. It was used to advertise the new journal widely: as Marie-Jeanne Roland said, it was distributed and pasted throughout Paris, and the next day, published in Brissot's journal, *Le Patriote François*. Although Paine wrote the text – it was signed by Duchatelet. As Paine wrote in English, the text also had to be translated. Duchatelet first approached Dumont, who refused, on the grounds that he felt it was foolhardy to advertise oneself as a republican without the backing of the Assembly and that it was not a good idea for Duchatelet to sign his name to a text by Paine. He describes the enterprise as one between 'an American and a young fool from the French aristocracy who put themselves forward to change the face of France'.[6] Given that Dumont refused to participate, Duchatelet had no choice but to turn to the Condorcets. Sophie, an experienced translator, was probably the one who ended up with the job (Condorcet's English was passable, but not up to a work of philosophical translation).

Despite refusing to co-operate with what he saw as Duchatelet's hare-brained scheme, Dumont seems to have agreed, in the first instance, to give his support to *Le Républicain,* but decided to withdraw it, upon receiving the first four issues (which turned out to be the only issues). He explains why in his *Memoirs*.

> I had written a piece for that republican journal he writes in his memoirs. It was published in the first two issues, but in my absence, after my departure and with alterations that were unfaithful. These alterations were additions and suppressions injurious towards the King, which did not conform to either my opinions or my character.[7]

In any case, he continues, it was his opinion that now the king had returned to Paris, the time for Republicanism in France had passed. The French would have to make do with a king and a constitution. Dumont wrote in his *Memoirs* that he conveyed these thoughts to two friends. The first was Etienne Clavière, a banker from Geneva, who sympathized with the Girondins and committed suicide in prison in October 1792. The second was Sophie de Grouchy, whom Dumont mentions several times when he talks of his involvement with *Le Républicain*.

If we are worried that Dumont's *Memoirs* are not reliable – it's not clear that anyone would want to tell the whole truth about their revolutionary activities in the aftermath of the Terror – we may turn to four letters that Sophie wrote to him between the summer of 1791 and the spring of 1792. The first discusses *Le Républicain*, but the others discuss either her own writing (she asked him to comment on an early draft of the *Letters on Sympathy* – he seems not to have obliged, at least at first) or the political situation in France (the disputes between factions and who wrote what).

Grouchy's correspondence with Dumont also tells us something about the early demise of the journal after only four issues and barely one summer. The decision to end the journal was taken after the Champ de Mars massacre. Sophie was there with her daughter when the army, led by Lafayette, shot at the crowds, causing many deaths.

Duchatelet and Grouchy both wrote to Dumont explaining why the journal had to close. According to Duchatelet, the suspension of the journal was only temporary, against his judgement and entirely Condorcet's doing.[8] Grouchy tried to shift the responsibility away from her husband and said that 'Brissot was forced to suspend the publication of *Le Républicain* because they could not bear to have any of its contributors locked up, even temporarily, and that people are being arrested, under the pretext relative to the Champs de Mars affair'.[9] Later, Condorcet himself wrote about how profoundly shocked he had been by the fact that his wife and daughter had been present during the attack. Marie-Jeanne Roland thought Condorcet a coward – and maybe this is the episode that prompted this judgement. But for a loving husband and father, the benefits of printing more issues of a publication that had already made its point, and made it well, was not worth putting his family at risk.[10]

3 Political journalist

Sophie de Grouchy's participation in the journal did not end with editing and translating. Two of the articles, both unsigned, may be attributed to her. These attributions cannot be made categorically, and because we have so little material from Sophie de Grouchy, it is not possible to use stylometry, the statistical analysis of literary style. Nonetheless, there is good stylistic and anecdotal evidence that it was she who penned these pieces.

The first one is very short. *A Letter from a Young Mechanic* announces itself as from a young mechanical inventor who is a student of the famous Vaucanson. The article proposes that a set of automata be built to replace the royal family and its entourage.[11] Even though such machines are expensive, it says, they will cost a fraction of what the French people are spending on their actual king. And what's more, the mechanical king, far from being a tyrant, will raise its pen and sign everything its government wants it to! Jacques Vaucanson, the putative teacher of the fictional author, was a famous inventor and one whose inventions Condorcet had praised in his works as an example of the sort of technical activity that could be just as inspirational as theories.[12] Automata were generally meant to be humorous rather than impressive scientific inventions or serious art. Vaucanson had created many impressive moving statues, including that of a musician who could play twelve songs on two sorts of flutes. But his most celebrated piece was a copper duck who could pick grain, swallow it and defecate them. Vaucanson claimed the duck could also digest the grain – this, however, was discovered to be untrue in an autopsy conducted in 1844 – the 'excrement' was stored in a different part of the duck's body, not metabolized from the grain it swallowed. Given this, the idea of the king and his family being replaced by automata was not simply insulting in that it reduced them to impotent machines. But it was also a cruel joke at their expense: the royal family, though they were used to perform their private functions in public, did not do so on demand!

Although Condorcet was a great admirer of Vaucanson, it is unlikely that he wrote the 'Letter': the style of the text is very unlike his. Condorcet could write lyrically, and he could appeal to his readers' emotions as well as to their reason, but rarely to their sense of humour or ridicule. Sophie de Grouchy, although she too was reputed for her seriousness, was not above the use of sarcasm when it was for a good cause and when it came at the expense of those she saw as the oppressors. Whereas Condorcet tried to remain respectful, even when he was highly critical, his wife had no qualms about being sometimes downright insulting. And indeed, the *A Letter from a Young Mechanic is* insulting: it reduces the function of the royal family to no more than a shiny display and a few symbolic gestures that an automated doll could fulfil just as well, and it associates them with a defecating duck!

A recurrent theme both in the *A Letter from a Young Mechanic* and the second piece, *Observations on the King's Letter,* is that of the financial cost of maintaining a royal family. Grouchy, who had lived for some years in the Hotel des Monnaies, while Condorcet was the inspector general of the Monnaie de Paris under Necker, had some knowledge of economics.

Condorcet himself advocated a liberal economy, much closer to his previous superior, Turgot, a physiocrat who believed in a *laissez-faire* economy. Together Turgot and Condorcet had attempted in 1774 to solve the problem of the growing price of bread by letting the farmers decide how they sold their flour instead of controlling the market. Unfortunately, their reform was followed by a draught and later severe hail storms so that whatever grain had managed to push through the dry soil was destroyed before it could be harvested. The king, rather than following Turgot's advice and wait for his reforms to have their effect – after all, no amount of reform could change the weather – sacked Turgot and gave his job to Necker. This did nothing to prevent the people from starving, and France found itself in the midst of the 'flour wars' with riots in Paris and pillages in the countryside by people who could no longer afford to buy bread or who spent their entire income on it, leaving nothing for clothes or housing. The price of bread never truly recovered from the mid-seventies' crisis, but it plummeted again just before the Revolution when the flour was coarse and black as well as scarce, and beggars were leaving the countryside to come to Paris, which was already full of starving people.

At the time of Turgot's dismissal, Condorcet asked to be let go too, but the king, perhaps sensing that he would not keep Necker long and that it would be good to have some continuity in the country's finances, refused.

Given the importance that the price of bread and the conditions of life of the farmers who produced the flour played at the beginning of the Revolution, it is no surprise that economic considerations should have played a role in Condorcet's political arguments. And this concern is also visible in both of Sophie's articles in *Le Républicain*. One of the main arguments in the *Letter from a Young Mechanic* is that the cost in taxes for a mechanical royal family would represent a fraction of the cost of the actual king. The author estimates the cost of producing a court of two hundred machines and the annual cost of maintaining the machines at half a denier per person. This was very little indeed. A casual labourer made 12 sous per day. This was also the cost of six pounds of bread (an amount barely sufficient to feed a family of three for a few days). A denier was one-twelfth of a sou, so half a denier per year would represent very little indeed for even the poorest of the French.

The *Observations on the King's Letter* is very different from the short and humorous *Letter from a Young Mechanic*. It is a long and very critical piece on the king and the mechanisms of his government. This article, it seems, was originally to be written by Dumont, but when the king and his family were arrested and brought back to Paris, he had withdrawn it. Dumont, however, had left a set of notes at the Condorcets' and these notes somehow turned up in the form of a two-part article in issues two and three of the journal.

Dumont, we saw, complained about this in his memoirs on the grounds that the alteration to his draft 'were injurious towards the King' and 'did not conform to either [his] opinion or character'.[13]

The *Observations on the King's Letter*, in two parts, is a commentary both of the king's speech at the opening of the meeting of the Estates-General, in the summer of 1789, and on a *Letter to the Nation*, that Louis had left behind when he attempted to leave France, in which he complained about the ungratefulness of the French people, whose happiness, he said, had always been his priority. The *Letter* had been published, and all members of *Le Républicain* had read it. Nearly all of them had also been present at the opening ceremony of the estates meeting which the *Observations* also discuss. Condorcet and Grouchy were there as spectators, as Condorcet had tried and failed to get elected as a representative. Dumont and Duchastellet were there to support Mirabeau, a representative member not of the Aristocracy but of the Third Estate. Brissot was there in his role as publicist – his journal, *Le Patriote Français* was just beginning. He had published one issue and was wanted by the king's police for it, so he would have had to keep a low profile. But what better hiding place than in the crowds coming to Versailles for the meeting!? Thomas Paine alone was absent – he was still in England and would not travel to France until the following year. So all but Paine would have been in a position to rewrite Dumont's text.

There is good stylistic evidence that the person who 'rewrote' Dumont's piece was, in fact, Sophie. In particular, an image she uses in her *Letters on Sympathy* can be found in the article, that of the king (and monarchy) as a rattle designed to amuse the immature French people, to distract them from the fact that they are not free. But more than that, the *Observations* seem to be a continuation of the economic theme of the 'Letter', which denote a preoccupation with the financial aspect of liberty that was not Paine's nor Duchastellet's, and could have been Dumont – had Dumont not denied being the author.

The costliness of kings, which is central to the 'Letter', is also present in the 'Observations on the King's Letter'. In the first part of the text, the author observes:

> King's palaces are out of proportion with human nature; the greats of nations fulfil the vilest offices for them; citizens vilify themselves in their presence and become mere subjects; our imagination turns them into gods to adore, and to who we sacrifice human blood. For the brilliance of the throne, two hundred thousand men cut each other's throats. The crown's honour is the scourge of nations, and when kings talk of their glory, the earth is covered in mourning.

But here, the cost is not just financial: it is also moral – subjects lose status and dignity – and physical – lives are wasted under a king because those that would serve the nation through their greatness become mere lackeys and those that would provide the workforce, kill each other.

After decrying the waste that the king's palace represents, the author of the 'Observations' argues that it is absurd to impoverish a nation merely to enrich its representative. The king's requirement for the continuation of his liste civile – that is an annual sum funded by taxes to support the royal family, and their entourage, and in particular Marie-Antoinette and her favourites, in luxury – means for the author, that the king is not willing to act as a paid servant of the state. And yet, that is precisely what he ought to be: 'A king is paid like any public employee; the principle that directs the cost of the salary is the usefulness of the work and the costs related to the office.'[14] Instead, the king wishes to carry on ignoring the nation's interest. The financial abuse is held up as a symptom here of the political unfitness.

4 Moral philosopher

When *Le Républicain* closed down, Sophie did not stop writing. Perhaps she had written before – we only know of her translations. In any case, in the spring of 1792, she had a complete draft of her *Letters on Sympathy* and fragments of a piece of fiction. By 1794, we know that she had also written at least one other text on moral philosophy. Unfortunately, we only have her *Letters on Sympathy*, which she eventually published in 1798, alongside a translation of Adam Smith's *Theory of Moral Sentiments*. Why did she wait so long to publish? And what happened to the other works?

As far as the first question is concerned, we have one clue as to why she published when she did. According to her daughter, she needed the money. In the last couple of years of the eighteenth century, Sophie was still fighting to retrieve her assets, which had been confiscated when her husband had been made an outlaw in the autumn of 1793. She made a living selling portraits she painted, but that was not enough to feed herself, her daughter, sister and other dependents. So she turned back to translation, picking a work by a highly popular author, which had been hitherto badly translated. This would sell. Her eight letters on sympathy were a commentary on Smith's *Theory of Moral Sentiments*, so it seemed apt to publish them together with her translation. It was also an excellent opportunity to publish her own work without making too much of a fuss about it, and perhaps, like Marie-Jeanne Roland, Sophie de Grouchy worried about the effect on a woman's reputation publishing could have. This would explain why she had not previously published her

Letters, even though they were written six years before they were published, and Condorcet thought enough of them to recommend them to his daughter in his *Testament*.[15]

In his *Theory of Moral Sentiments*, Smith argues that morality arises from our reactive attitudes and sympathy but that moral principles can only be developed through reason to become a system of moral rules. Neither reason nor sentiment by themselves can give us morality, Smith says. The *Letters on Sympathy* engage with Smith's philosophical analysis of sympathy, but more than that, they bring a valuable political perspective on Smith's theory. Grouchy wants to know how understanding the mechanisms of sympathy could help rebuild the social and political institutions of France after the Revolution.

Grouchy is enthusiastic about Smith's views – she agrees with him that moral sentiments and judgements can be derived from sympathy and that we need to develop our rational abilities to render this capacity at all useful. But she takes issue with certain aspects of them. He has not, she feels, dug sufficiently deep to understand what sympathy is: he has noted 'its existence, and its principal effects', but not gone back to 'its first cause, and show, at last, why sympathy is the property of every sensible being susceptible of reflection'.[16] She traces this first cause back to infanthood and the very physical relationship of a baby with its nurse. Grouchy does not talk about mothers there. She is careful to distinguish between the physical relationship – skin on skin, feeding – and the moral one – the duty a mother may have to nurture her children and the duties of the children to love and respect their mothers. She differs from her contemporaries, Marie-Jeanne Roland and Mary Wollstonecraft, who thought that an infant needed to be fed by his mother to flourish morally. Grouchy is looking for a physical trigger to the sensations of pleasure and pain that will eventually give rise to sentiments of sympathy. This trigger has to be common to all human beings to account for the ubiquitous presence of sympathy in human societies. Every baby that survives to an age where they may develop sentiments will have been fed by another human, and there will have been no previous universal experience suited to stimulate the sensations that can lead to these sentiments. Grouchy not only traces sympathy back to its origins, but also her account is distinctly naturalistic.

Although the *Letters* read more like a treatise than a record of correspondence (there is in fact only one letter writer involved), each chapter is set out as a letter to someone addressed as C***, announcing the topic of discussion, linking it to the previous one, and at the end, drawing out the conclusions to be taken forward to the next chapter. C*** is also an excuse for considering objections to Grouchy's arguments, with many paragraphs starting with formulas such as

'No doubt you will tell me, my Dear C***'. So C*** is very much a philosophical interlocutor, the Platonic touchstone to Sophie's Socrates.

So who is C***?

The obvious assumption is that it is Sophie's husband, Condorcet.

But there are reasons why this is probably not true. First, her husband was dead by the time the *Letters* were prepared for publication. Second, if Sophie were to record a fake dialogue with a real person, she would probably have picked someone she actually corresponded with – in 1791 and 1792, when the letters were presumably written, Sophie and her husband were not apart long enough to correspond.

But there were at least two more Cs in Sophie's life, to whom she was very close, with whom she did correspond and who were still alive when the *Letters* were published.

They were her sister Charlotte and their close friend, Pierre-George Cabanis. Of the two, C*** cannot be Charlotte, as 'My Dear C***' in French is '*Mon Cher C****', which is masculine. So Cabanis is more likely.

Cabanis, as it happens, did correspond with Grouchy on topics very close to her *Letters*, on physiology, a materialist science aiming to understand human beings through their bodily organs. In 1802, Cabanis published his *Rapports du Physique et du Moral de l'Homme*, in which he explored the relations between bodies and morality, discussing, for instance, the influence of weather and digestion on mood and decision-making. According to Grouchy's biographer Guillois, Cabanis corresponded with Sophie and had long discussions with her on the subject. Physiology is also central to the *Letters on Sympathy*, as Sophie argues that our moral feelings are born out of the physiological response that ties a newborn to the person that nurses her and holds her.

Although Cabanis and Grouchy were close, there is no reason to suppose they were romantically involved. In fact, it was with Sophie's sister, Charlotte that Cabanis was involved. He and Charlotte de Grouchy became lovers during the Revolution, and in 1796, they were married.

Cabanis had come to the Capital as a boy to study medicine and had met the influential saloniere, Madame Helvetius, there. The two had become very close, so that he considered her his adoptive mother. A medical doctor by profession, he did not practise regularly. But he did practise and had been Mirabeau's physician during his final illness. Some say that he was a spy, not a doctor. But Cabanis was much more interested in how science and philosophy could bring about political reform. It was he who gave Condorcet a dose of poison to hide in a ring, calling it 'the brother's bread'. And this poison, in some accounts of Condorcet's death, is what he took to kill himself when he was captured in March 1794.

Although Grouchy's *Letters on Sympathy* were only published in 1798, we have evidence that they were drafted several years earlier, perhaps as early as 1790, and definitely by 1792. The evidence for the earlier draft comes to us via Charles Roederer, who notes both in his *Memoirs* and in his review of Grouchy's translation of Smith the existence of an earlier manuscript which he had seen in the hands of Sieyès in 1789 or 1790.[17] It's possible that a draft existed then, but Roederer's hesitation about the date, and the fact that he refers to it nine years later, should make us suspect that his memory is not all that reliable.

The evidence we have for the *Letters* having already existed in some form in 1792 is more reliable as it comes from an exchange between Grouchy and Dumont in which Sophie sent her friend some manuscripts and asked him for feedback.

> Here are the inchoate manuscripts I mentioned to M.Dumont, or rather the indecipherable sketches. I have lost the eighth letter on sympathy. As to the other mess, it contains as yet only a few weak traces of development of character and passions, and that is not yet strengthened by any of the circumstances that make a novel interesting. One of the main causes of my laziness when it comes to working on it is 1) difficulty in obtaining good advice (will some arrive from overseas!) 2) the fear of not having the means of executing the ideas, which, in other hands could enrich the subject matter, but in mine, will probably make it less.
>
> If M. Dumont were to dine here this Tuesday, I would be in a better position to take heed of his advice, but also, they might be more honest if they are in writing. There is no need, I know, to ask him to speak to no-one of that which I send him.[18]

Dumont did not reply, and either he did not come to dinner, or the conversation did not turn to Sophie's writings, as her following letter read:

> You are a ruthless man towards unfortunate authors, especially towards such a pitiful female author. What would it have cost you to tell me whether what you'd seen from my drafts deserved to be developed? I give you my word you would have had no grief from it.[19]

Why did Dumont not reply? Perhaps, despite his friendship with Sophie, he was not entirely persuaded that women should waste their time in literary pursuits or that their contributions would be particularly good. Or perhaps he did not wish to spend his leisure time doing for free what he did for a living! Fortunately, the *Letters on Sympathy* were already fully drafted, and six years later, she published them, together with her translation of Smith's *Theory of Moral Sentiments*. Unfortunately, we know nothing of the novel. Was she discouraged by Dumont's refusal to talk about it, and did she give in to the laziness she refers to in the first letter?

5 'An inflamed head'

As we saw in a previous chapter, eighteen-century journalists were not always kind to women who took part in the Revolution on one side or the other. One particularly unpleasant royalist pamphleteer, Francois-Louis Suleau, had written a nasty piece in which he condemned aristocratic women who'd taken the side of the Revolution, with Grouchy in 'the lepers' infirmary', 'infertile and covered in ulcers, mange, gripe, ringworm, the clap, sores, yaws, farcy, bleb on their necks, suction cups on their chests, poultices on their thighs, and plasters everywhere'.[20]

Grouchy was also the subject of obscene caricatures, such as the one reproduced earlier, where, along with other women, she shows her bottom to the royalist army to scare them away. She had acquired early on a reputation as an extremist and was blamed by the royalist press for Condorcets' adherence to republicanism – Condorcet was a reasonable man, a shy mathematician and an aristocrat, why would he turn revolutionary? She was blamed, not only for inciting her husband to Revolution but also for various other men who were claimed to be her lovers. And because she could not become a revolutionary through reflection – she was, after all, a woman – there had to be some reason, and that reason had to be fitting to a woman's character. So it was decided that Grouchy turned to the Revolution because she had been slighted by the queen.

It is Dumont who reports this piece of gossip even if he denies it:

> It is said about Mme Condorcet that she had been snubbed by the Queen and that her republican zealousness was but the result of a woman's revenge. I don't believe any of it. A serious character, a mind that flourished on philosophical meditations, republican readings, and a passion for Rousseau's works had inflamed her head.[21]

Note that Dumont also feels that Sophie's enthusiasm for liberty and equality has to be explained: too much Rousseau goes to a woman's head!

Sophie de Grouchy's works also received praise, including, according to Roederer, who himself reviewed her *Letters* and translation very positively, from Sieyès. One very enthusiastic reader was Madame de Staël. She and

Grouchy moved in similar aristocratic and international circles, but they were not friends. Germaine de Staël was the daughter of Jacques Necker, the Swiss banker appointed by Louis XVI as finance minister in 1777 to replace Turgot. To the French people, Necker came across as something of a quiet hero of the Revolution, a man who did his best to resist the decadence of the French regime and serve the nation. This was undoubtedly how his daughter saw him. However, Grouchy would have seen him differently. People in Turgot and Condorcet's circle believed that Necker had had a hand in Turgot's dismissal, deliberately misrepresenting to the people and the king what Turgot was trying to do.

With this background of political squabbling, it is no surprise that Grouchy and Staël never became friends. Each was loyal to her husband or father. The rift grew bigger when the Condorcets' close friend and ally, Mirabeau, took over from Necker in the heart of the French people. Necker left France, and after 1789, had no role to play in Revolution. But as influential figures in French literary circles, Staël and Grouchy could not ignore each other. And when Grouchy's *Letters on Sympathy* came out in 1798, Staël wrote to her, admitting that she envied both her style and the depth of her analysis.

It is not clear whether Sophie de Grouchy took the homage seriously or whether it was meant as such. Wilhelm von Humboldt, who visited Sophie in 1799, talked about the letter in his *Journal Parisien*. 'She showed me a letter which Madame de Staël had written about her book to which she gave exaggerated praise'. Was this also Sophie's view? Or did she accept Staël's praise at face value? It is possible, in fact, that Humboldt did not think the book deserved great praise and that this explained his judgement of the letter.

6 'No time for emotion': Philosophical reflections on the guillotine

As was the case with Olympe de Gouges and Marie-Jeanne Roland, Sophie de Grouchy's political thought was also influenced by the political situation in Paris at the time of her writing. In particular, some of the material in the *Letters on Sympathy* can be read in part as reflections on the guillotine.

Before 1789, there were several ways in which the law could kill its criminals depending on the kind of crime they had committed and on their station. Capital punishment differed and varied in cruelty depending on the rank of the accused. Aristocrats were decapitated with a sword. This was regarded as the most honourable death, although it was not always the least painful or horrible. Count Lally-Tollendal, who received the death penalty in

1766 for having betrayed the king's interest at war, had to be hit three times by the sword before his neck could be broken and the head detached. Sanson, the executioner of the Revolution, cited Lally-Tollendal when defending the proposed new machine that would cut heads off neatly and instantly.

Nonetheless, decapitation carried less infamy than the sentences reserved for commoners of death by hanging (murderers) or the Catherine wheel, a wooden wheel on which thieves and highway robbers would be tied, and broken by beating. A death considered infamous had repercussions for the family of the person executed so that the social respectability of the family of an aristocrat who was beheaded suffered less than that of a commoner who was hanged. Not only was the family of the beheaded aristocrat not touched by infamy, but had they been, they would have been able to retire to a secondary residence until such a time as the royal family would bestow their approval on them by inviting them to court. In the case of the family of a beheaded poor, the nature of the execution, the fact that the crowds were encouraged to attend and throw insults or rotten fruit at the condemned while they waited to be hanged, or while they were tortured on the wheel meant there was time to develop popular feeling against them. This was then passed on to the family of the condemned, and being rejected by their community meant, very often, being cut off from any means of economic survival.[22]

When, on 10 October 1789, Dr Guillotin proposed a practical plan for equalizing punishment, his argument was that the shame inflicted on the families of commoners was intolerable and that the only way to remedy this injustice was that all should be given an equal death. The only way to remove all the prejudices attached to death penalties other than decapitation, Guillotin said, was to get rid of those penalties. And to make decapitation itself less painful, more humane and – presumably – less work for the executioner, he proposed a machine be created that would render the execution itself mechanical. But also, this new type of execution had no class connotation and would not shame anyone by bringing them to the level of someone else. Everyone was *a priori* at the same level – that of the blade.

Many revolutionary reformers of punishment were much influenced by the writings of Milanese criminologist Cesare Beccaria.[23] Beccaria's short treatise, *On Crimes and Punishment*, was published in 1764 and translated in French that same year with a lengthy commentary by Voltaire.[24] Not only was Beccaria's book immediately successful, but it had a lasting influence, at least until the drafting of the 1791 Penal Code, which followed its principles closely and, in particular, abolished torture. Beccaria denounced inequalities in the penal law and the use of torture as punishment as unjust but also liable to encourage rather than discourage crime – if one could be convicted by a corrupt judge and tortured no matter what one did, then one might as well be a criminal. For him, punishment had to serve a purpose, reduce crime so as to increase general happiness, without at the same time causing unnecessary suffering.[25]

Beccaria also believed that to be efficient punishments ought not to be too severe – both because too much severity will defeat the imagination and prevent the public from thinking of consequences that would befall them in similar circumstances, and because it also gives potential offenders the sense that they have nothing to lose. The point of punishment, he says, is not to torment nor to undo the crime but to prevent future crimes and provide reparation if possible. But torture is not reparation, and death cannot undo a crime.

Generally speaking, Beccaria saw the infliction of pain as a mode of punishment that is favoured by tyrants, who cannot rely on the appeal of justice to keep their population from crime:

> Is it possible that torments and useless cruelty, the instruments of furious fanaticism, or of the impotence of tyrants, can be authorised by a political body?[26]

The rule of law, he argues, following Montesquieu, is what a strong state will rely on to keep a population honest, as this will both appeal to the reason of free citizens and put a halt to the sort of debauchery that is encouraged by tyranny, and that leads, for instance, to the crime of rape, as he argues in the chapter on infanticide.

> Do you want to prevent crime? Then make sure the laws are clear and simple and that the whole strength of the Nation is concentrated on defending them, and that no part is used to destroying them. Make sure that men fear the laws and only the laws. Fear of the law is salutary, but man's fear of his fellows is fatal and productive of crimes. Slavish men are more debauched, more barbaric and crueller than free men.[27]

Revolutionary reformers were impressed by Beccaria's humanitarianism, by his frequent references to tyranny and freedom, which matched their own republican ardour, but also by his confidence that good laws could be successful with milder punishment. Voltaire's involvement in the French publication of *Crimes and Punishments* also enabled that trajectory. Voltaire had been involved in high-profile cases of cruel and arbitrarily dispensed punishment. His mentee, Condorcet, had followed suit by fighting on behalf of three men wrongly and cruelly condemned to the wheel in Chaumont.

The men had been pronounced guilty by a 'partial' magistrate and not judged according to the law, thus going counter to Beccaria's injections that we should fear the law, not men. The case of the three men was fought and lost with Condorcet's help by Charles Dupaty in 1785.[28]

Beccaria's claim that infamy was a punishment of itself and ought not to be attached to any other person than that deserving that punishment was the inspiration for the first article of the Constitution of 1791, which abolished aristocratic privilege in the face of punishment. The Abbé Sieyès, leader of the Third Estate, and one of the principal authors of that constitution and of the *Declaration of the Rights of Man*, called the use of privilege in punishment an 'abominable distinction':

> Why do the privileged, when they commit the most horrible crimes, nearly always escape punishment, thereby stealing from the public potentially most effective examples? [. . .] The law dictates different sentences for the Privileged and he who is not. She seems to follow the Noble criminal with its tenderness and to want to honour him even at the scaffold.[29]

Sieyès recommended that privileges in criminal law be among the first to be abolished. There could be no distinctions made between rich and poor when deciding which sentence to apply for the same crime.

There were several indirect connections between Beccaria, Cabanis and Grouchy.[30] First, it was Condorcet's mentor, Voltaire, who published the French edition of *On Crimes and Punishment*. But also Beccaria came to Paris and spent much of 1776 in Madame Helvetius's salon in Auteuil. His influence was no doubt still present some years later when the Marquis de Condorcet, Cabanis and later Sophie de Grouchy herself became frequent visitors. Perhaps Grouchy would have developed intellectual affinities with Beccaria's views even without these influences. In any case, the affinities are clearly there, and she understood the value of punishment to rest at least in part in its efficacy, that is, reducing crime and increasing happiness. So in her *Letters on Sympathy*, she wrote:

> For the fear of a sentence to be effective and beneficial, the sentence must not outrage. Its justice must be perceptible to average reason, and it must especially awaken the conscience, at the same time as it punishes its silence and slumber. But this will not be so [. . .] if a judge can arbitrarily harden or soften a sentence; if there are privileges, hereditary, personal or local which offer a legal loophole, direct or indirect.[31]

For Grouchy as for Beccaria, the effectiveness of a sentence is inseparable from first, the question of equality – all must be treated equally by the law – and second, lack of cruelty – a cruel or excessive punishment will fail to appeal to anyone's moral sense, it is tyrannical, so does not require the approbation of free citizens but the unwilling compliance of slaves.

Nobody who is at all humane or reasonable, she says, will denounce a servant for theft if that denunciation will result in the servant's death. And given that minor crimes are often too severely punished, this means that they are not often reported. Added to that, she also concurs with Beccaria that severe laws, rather than acting as a deterrent from crime, in fact, create incentives for greater crimes: why steal an egg if it carries the same sentence as stealing a chicken? Criminal laws, through their severity, and civil laws, because they favour inequality, are therefore the cause of impunity for lesser crimes. And they can also be considered the cause of greater crimes since it is the impunity of the former that inspires the confidence needed to commit the latter. The poor, she concludes, are punished too severely for minor crimes, which leads to a disinclination to prosecute among more humane employers. The injustice of the law leads to it being disregarded and thus doesn't serve utility.

In the light of Beccaria's evident influence on Grouchy's theory of punishment, we might be tempted to assume that she would have welcomed the advent of the guillotine. The instrument was proposed, after all, because of its equalizing properties – no one suffered more or less infamy from a death sentence because of their class – and because it killed swiftly without the infliction of pain. However, this would be a mistake. First, she does not mention the guillotine. Granted, the *Letters* were drafted before it became the official tool of the death penalty. But she could have chosen to add her reflections on the guillotine before publication, and she did not. Why leave it out, given that two of the eight chapters of the letters dealt with the law and punishment? One possible answer is that she did not think the guillotine was a good form of punishment but did not yet feel safe criticizing the government – after all, many of her friends and colleagues had died at the guillotine. Grouchy did try to qualify the form that egalitarian punishment should take, and the guillotine would have been found wanting on the grounds that had little to do with Beccaria's proto-utilitarianism and all to do with her own theory of sympathy.[32] This was expressed by Cabanis, who did write about the guillotine, and possibly had in mind his friend and collaborator's theory of sympathy when he wrote the following:

The guillotine's work is done in less than a minute. The head disappears and the body is put away immediately in a basket. The spectators do not see anything; there is no tragedy; no time for emotion. All they see is the blood flow. If they draw any lesson from it, it is only to harden themselves to draw blood with less repugnance, when they are prey to furious passions. Instead of that, our institutions and all our public acts should nurture that most precious of sentiment of the human heart, compassion for the suffering and destruction of our kind.[33]

The last sentence appealing to 'the most precious sentiment of the human heart', the ability to feel another human being's pain, and react to it as if it were one's own is quite clearly a reference to Grouchy's theory of sympathy and in particular of the need to educate the moral sentiments.

But is pain a spectacle, and is an execution a tragedy that can educate our sympathy? This is certainly something Grouchy contemplated:

Finally it is because the point of tragedy is in great part to make our sympathy for the misfortunes of other seem pleasant to us by stimulating our sensibility progressively, and not by suddenly confronting it with the heartbreaking sight of physical pain – a sight we cannot stop thinking about if it moves us, and which turns into ridicule if it doesn't.[34]

The spectacle of pain is necessary for the growth of the natural sympathy we feel for those who care for us to other human beings, and in that sense, tragedy is useful to moral development. But this passage also contains an objection to the educational potential of tragedy: there are limitations to what an actual spectacle of pain, theatrical or real, can achieve in terms of educating our emotions. Unless we are exposed to suffering gradually, Grouchy says, the sight of pain will not have the desired effect – it will wash over us or make us laugh.

A second limitation of tragedy as enabling sympathy is that it lacks the 'enlightened hand' of the parent or teacher and exposes us, instead, to the influence of the crowd. The fact that a spectacle, whether a tragedy or a public execution, is something we perceive as part of a crowd, and not privately, also has an effect on the sort of emotional and moral consequences of seeing pain. When we are together with other spectators, we tend to be guided by their emotional reactions so that the very propensity that helps us develop as moral individuals can also make the spectacle of suffering appealing in a way that will not lead to improvement:

Amongst the effects of sympathy, we can count the power that a large crowd has to affect our emotions [. . .]. Here are, I believe, a few causes of these phenomena. First, the very presence of a crowd acts on us through the impressions created by faces, discourses, or the memory of deeds. The attention of the crowd commands ours, and its eagerness, forewarning our sensibility of the emotions it is about to experience, sets them in motion.[35]

Crowds pull us in against our better judgement sometimes. Why is this? Grouchy tried to pinpoint the reason. It is the overwhelming presence of living bodies, all in one place, all speaking, moving, twitching in their own way, but at the same time all focusing their attention on the same point, which both confuses us and takes over our own sense of direction: we too want to look where they look, and we too are getting excited with the anticipation of what will happen there.

So does the spectacle of pain, whether at the theatre or around the scaffold, have any potential to educate one's emotions and teach us to manage them in such a way that we will become compassionate? Grouchy seems to think that it sometimes does:

> In any case, we know that the spectacle of physical suffering is a real tragedy for the masses, a tragedy they seek only through a dumb curiosity, but whose sight sometimes arouses the kind of sympathy which can become a passion to contend with.[36]

It's clear that Grouchy had the spectacle of the public execution in mind when she wrote this. When she first drafted the *Letters*, executions were most commonly hangings, and they were always public in France as elsewhere. People came to watch and bought snacks and souvenirs, as they would at the theatre. A year and a half later, during the height of the Terror, she became more closely familiar with public executions. Her husband was in hiding, and she was living in Auteuil, just outside Paris. In order to visit Condorcet without giving away his hiding place, she would come on foot, dressed as a peasant and follow the crowds to the guillotine before turning off to join her husband on the other side of the river. Then she would have seen how the speed at which the guillotine was operated meant that there was, literally, nothing to see. Sanson is said to have executed twenty-two Girondins in less than half an hour – there was no time for showing off there! But sympathy, Grouchy tells us, takes time. It takes the time of a tragedy, and this was butchery. The death, the suffering, has to make an impression on the spectator – but this barely registers on their senses, and there is no time for them to delve into the emotions they experience or witness.

Did public beheadings arouse the emotions of the crowd? In some cases, they certainly did. Cabanis cites two high-profile executions that did move spectators. The first was that of Madame Dubarry.

Madame Dubarry's shrieking, pleading and sobbing deeply affected those who followed her cart in the streets, and nearly everyone who was at the Place de la Revolution left with tears in their eyes. But brave men cannot lower themselves to such cowardly despair in order to encourage the people to feel deeply: virtue cannot go that far.[37]

Yet, virtuous behaviour at the scaffold could also act as a prompt for popular emotion: the slapping of Charlotte Corday's cheek after she was beheaded led to great indignation, as well as to the probable myth that her face reddened from the outrage.[38] But otherwise, he notes, the people watch executions with bored indifference, and so the spectacle of pain, when it is shown with the purpose of demonstrating the power and justice of the republic profoundly, fails to educate the citizens who constitute its audience.

7 Lost papertrail

All we have left of Sophie, save for a few letters to Dumont, to her aunt, to her grandchildren and to the men who were her lovers after Condorcet died, Mailla Garat and Claude Fauriel, are her *Letters on Sympathy*. Yet we know from the *Testament* Condorcet wrote for his daughter, and from a letter Sophie wrote to Dumont, that there was more: more texts in moral philosophy and a fragment of a novel. Was the novel ever completed? What happened to the other philosophical texts? They are apparently lost, along with her manuscript of the *Letters*.

In the summer of 2019, I visited the Bibliothèque de l'Institut in Paris, on the Quai de la Monnaie, where Condorcet and Grouchy used to live, and which now houses all the papers related to the Académie Française. I was hoping to find some trace of her papers. I found her will, stating that she left her papers to her daughter, Eliza, and her sister, Charlotte Cabanis. Her executor was Madame de Lasteyrie, Lafayette's daughter. Eliza appears to have donated all that she had to the Institut, perhaps when the Academician Louis Arago, together with Eliza's husband, was re-editing Condorcet's works. But there is very little in the Institut that pertains to Sophie herself – a short account of her life written by her daughter and some love notes to Fauriel, her botanist boyfriend, and her will. Perhaps she gave her personal papers to her sister? In which case, they might be found in the papers of some male heir of Cabanis – or perhaps they are lost. In her correspondence with Fauriel, after Sophie and Cabanis's death, Charlotte only ever mentions her husband's papers, never her sister's.

The women on the other side of the channel

1 England's influence

The members of the English Parliament are fond of comparing themselves to the old Romans. *Voltaire*, Lettres Philosophiques, *VIII*.

At the time of the Revolution, many French political thinkers looked up to Great Britain. They thought of it as a political model: England had achieved some political legitimacy without excessive violence by establishing a parliament to rule alongside the king. Before the American Revolution, many saw this as the best thing republicanism could offer. In the early days of the French Revolution, a parliamentary monarchy seemed more plausible than a democracy.

There were other reasons to look up to England. First, a tradition of religious tolerance had allowed for the flourishing of religious sects such as the Quakers, the Radical Dissenters. And these had interesting political and educational views. Second, freedom of the press, if not perfect, was at least greater than in France. In his visit to England in the 1730s, Montesquieu had observed that the English lack censorship which worked like a form of tax: 'The King levies a duty on all periodicals, and there are about fifty of them, so he gets paid every time he is insulted.'[1] In France, authors needed their books to be preapproved by church and king. Books were submitted to censors who would offer, or not, approvals. Authors could also be asked to submit corrections. In a sense, this worked much as a referees system, except that it was not blind, and it was – because of its allegiance to the Catholic Church and the king, extremely prejudicial.[2] Many French authors resorted to printing their books abroad, in London or Amsterdam. The books could then be sold in France, and especially if the author retained their anonymity, this was a reasonably safe process. Otherwise, authors who published against censorship could end up in the Bastille. Voltaire had been sent to the Bastille for writing a satirical piece on Philippe d'Orleans. The Marquis de Sade was famously interned there until July 1789, and it was during this time that had he penned his *120 Journées de Sodome*. In his case the sentence did not operate as a deterrent.

Jacques-Pierre Brissot, the Girondin journalist, had moved to England in 1782 to avoid French censorship. Brissot seemed to have had little patience for the scandalous authors of pamphlets who run away to England to keep out of the Bastille, such as Morande, an unscrupulous Frenchman, permanently residing in London. But Brissot himself came to London to avoid censorship, so what was the difference? Brissot wanted to publish a periodical condemning the French government and disseminating new ideas. And he thought that he could do that better if he were not under the constant threat of arrest.[3] Unfortunately, he quickly found out that the cost and the effort involved in publishing a periodical and smuggling it for sale in France did not make the enterprise worth the exile. In 1784, he returned to Paris and was arrested for the publication of a pamphlet on criminal law (published in Berlin). He spent a few weeks in the Bastille.

2 Travelling in the Republic of Letters

British women, much like their male counterparts, travelled enthusiastically in the eighteenth century, writing about their experiences as they discovered new cultures.[4] The most famous perhaps is Lady Mary Wortley Montagu, whose Ottoman letters Voltaire admired.[5] Some women followed their husbands like Montagu or Hester Piozzi, who travelled to France and Italy with her musician husband. Some travelled alone, notoriously Mary Wollstonecraft. She travelled to revolutionary Paris as a journalist, and before that, to Ireland and Portugal. Later she also travelled to Scandinavia to trace a lost silver shipment, armed with a toddler, a French maid and a power of attorney.

Wollstonecraft's role model, Catharine Macaulay, also travelled alone, visiting France and America for work. But the freedom to discover new cultures, even by tagging along with one's husband was not shared by French women at that time. When Voltaire came back from his stay in England, he introduced his lover and collaborator, Emilie du Chatelet, to the works of Newton. Newton became central to her life: she translated, commentated and explained his works. She dreamed of visiting the country where he had grown up and worked. But her husband, who was happy to tolerate her living with Voltaire as a couple in his country house at Cirey, did not think it would be respectable for her to travel to England.[6]

A few French women travelled to England: Marie-Jeanne Roland accompanied her husband on a fact-finding trip for the encyclopedia of textile manufacture they were writing for Panckoucke. And the Revolution forced others to go abroad: Elizabeth Vigée le Brun left early on. She went to England to join the community of temporary émigrés. Those who planned to stay gone travelled further to America and became settlers rather than exiles.

Though lengthier and less comfortable than it is now, the journey from France to England was not extraordinarily demanding. The crossing from Boulogne to Dover took less than ten hours in good weather – nowadays, the ferry takes approximately four hours to cover the same distance. The rest of the trip could be conducted by land or river, depending on where one was starting from (Marie-Jeanne Roland took a water coach on the Somme – a slow and tedious way to travel, she said). The better off had private carriages. Otherwise, one would go by stagecoach, first or second class. There would be stops for the night in inns or at friends' houses. Marie-Jeanne Roland noted that English Inns were much cleaner than their French counterparts and remarked that the English travelling to France 'must find us horribly dirty'.

Women who did not travel could still maintain an up-to-date connection to other countries via letters – one could expect a letter from London to arrive in Paris in less than a week. Sophie de Grouchy did not travel to England – she never left France, despite marrying her daughter to an Irishman – but she was well apprised of its culture and politics via her friend Etienne Dumont, who wrote regularly. She knew of the struggles of the Dissenters, getting news of the Birmingham riots and the persecution of Priestley just two weeks after they happened, and other details that one could not obtain from reading Voltaire and Montesquieu. It's likely that Dumont also introduced her to the philosophy of Bentham (whose translator and editor he was at the time of their correspondence) and possibly even Wollstonecraft – Grouchy alludes to a book he sent her, which leads her to dream of a world in which women can live alongside men as fully developed human beings.

Men who travelled, provided they were on friendly and mutually respectful terms with women, were generally a great source of information. Jacques-Pierre Brissot, who had travelled twice to Britain and to America, was particularly useful for disseminating knowledge, especially about abolitionist movements. Some of the arguments he published were influenced by his study of Quakerism and the Clapham Sect. Brissot was also instrumental in bringing Macaulay's work to France, having met her in England and brought back copies of her History of England.[7] While English women travelled to France, this was no guarantee that they would meet French women, who did not move between salons with the same ease as their male counterparts. Mary Wollstonecraft, who was friendly with the Girondins, may have met Grouchy or Gouges – but we have no record of it – and according to her husband, she knew Roland well. When Macaulay came to Paris, she met Turgot and so may also have met Condorcet, who was working with him. But she did not meet his wife: Grouchy was thirteen years old, Marie-Jeanne Roland, aged twenty-three, was still living at home, and Olympe de Gouges had not yet begun to write. Macaulay did not come back to Paris later.

In several indirect ways, therefore, a connection was established between the women philosophers of France, our three included, and those of England. This connection came to intellectual and political fruition, as revolutionary women on both sides of the channel learned from their counterparts what may and may not be achieved or hoped for in a revolution.

The following section will look at Marie-Jeanne Roland's trip to England – she is the only of the three who left France – highlighting how even then, she was looking for signs of the superior social arrangements that political freedom brings. Then I will turn to two republican women from Britain who had close connections to the women of the French Revolution, in one way or another: Catharine Macaulay and Mary Wollstonecraft.

3 Marie-Jeanne Roland travels to England

In July 1784, Marie-Jeanne travelled to England with her husband, who was to meet professional contacts there, to help with his project of writing an encyclopedia of textile manufacture. His wife was closely involved in the project, helping conduct research, revising her husband's texts and sometimes writing them herself, so it made sense for them to travel together. Moreover, the Roland marriage had more equality than most, and the husband did not object to the wife travelling. Just before their trip to England, Marie-Jeanne had spent some time in Paris and Versailles, petitioning for nobility papers on behalf of her husband, while he stayed home in Amiens to care for their daughter.

When the Roland couple travelled to England, little Eudora stayed home – the trip would only last three weeks. But Marie-Jeanne recorded her impressions of England in a diary inscribed to her daughter.[8] They travelled by water first, taking a riverboat from Amiens to Boulogne, and then a ship with 'two rooms and six beds' for a ten-hour crossing to Dover. From there, they made their way to London, stopping on the way as tourists would. From Dover, where they arrived in the middle of the night, they went on to Canterbury, and a few days later to London.

Marie-Jeanne was enthusiastic about what she saw. The English countryside was pretty, clean and welcoming to travellers, with walking paths readied and lands separated with 3-foot hedges rather than 12-foot walls as they were in France.

In London, she found the Strand, with Somerset House nearly finished, to be a most beautiful avenue. And unlike Montesquieu, who fifty years earlier had found London to be extremely dirty, she described it as clean – even the market displays of fish and meat were tidy and appealing, with window panes allowing customers to see what was in the shops from the street – a practice copied a few years later at the shopping arcades of the Palais Royal in Paris. She saw London through tourist's eyes – she and her husband wanted to see a seventy-cannon ship but were told that they may not and that the penalty for getting too close was a cannonball. They visited the Tower of London, its display of torture instruments, the queen's house in Greenwich, and saw the place where Charles I had been executed. During their tour, they were delighted to spy a Scottish regiment in traditional garb.

St Paul's cathedral was like nothing she had ever seen, and she loved Westminster, the Abbey and the Palace. The British Museum, with its displays of insects, organized according to the Linnaean classifications, and its collection of Egyptian mummies was fascinating. The Rolands also sat-in during a parliament session and heard Pitt the young and Fox arguing. They travelled to Kew and saw the gardens there – Marie-Jeanne recorded that Ermenonville, where Rousseau was buried, was a poor copy of the natural beauty of Kew.

Her stance in the diary is not just touristic or even aesthetic, but her reflections comprise some social commentary. While she describes the prettiness of the English countryside ('to each cabbage, a rose'), she also takes care to note the implications that the landscaping has for the quality of life of its inhabitants: 'One feels that a man, no matter whom he might be, counts for something here and that a handful of rich men does not make a nation.'[9] The properties she sees are separated by short hedges, which give a full view over the beauty all around, which in France is prevented by ubiquitous high walls designed to prevent thieves and poachers from entering. This, she notes, is a sign that the rule of law is more powerful in England than France: 'In a country where it is the law that commands, much more than pains prevent, property is respected.'[10] Later on, when she visited St James' Park, she was struck by a similar thought, though this time, it was inferior beauty (of the statues in the park) that she read as a sign of superior politics. 'We have beautiful things in France', she says, 'but all are made by the Prince at his subjects' cost, subjects who, arbitrarily dominated, are miserable in their provinces from paying for the goods they only know from their sweat and pains.'[11]

Marie-Jeanne Roland's social observations also turn to women. She notes with interest the different ways women live in England and, in particular, how they are often separated from men. Men go to clubs, she observes, and debate public policy. Women stay home and look after their children. They meet other women for tea and take walks. But they take pride in the fact that the domestic world belongs to them and that it is their responsibility to bring up children. Boy children, however, she notes, are sent out to school, so it is mostly the education of daughters that women are responsible for. Roland notes that for those daughters who cannot be educated at home, there are, in the suburbs of London, excellent establishments, superior to French ones, where girls may board.[12]

English women, Roland also observes, are also more modest – and cleaner – than their French counterparts. They often wear white, and cover their décolleté – which is not too low – with a scarf, and wear a kerchief under their bonnet at all times. Young women are not shown in society till quite late, and they do not powder their hair until they are between fifteen and eighteen years old.

But even in this picture of domestic simplicity, Roland is able to read something akin to a republican stance (as she did when she wrote her essay on Spartan women for the Academy of Besançon). Women are in charge of bringing up children, and in doing so, they follow only two rules: cleanliness and liberty. Children are bathed every day, from head to foot, but otherwise, they are let to do as they wish. As they mature, they are able to shape their character simply through observing what suits their surroundings, but at no point are they oppressed by the learning of etiquette.

> Liberty and cleanliness: here are the two laws of early childhood. Children are washed every day, from head to toe; they do as they wish, as long as they cause no harm. We would be surprised to see at the table of a Duke, his children, aged 8 or 10, pushing their plates in front of them, putting their elbows on the table and resting them on their hand, or other such things. They do not pay attention to such trifles as they know that later, the child will notice that these things are not done and will correct themself for the sake of their own well-being. From this method in general it follows that children are themselves in front of their parents, they do not feel embarrassed by their presence, and their parents know them better. It also follows that children are more natural, free, and confident in their movement, their demeanor, which becomes permanently imprinted and suits well the pride of a republican and the independence of a man.

Marie-Jeanne Roland was overall very impressed with England, and while she did not approve of their government by constitutional monarchy, she felt that England provided the right atmosphere for thinking about liberty. Indeed, her favourite republican author, the one she held up as an example of herself in the days before she died, was British historian Catharine Macaulay, the subject of the next section.

4 Macaulay

Catharine Macaulay (1731–91) travelled to Paris seven years before Marie-Jeanne Roland travelled to London. She was travelling for her health, not pleasure, having been advised to go to the south of France and hope that the weather there would cure the ailments that had troubled her for several years. Her doctors, she said, were at their wits' ends and wanted to send her off so that she did not die under their care. She had tried conventional medicine and turned to the very unconventional Dr Graham, who was considered a quack by much of British society, and whose younger brother Macaulay had married. She travelled to Paris with great difficulties, complaining about the state of the accommodation between Calais and Paris. Once she arrived in the Capital, doctors advised her not to go any further, as she might die on the road. She stayed in Paris for a short while, as she found that the food in France did not agree with her:

> [T]heir meat is carrion [*sic*], their poultry and even their game insipid and their cookery most detestable. They have no good spices to season their meats with, and they use them too sparingly; their made dishes are a collection of gravy made from bad meat, fat, etc., without other flavour but what a little onion gives [. . .] all their wines turned sour upon it.[13]

But aside from the hotels and the food, Macaulay had nothing but praise for France. She found that everyone did their utmost to be kind and pleasant to her and enjoyed the visits and the dinners held in her honour. She also enjoyed the admiration she received for her 'genius' and 'literary powers' and was pleasantly surprised that being 'a hater of kings' also spoke in her favour.[14]

She found that no one in society spoke about the royal family, even though the young queen was reputed to be very beautiful and accomplished. She also found a lot of support for the American Revolution, noting that although for the 'vulgar', it was mostly an expression of hatred for England, among the enlightened, she detected a genuine interest in republicanism.

> In regard to the part they take in our civil wars, they are all American mad; and I do assure you, my Lord, that even your lordship would not be

well received in France if you were not an American. All the enlightened French wish ardently to see a large empire established on a republican basis to keep the monarchies of the world in order; and all the vulgar may have the same earnest desire, through hatred and jealousy of the English.[15]

Macaulay's republicanism predated the American Revolution. She grew up an admirer of Milton, Sydney and Needham, who had first revived Roman republicanism in England. She was particularly sympathetic to Milton's stance on regicide, and his claim that liberty was the true republican principle, while licence was the product of tyrannical government.[16] The first volume of her History of England, published in 1763, lauds the republican factions of the English civil war. Macaulay collected Leveller texts in her private library.[17] Brissot even considered that her expertise on the Levellers had been instrumental in shaping the principles that led to the American Revolution. According to him, both the English Revolution and Macaulay's *History* were a significant influence on the American Revolution:

> The Americans lit their reason with the torch of those men, who were enlightened in a century when nobody was. It is enough to be convinced of it to read the excellent History of Miss Macaulay and compare what this excellent woman says about the *sevellers* [*sic*] whose principles she set out so well to all the public writings of Americans during the troubles.

According to Karen Green, Macaulay's egalitarian views became clearer in the third volume of the *History*, in which she begins to criticize privileges as counter to the 'Freedom of society'. As was true for many of her contemporaries and compatriots, including Wollstonecraft and Paine, Macaulay's republicanism was grounded in principles of liberty, equality and rights, but also on certain religious beliefs which precluded a wholly pessimistic view of human progress. Humans were born free because they were made in God's image, and God had made them such that it would be possible for them to live fruitful and happy lives by acting on that innate freedom. This meant that we would be able to respect each other's freedom, and be capable of living together in some form of harmony, provided we were governed legitimately. Any form of tyrannical government would not only take away the freedom that is our birthright but also prevents us from forming the social binds necessary for a flourishing society.

Although Macaulay had visited Paris in the late seventies, it was not then that she acquired the fame and influence that led Marie-Jeanne Roland to write, in her prison memoirs, that she wished she could have become the

Macaulay of France. She was already known as a republican – she had then published the first five volumes of her *History of England*, but they had not yet been translated into French. She then took a long hiatus, and the eighth volume was published around the time she met Brissot in 1784. Brissot initiated the translation by bringing the eight volumes back to Paris with him.[18]

Catharine Macaulay was only fifty-one when Brissot met her, and according to him, she was one of the few natives who did not snub him.[19] They met shortly before she left England for America, but they seem to have taken to each other and developed a strong respect for each other's work. In a short letter inviting him to tea, Macaulay told Brissot that 'she has read with much pleasure and profit Monsieur Warville's [Brissot] *meditations sur la verité* and she expects great things from the work he has announced to the public under the title of *Correspondence Universelle* etc.'[20]

Brissot himself makes numerous references to her work in his own and, as we saw, thought her an important source for the principles that led the American Revolution. Friendship and admiration did not stop him, however, from taking the same unkind stance to her marriage to a younger man, as most of her acquaintance had. He describes Macaulay, then aged fifty-two, as a very old woman:

> Imagine a woman with lead on her face, missing teeth, wrinkles badly hidden with rouge, and whose decrepitude showed beneath her always fashionable and elegant get up. Next to her the brilliant figure and freshness and health of her husband, still adolescent! It looked as if a child was attached to a corpse.[21]

Macaulay's marriage to a twenty-one-year-old (twenty-six at the time Brissot met him, so hardly a teenager!) had of course been badly received, and even Brissot, who admired her greatly and found her *History of England* remarkable, had trouble accepting that her marriage was not a sign of folly. Brissot thought that work remarkable and believed wholeheartedly that Macaulay deserved the laurels she had taken off Hume. To objections that she could not, as a woman, really be the author of that work, he replied that the evidence that she was laid in her conversation: 'It has all the characteristics, he said, of the dignity, the republican energy breathed by her History.'[22]

Although he did not translate the work himself, Brissot is responsible for having introduced Macaulay's *History* to revolutionary France. In his memoirs, he recalls telling Mirabeau about the work:

> As I was talking one day with enthusiasm to Mirabeau about this History, he suggested that we should translate it. I replied that it would be a very

difficult piece of work, as literal translation was both hateful and boring for the French. We would have to write a new work, adapted to our taste and our needs, and only look at Macaulay's History as a depository of precious materials. Mirabeau did not, however, give up on this idea. Jealous of any sort of glory, he engaged Debourge, who had several times already lent him his pen, notably for his 'Avis aux Bataves' to produce this translation. Debourge talked to me beforehand, I gave him the same objections, but this did not stop him. He first wrote the preliminary discourse, which is entirely his, and he abandoned the translation. Guinguené took over next, or rather, paid a mercenary author who charges by the page to do it. Such is the origin of the hateful translation published after the death of Mirabeau, under his name. He had nothing to do with it. He did not speak English and his name was only used to sell the work.[23]

The translation, as bad as it was, was immediately praised and hailed as the most important work since the Revolution:

All history lovers, and especially free souls, must hurry and buy these two volumes and wait impatiently for the next six. This book is one of the most important ever to be published since the Revolution.[24]

Fortunately, a new translation was prepared very soon after, better because more time was given to it, and the French were able to read what Macaulay had said, rather than a French commentary with a few passages in literal translation. Still, those who could read English tried to read the original. Marie-Jeanne Roland borrowed Brissot's copies of the first few volumes. Unfortunately, by the time she had read these and wanted more, she was in prison, and Brissot was about to be arrested.

While Macaulay's popularity in her own country declined after her second marriage, she remained influential not only in France but in America too. She was part of an intellectual and political correspondence circle. She exchanged letters with Benjamin Franklin, John and Abigail Adams and Mercy Otis Warren and George Washington. In 1784, taking her husband with her, she decided to visit the friends who had admired her from afar, and she sailed to America.

According to Brissot (who did see her just before she travelled), Macaulay, encouraged by the warm friendship of her correspondents and the success of her History in America, had decided to travel to that country for the purpose of writing about the American Revolution. During that time, she was hoping to gather material for her book and find support for publishing it. In that, Brissot tells us, she was disappointed:

She was admired everywhere she went, but no one paid a subscription for her History. Deceived in her speculation and in the support she had excepted, she came back disgusted by the Americans. Her anger was unfounded. At peace, impoverished Americans only thought of rebuilding their farms and cultivating their lands. They only read newspapers, which, despite their cheapness, they could ill afford. Few books, aside from the Bible, were being sold in America, and if you look at the list of subscribers for Gordon's *History of America*, you will be surprised to find that three quarters were English.[25]

One might be tempted to think that she would have received more support had she been a man – she could, like Paine, have become the cosseted darling of the Americans. However, Paine went to America before the war, before the Americans became strapped for cash. Brissot experienced something similar to Macaulay – when he travelled to America to find a place to settle with his family, he tried to enlist patrons, people who would help him establish himself there as a writer. He too came back disappointed, and perhaps, for this reason, makes more than there was of the failure of Macaulay's trip, noting that she died shortly afterwards (she died in 1791, so several years after her trip, in fact). He does not perhaps realize the extent to which Macaulay's trip was about meeting with those people she had corresponded with, deepening the relationships and adding a conversational element to their correspondence on political matters. In that sense, the trip was a crowing success to her career as a republican thinker.

5 Wollstonecraft in Paris

In December 1790, six months before Catharine Macaulay died, at the age of fifty-nine, she received a volume and a letter addressed to her from a 29-year-old woman who was yet unknown because although she had published books, she had done so anonymously. The book, *A Vindication of the Rights of Men*, was a pamphlet written in response to Burke's attack on the French Revolution and the Reverend Richard Price who defended it. Its author, Mary Wollstonecraft, was moved both by a strong republican stance and loyalty to Price, who had befriended her some years previously in the London suburb of Newington Green, where a community of Radical Dissenters led by Price, was thriving. Burke had accused the French of overthrowing, with their king, all social equilibrium and let France, the victim of unattractive and violent peasants and paupers who would inevitably bring about its destruction. His pamphlet, *Reflections on the*

Revolution in France, was published as a direct response to Price's speech, given on the anniversary of the fall of the Bastille, praising the English Revolution and defending republican ideals. As soon as Burke's pamphlet was printed, responses began to arrive, creating a pamphlet war. The first response, written in under four weeks, was Wollstonecraft's. The two best-known ones that came afterwards were Thomas Paine's *The Rights of Man* and Catharine Macaulay's *Observations on the Reflections of the Right Hon. Edmund Burke on the Revolution in France*. The pamphlet war was evidence of a divide of opinion in England about the French Revolution, as Macaulay noted in the introduction to her response to Burke:

> Two parties are already formed in this country, who behold the French Revolution with a very opposite temper: To the one, it inspires the sentiment of exultation and rapture; and to the other, indignation and scorn.[26]

When Wollstonecraft wrote to Macaulay, it was to present her with the second edition – which was going to bear her name as author – of the *Rights of Men*. Macaulay responded by asking her editor to send her the text of her *Observations*. When a little over a year later, Wollstonecraft had drafted her second *Vindication*, she much regretted that she could no longer seek Macaulay's feedback and approval, as she was no longer alive.

Wollstonecraft, like Macaulay, was definitely on the side of those who were passionately enthusiastic about the French Revolution, not merely because of the overthrow of tyranny and the making way for republican principles of government, but because she saw it as an opportunity for these principles to be applied to women as well as men. Nowhere is this clearer than in the first pages of her *Vindication of the Rights of Women*, which she dedicated to the Marquis de Talleyrand. Talleyrand was at the time charged with reforming the French educational system. Although he'd made a glib remark or two about equality of the sexes, his new system mainly was a reform for the education of men – women would presumably have to make do with learning to embroider with republican patterns. In her dedication, Wollstonecraft makes a strong case for including women in the reform, arguing that not only are women as capable of being educated as men, but also they are rational beings capable of virtue and that not to educate them would result in preventing the flourishing of the country as a whole:

> Contending for the rights of woman, my main argument is built on this simple principle, that if she be not prepared by education to become the companion of man, she will stop the progress of knowledge and virtue;

for truth must be common to all, or it will be inefficacious with respect to its influence on general practice.[27]

Wollstonecraft came to Paris in December 1792, just three months after the Parisian mobs had butchered aristocrats in their prisons, priests and nuns in convents and monasteries, supposedly on the order of Danton. She'd travelled alone, against the advice of friends, to step away from a situation that could not be resolved – she had wished to enter into a menage a trois with the painter Henry Fuseli and his wife. The couple had not been amenable.

Wollstonecraft was used to travelling – she had been all over England and Wales as a child, travelled to Bath as a lady's companion, to Ireland to work as a governess, and to Portugal to assist a friend in giving birth. She took a stagecoach from London to the coast, which took twelve hours. The crossing was made in good time, which could mean between five and ten hours, but then she had another two days by coach before arriving in Paris.[28]

The first few weeks of her stay were momentous: the king of France was tried by the people, condemned to death and executed. She saw Louis drive past her window on the way to his trial, just a couple of weeks after she had settled in Paris. But even without the growing atmosphere of terror, Wollstonecraft would have found it hard to settle in Paris: her French, while good enough for reviewing and translation purposes, was not really up to making conversation, and she was here alone despite having originally planned to travel with friends.

Given all that, perhaps it is not surprising that her first impressions should be negative, bordering on the depressive. She had travelled to Paris with a commission to write a series of letters on the French Revolution. However, upon arriving, she was quickly discouraged by the turn the Revolution seemed to have taken, wondering whether the principles of 1789 survived at all or whether the aristocracy of nobility had been replaced with one of wealth.

Wollstonecraft abandoned the letters, but not the work: instead of an account of what was happening in France right now, she decided to write a history of the French Revolution. In the spring of 1793, she wrote to her sister that she had begun this 'great work'. The first volume was published in 1794. The other planned volumes were never written. The long volume in which Wollstonecraft compiles and summarizes various accounts of events and speeches given in the early days of the Revolution by Mirabeau (or Dumont) and others also reflects her ambivalence towards the Revolution. On the one hand, she felt that dreadful, criminal mistakes were made because the Revolution happened too quickly. On the other, she remained confident that things would get better, that mistakes would not be repeated, and that the Revolution, on the whole, was progressive.

The great work must have occupied most of Wollstonecraft's work time during the two and a half years she spent in Paris. It is a large book, and even if a significant proportion of it reproduces the works of others, gathering these documents, choosing and ordering them into a coherent whole, then summarizing them (and perhaps in some cases translating them) would not have been a trifle. Although only an 'observer' of the revolution, she still would have had to worry about her safety as England and France were now at war. She even went so far as to hide her nationality from the French government, her American lover, Gilbert Imlay, registering her as his wife at the American Embassy so she did not risk arrest. But despite the genuine risks to her freedom and life, Wollstonecraft stayed in France till 1795. She spent her first year in Paris and became pregnant with her first child Fanny. But at the end of 1793, when the Girondists, with whom she sympathized were all dead, and her English friends Paine and Williams in prison, she moved to the suburbs. In 1794, after her and Imlay's daughter was born to the relative safety of le Havre.

When Wollstonecraft was in Paris, she mostly visited English nationals, such as Helen Maria Williams, and Johnson's associate, Thomas Christie. She was close, ideologically, to the Girondins, some of which were fluent English speakers, such as Brissot and his wife, Félicité, Marie-Jeanne Roland, who had taught herself at the beginning of her marriage, and Sophie de Grouchy, a fluent English speaker and writer, whose salon in the early years of the Revolution attracted foreign luminaries such as Thomas Paine and Jefferson. Is it at all possible that Wollstonecraft had met either Grouchy or Roland or even Olympe de Gouges (the only one of the three who did not speak English)?

Wollstonecraft's biographer, Janet Todd, suggests that Wollstonecraft may have been contacted in 1792, shortly after her arrival, by Condorcet and Paine to help rework the plan for educational reform that Talleyrand had started in 1791. We do not know whether Wollstonecraft considered taking them up on the offer or whether she felt she had enough work on her hands with her writing. But she was invited to present a paper to the committee and accepted, but the paper was not, in fact, given.[29] But the fact of the invitation suggests that she might have met Condorcet's wife, Sophie de Grouchy. Despite the fact in her letters from France, Wollstonecraft mostly speaks of her English and American friends, William Godwin, who married Wollstonecraft in 1796, wrote in his biography of his wife that she knew most of the leaders of the Revolution, associated with the Girondins rather than the Jacobins, and was particularly close to Madame Roland. Wollstonecraft would probably have met Marie-Jeanne through one of her Paris acquaintance, the poet Helen Maria Williams, who often accompanied Marie-Jeanne Roland to the Jacobins' club.[30]

Another question worth asking is whether the women of the French Revolution were acquainted with Wollstonecraft's writings. Again, there is no direct evidence that they were. But we know that Wollstonecraft's *Vindication of the Rights of Woman* had been translated into French before she came to Paris and that it had been well received. Before travelling, she wrote to her sister: 'I shall be introduced to many people, my book has been translated and praised in some popular prints.'

La Défense des Droits des Femmes was translated anonymously. Wollstonecraft's most recent translator, Isabelle Bour, suggested that this first translation might have been done by a member of the Girondin circle. This is entirely plausible as we know that the Girondins did defend women's rights to some extent. Condorcet published an article arguing that women should be given equal political rights to men in 1791 so that Wollstonecraft's book would have struck him as important and topical.

The French translation of Wollstonecraft's *Vindication of the Rights of Woman* was published before she arrived in Paris in the winter of 1792 and reviewed favourably in at least four reviews, including one, *La Chronique de Paris*, edited by Condorcet.[31] The translation is a good one: it contains spelling mistakes rather than mistakes in the translation, which suggests that it was done in a hurry by someone who knew English well. It is also annotated in a way that suggests familiarity with English culture and literature and a desire to defend 'Papist' France against the allegations of a protestant writer while at the same time poking fun at Wollstonecraft's old fashion religiosity.

The translator seems thoroughly on board with Wollstonecraft's defence of women, until, that is, we reach a footnote to Chapter 11 (which primarily concerns the education of women) where we get a peek at the translator's insidious sexism:

> Here the author is talking about France. It is true that the Revolution is allowing us to pay attention to women who for too long were treated with superficial respect and deep contempt. We owe them a better education; because mothers are the first teachers that nature and society offer children. We owe them divorce, which only the tyranny of priests was able to take from them. A large number among them have proven that they were worthy of liberty; they only need to be enlightened. More enlightened, they will become more virtuous and happier. We owe them reparation for all the gothic crimes of feudality against them, for inheritance, etc., *for if nature seems to refuse to grant them political rights, they have as many claims to civil rights as men.* In a word, it is up to them to give the new regime the firmness it needs. Since the French nation has shaken off its yoke, we have heard much about a counter-revolution.

Legislators! Don't deceive yourselves: if there is to be a counter-revolution, it will come from the influence of women. So let the Constitution concern itself with them; what you do for them will not be lost. What you have deposited in the hands of the paterfamilias really belongs to them, as they will transmit it to future generations.[32]

The translator accepts what Sieyès proposed in the draft of the constitution, namely that women should be only passive citizen, that is, enjoy civil but not political rights.

The translator is also quite clear that the main reason why we should grant women any rights is that they are mothers to future citizens. But although Wollstonecraft does emphasize the importance of the role of women as mothers in a republic, she by no means reduces their citizenship to that, indeed, takes pain to say that women need not marry nor have children, but that they still deserve to be treated as full citizens. To attempt to confine women to their domestic role, she says, will have a negative effect on politics, as they will inevitably attempt to participate. Indeed, Wollstonecraft suggests that women's nature, just as men's is to be political, thereby directly contradicting the translator's note:

I have repeatedly asserted and produced what appeared to me irrefragable arguments drawn from matters of fact, to prove my assertion that women cannot, by force, be confined to domestic concerns; for they will, however ignorant, intermeddle with more weighty affairs, neglecting private duties only to disturb, by cunning tricks, the orderly plans of reason which rise above their comprehension.[33]

What the translator's note on Wollstonecraft's *Vindication* shows is that the readiness of revolutionary men and women to bring down, if not dismiss women's aptitude for holding political rights, and for participating actively in the running of the republic, was salient even among those who defended women, even while they defended them.

We have no evidence that the women we are interested in, Grouchy, Roland or Gouges, had read the translation of Wollstonecraft's *Vindication*. But a letter dated 20 August 1791 from Sophie to her friend Dumont suggests that perhaps she may have come across one of Wollstonecraft's earlier books – perhaps her *Thoughts on the Education of Daughters*. Sophie thanks Dumont for sending her books and political news from England and says:

Until I receive more news from you, I will be busy reading the book you sent me and dreaming about the best way to raise reasonable women who can live with men who are not and will not be reasonable towards women for a long time from now.[34]

This could, of course, be a coincidence. But it does suggest that the book Dumont sent her and Sophie's dreams might be related. And who, better than Wollstonecraft, could be the inspiration for such dreams?

The American dream

From republican model to asylum of freedom

Before the Revolution started, England held a strong attraction for the republican-minded French man or woman. Its constitutional monarchy proved that it was possible to establish a government that served the interests of all. It showed that religious tolerance could help advance causes like abolitionism or women's education. But after the Revolution, England quickly became an enemy nation and republican France had to look elsewhere for inspiration. America was the natural choice. The French had helped fight and pay for the war of independence against England. This gave it extra value in their eyes. Also the Marquis de Lafayette, already hailed as a hero of the American Revolution, was on his way to becoming one in France too. Soon, America took England's place as an aspirational model for the republican French.

In the early years of the French Revolution, America was often held up as a model for what could and could not be achieved in France. This was a model created by French travellers to the United States and American visitors to France. The Girondins, in particular, were inspired by America. The Jacobins' preferred model was ancient Rome. This led to some heated debates between Brissot and Robespierre at the Convention.[1] Brissot had travelled to America and brought back thoughts on abolitionism, which led to the foundation of the Société des Amis des Noirs. This, in turn, led to friendship and collaboration with Olympe de Gouges. His travels also influenced French immigration to America. The Roland couple's plans for a republican colony were inspired by Brissot's travels to America. Brissot's travel book also attracted the attention of Mary Wollstonecraft, who reviewed it for Johnson's *Analytical Review*. She found interesting parallels between his views on republican morality and hers on gender equality.

Among visitors from America who influenced philosophical thinking about the Revolution, Thomas Paine stands out. He became a close friend and collaborator of the Condorcet couple, and with them was instrumental in bringing republican ideals to revolutionary France. Paine's influence extended beyond politics. Like many Americans, he believed that good republican politics did not necessitate atheism. Despite their admiration for some of the religious sects of America, in particular the Quakers, the Girondins tended towards atheism. This sat uneasily with their American and English supporters. Mary Wollstonecraft joked that her stay in Paris had not turned her into an atheist. Paine argued against French atheism from his Luxemburg prison where he wrote *The Age of Reason.*

1 Republican morals

In November 1792, the Girondins accused Robespierre of attempting to take over the government through his new role as leader of the Paris Commune. Robespierre responded by mocking his accusers for mixing their Roman history references (did they think he was trying to become a dictator, a tribune or set up a triumvirate?) and in turn by justifying his actions by comparing himself to Cicero, who when he stopped Catiline's conspiracy, went above the law. What the Revolution needs, Robespierre says – unless it wants a revolution without a revolution – is a leader whose virtue means that he can act above the law for the good of the 'Patrie'. In times of legal uncertainty, when one system is being overthrown, and the new one is not yet established, virtue is everything.[2]

Robespierre was not unusual in his appeals to Roman virtue. Olympe de Gouges, attacking Robespierre for his justification of his role in the Commune, and the many arrests that came from it challenged him to a show of virtue:

Robespierre! Have you the courage to imitate me? I suggest we take a bath in the Seine, but in order to wash away all the stains you have acquired since the 10th, we will attach cannonballs of sixteen or twenty-four to our feet; then, together, we will rush headlong into the flow. Your death will calm minds, and the sacrifice of a pure life will disarm the heavens. I am useful to my country, you know, but your death will at least free it of its greatest scourge, and maybe I will never have served it better: I am capable of such extreme patriotism. Such is the courage of the great characters that you yourself describe without ever knowing any. 'One can outrage virtue, but memory lives on forever,' you are right. 'The small-minded and facetious never last, only the great live on.' It is too marvellous that you yourself should write their defence and your proper accusation! Mediocre and boastful compared to your superiors in merit and talent; a cringing impostor to the people: there is your portrait. Tell me, what, actually, will be your place in the pages of history; lift up your eyes, if you dare, and see the ideal philosopher and people's magistrate.[3]

While the American Revolution was also a virtue-led political movement, the relevant model was somewhat different, tied to the Protestant ethics of its leaders, and intended to be applicable to life in the New World. The contrast between the two sets of virtue beliefs showed up in the conflict between the Jacobins, enamoured of Roman history, and the Girondins, who looked to America as their model.

1.1 Virtue and the republic

The French Revolution was shaped by a culture of classical education. Robespierre, Desmoulins, but also many others, including Marie-Jeanne Roland, had been brought up on Roman republican texts and had developed a strong admiration for Roman virtues and politics. Cato was their model, and like him, they placed the 'Patrie' above everything personal, including their own family and disdained luxury and private benefits of any kind.[4]

As well as being willing to sacrifice everything for the republic, a good revolutionary – and Danton was the notable exception whose sins had to be constantly forgiven because he was clearly so devoted to the people – was expected to model Roman or even Spartan virtues. This is why, for instance, Brissot made it known, in his reply to accusations of anti-revolutionary activities, that he had no personal ambition, that he led a simple, Spartan life and therefore could not be charged with being open to bribery.[5] The same reasoning explains why Marie-Jeanne Roland, when she started her Parisian salon, made sure to serve very simple meals – one course only! – no alcohol, but instead sugared water. She also did not invite women, lest the conversation turns to gallantry rather than policy. This seems unduly suspicious of her own sex: many of the women she socialized with and could have invited, such as Louise Keralio-Robert, Louise Pétion, Félicité Brissot, Helen Maria Williams or even Mary Wollstonecraft, would have had no more compunction to flirt than the men guests, and perhaps even less. But allowing women to come, Roland knew, would give men like Danton and Dumouriez free rein to bring their mistresses to her home and turn her gatherings into debauchery.[6] Marie-Jeanne Roland wanted to make sure that the virtue of her 'little committee' remained safe from their influence. And in order to show her dedication to the single-sex nature of her salon, she never joined in the debates herself but sat apart, at her work table, with a piece of embroidery, demonstrating the sort of female virtue also praised by the Romans and expected by her contemporaries.[7]

1.2 A revolution in manners

When Brissot travelled to America in 1788, he was travelling from a monarchy – France – and had previously lived in a constitutional monarchy – England. America was a clear improvement in terms of freedom and something for a republican such as he to use as a model. But by the time he got down to writing up his travel notes, published in 1791 – under the title *Nouveau Voyage Dans Les Etats-Unis de l'Amérique Septemtrionale, fait en 1788, par J.P. Brissot (Warville) Citoyen François* – France was no longer a monarchy. This made a difference to the value of his observations. America could still serve as a model, Brissot said, not to teach the French to become free, but to teach them how to preserve their newly won freedom: 'We have no need to learn from Americans how to attain the blessing of liberty', he wrote in the preface to *Voyage*, 'but we have to learn from them the secret of preserving it'.

The key to preserving liberty, Brissot claimed to have learned from America, was morals, which came down, he said, to the use of reason in every aspect of everyday life. Acting immorally, unreasonably or immoderately was tantamount to wanting tyranny back. So Brissot argued that the most useful way France could emulate America now that both were republics was to bring about a moral revolution. This argument struck a chord with one of his English reader, Mary Wollstonecraft, who had been tasked with reviewing his book for Joseph Johnson's Analytical Review.

In the late eighteenth century, the fashion in writing book reviews was to be harsh and critical.[8] Wollstonecraft's reviews were no exception, but she still found it in her to praise a fellow republican who, like her, thought that the way forward was through a moral reform. So while she applies gentle sarcasm to Brissot's 'energetic expostulations', she also noted that 'he writes like an enlightened citizen of the world, whose zeal for liberty appears to arise from the purest moral principles and most expansive humanity'. To those who would mock his enthusiasm, she replies that it is due to 'the sacred overflowings of an honest heart' and to 'common sense'. In particular, what Wollstonecraft admires about Brissot's book is the preface and his claim that if one can obtain liberty without virtue, it is not possible to keep it. She approves of his main purpose in travelling to America being to find out what 'manners' the American people have developed to protect their republic.

This point of view is very close to the one Wollstonecraft herself developed in her *Vindication of the Rights of Woman*, which she had already begun to work on when she read Brissot's book. Wollstonecraft called for a 'Revolution in manners' as a necessary supplement to any legislation about women's status.[9] Until women could learn to behave like citizens, rather than frivolous pets to their husbands, she said, and until men could learn to treat them as such, there was no point in hoping for equality.

Brissot's description of American women's manners certainly resonated with Wollstonecraft, and in her review, she quotes this long passage treating it as evidence that sensible moral reforms could bring about more natural relations between men and women:

> The simplicity conspicuous in the manners of every class, particularly the innocent frankness that characterizes the American women, and the consequent *friendly* intercourse that subsists between the sexes, when gallantry and coquetry are equally out of the question, must have surprised a Frenchman, who could not instantly forget the sensual effeminacy of European manners. Indeed there cannot be a purer proof of the purity of morals that still prevails in America than the easy, unreserved behaviour of the women. Men and women mix together like social beings; and, respecting the marriage vow, mutually improve their understandings by discussing subjects that interest the whole race; whilst in Europe, the conversations that pass between *gentlemen* and *ladies*, in general, consist of idle compliments and lively sallies; – the frothy food of vanity.[10]

If Wollstonecraft thought that her own country had much to achieve in terms of giving women back their reason and human dignity, she was quite sure that the rest of Europe, particularly France, trailed even further behind. As a Frenchman, she says, Brissot must have been very surprised to see men and women interacting so freely. Perhaps had France not been so far behind America in terms of gender relations, Marie-Jeanne Roland would not have hesitated to invite women to her salon. As it was, French 'manners' and underlying morals made it impossible for men and women to interact with each other 'as social beings' but only as potential sexual partners. Adopting American style manners would mean that the two halves of the population, rather than flirting with each other and plotting advancement through marriage, would be able to join forces and preserve the liberty that had been achieved in France. What Wollstonecraft does not yet say, but made clear when she wrote her Vindication of the Rights of Woman, is that another consequence of the Revolution in manners would be to bring this liberty to women as well as men – something which Brissot was perhaps not fully contemplating.

While Wollstonecraft does not specifically read Brissot as arguing for women's rights, she does note that his programme includes abolitionism:

> But his humanity is particularly conspicuous in the long account he gives of the treatment of slaves and the attempts made by the Quakers to abolish that infamous traffic.[11]

Indeed, Brissot did look to the American Quakers for ideas about how to develop his own abolitionist programme, spearheaded by the Société des Amis des Noirs, founded in early 1788 just before he set out to America. The impact of this society on Olympe de Gouges's own abolitionist work is discussed in the next chapter.

2 The asylum of freedom

Many French people who immigrated to America in the early days of the Revolution did so to escape the violence and the threat of the new regime. This concerned not only aristocrats but also the impoverished French who saw that the Revolution would only make them poorer by disrupting their ability to work regularly. But it was not just the violence that brought poverty. An anonymous letter written in 1790 argues that the Revolution had put an end to the excesses of the aristocrats and the clergy meant that a lot of people – who had been working to cater to these excesses – were now out of work. Those aristocrats could simply move out of France to nearby countries, with friends or families, waiting out the Revolution.[12] A group of early immigrants attempted to fund a French colony in Ohio: Gallipolis. The Scioto Company, who had sold them the land, had poorly organized the immigration so that a boatful of eighty-six women, men, and children travelled with provisions for fifty, and that once in New York, no one was there to take them to Ohio. Many came back to France or went elsewhere. Those who made it to Gallipolis never succeeded in making more of it than a small town of log cabins.[13]

For those who were in favour of the Revolution, and who did not foresee that harm would come to them as a result of it, America held a different sort of attraction: it represented what they wanted France to become. A number of French republicans, consequently, thought about immigrating to America before the Revolution. But once the Revolution took hold, the priority became to help make France into the republic they wanted it to be, and America went from being a destination to a model. A few years later, the wind turned again, and America once more became a destination for those French republicans who had become a target of the Terror.

A few weeks before her death, while she was incarcerated in Ste Pélagie, Marie-Jeanne Roland learned that Brissot and twenty-one other Girondins had been arrested. Others, including her lover, Francois Buzot, had succeeded in escaping. She wrote to Buzot:

> The fugitive deputies, alas! have they at length escaped from this inhospitable land, which devours the virtuous and the sage, and drenches itself with their blood? Oh, my friends! May propitious fate conduct you to the United States, the only asylum of freedom! My wishes would conduct you thither, and I ardently hope that you are now actually on your passage. But what remains for me? I shall see you no more, and while for your sakes I rejoice in your removal, I lament in it our eternal separation.[14]

2.1 Republican living

Brissot travelled to America in 1788. His observations were published in 1792 with a preface by his friend and fellow Girondin, Etienne Clavière. While we saw that the book itself was written to warn the French that they needed virtue to protect their liberty, the initial plan for the voyage had been to see whether he might make a living for himself and his family in America.

Brissot had several reasons for thinking of moving to America. His brother-in-law, Francois Dupont, immigrated to Philadelphia in 1789, followed a few years later by his sister, Nancy Dupont. The Brissots and the Duponts were involved in publicizing the land for sale in Ohio by the French company Scioto. Brissot, who was already thinking of immigrating to America in 1786, drafted a proposal for *A Society for Promoting the Immigration from Europe to the United States*, a proposal that included a house, somewhere on a European cost, where potential immigrants could come to purchase land and passage, but also to be vetted, so that only 'industrious, sober and healthy Europeans' who could help 'enhance the value of the land' would be allowed through.

Unfortunately, the Scioto Company turned out to be unreliable. As well as the failed immigration organized in 1790, the land they were selling in Ohio was worthless and impossible to cultivate. But the Brissots/Duponts continued to encourage immigration, alerting each other of potential newcomers. Félicité Brissot, writing to her brother in Philadelphia, warns him of the possible arrival of several men they know, and of their various moral failings – one is selfish, another stupid and a third so bad-tempered that he has alienated everyone who could help him. She adds, charitably, that they are young and that, therefore they may benefit from the move, but worries nonetheless about the effect of these men on the American communities (in particular the one she thinks of as intellectually limited, because he would, she thinks, encourage gossip).

Another obstacle to Brissot's removal to America was the lack of a market for writers – which he notes in relation to Catharine Macaulay's project of a history of the American Revolution. When Brissot travelled to America, he intended to make himself known. Brissot did not wish to give up his literary career, and if he were to move to an unknown country, he would need the support of influential people. In that sense, his trip was not successful – he did not feel he had made enough of an impact to risk moving his name and career to the other side of the ocean. But the dream remained. When he wrote up his travel notes, he emphasized what he saw as the parts of American life worth reproducing: the Americans, he thought, lived well because their lives were simple and virtuous, and everything in it arranged according to reason. This was the dream he was after, and with which he infected his friends, Marie-Jeanne and Jean-Marie Roland.

2.2 'Philosophy and agriculture'

For those who cared about the future of France and who thought that they were in a position to benefit the nation through their character, ambition and knowledge, the Revolution meant that they ought to stay and attempt to bring the American model to the new republic, rather than draining it of its most promising citizens in order to join those it has already rejected.

Towards the end of 1789, land and buildings that had belonged to the clergy were put up for sale to private buyers as a way of reducing the national debt. This was an opportunity for Brissot to put his plans for a colony into practice without leaving the country. There were several reasons why that might have seemed like a good plan to him. First, his trip to America had not been the personal success he had hoped it would be so that if he moved there, he would not be known as a writer and could not count on the help he would surely need to establish himself in that profession. Second, France was now a desirable place to be for the reason America was: it was on its way to becoming a republic, a land of freedom. And it was one in which Brissot could be of direct influence: in 1788, he had started his journal, *Le Patriote Français*, which quickly became one of the most important diffusers of revolutionary news and republican ideas. He had also been instrumental in the creation of the Société des Amis des Noirs. Brissot had a career in France that was not only successful but also useful, and he could not sacrifice to sail to America and seek a republican life there. The solution that suggested itself to him was to emulate the American republican lifestyle in France. This was not simply a matter of helping the Revolution along and waiting for the republic to be sufficiently well established that French life would be like American life. Brissot wanted to start a republican commune in France, where republican life and values could be modelled by a small group of French citizens for the benefit of others.

Brissot first approached his friends Louis Augustin Bosc d'Antic and François Xavier Lanthenas. The latter had some money and was enthusiastic about the idea – although he might have preferred the original plan of going to America. Bosc d'Antic and Lanthenas suggested they include the Rolands in the plan. Their current way of living, in an idyllic country house, Le Clos, together with their shared republican dreams, made them perfect for the project. Brissot was introduced, and the friends corresponded. It was decided that they would contact a few others and try to put together enough money, in instalments, to buy land and set up the commune.

Brissot drafted a plan for 'An agricultural society, or society of friends'. The aim of the society would be twofold: to 'regenerate' its own members by cultivating the earth; and to regenerate the local community through a 'rural education'. The first part of the plan would be to buy property, a land vast enough to house twenty families, each in its own simple and luxury-free house, and with room to grow. The land should be in the countryside, contain a wooded area and water, be close to a mountain and served by a large road.

The plan says nothing about how rural life would help 'regenerate' the members of the society. Maybe he felt there was no need and that anyone interested would already believe in the healing powers of the simple, rural life. This was certainly true of Marie-Jeanne, who even before she was married, and while she still lived in Paris, claimed that the Spartans led the best lives because they lived in the country, simply, without any luxury. She embraced, and sought to reproduce, whenever she could, the life led by Rousseau's Julie at Etanges, simply, luxury free, industrious and always with an eye to the needs and education of the men, women and children working the land she lived on. At Le Clos, she even participated in the Vendanges when the season came, picking grapes alongside her peasant neighbours, making friends with them and treating them as equals. When the Great Fear happened, and those who had locked their doors against those who did not, she was secure enough in her relationship with the poor of le Clos not to run away.

Another reason why Brissot may not have felt the need to explain what was in it for the colonists lies in the title of the document in which he details his plan: a society of friends. Brissot had ties with the Quakers of England, whose philosophy and way of life he admired, and when he travelled to America, it is the Quakers he sought, both because he regarded them as a model and because of their work against slavery. His brother-in-law had immigrated to Philadelphia, a Quakers town, so there were possibly ties to the sect from that side of the family too.

Another possible clue to Brissot modelling his proposal on Quakers communities is the content of the educational programme the colons were to dispense to the locals – one in which religion was taught but in very simple, rational terms. Members of the society, when they were not labouring the earth, or reading philosophy, would teach peasants 'the purest morals, the simplest religious beliefs and how to work with their hands'. Although the colons were to live simply, one thing they would not have to compromise about was reading materials. Brissot takes care to specify in his plan that the colony will house a good library held in common.

The purpose of the commune extended beyond the desire to experiment in republican living. The idea was to spread republican virtue by becoming a source of influence for the people living around them, teaching them the value of a virtuous life, to be more efficient in their work, and better citizens. At the same time, they had no intention of living among the peasants as equals or of integrating the peasants more closely into their communities. The community was one of the teachers, who would benefit from a more rural lifestyle, but not peasants. Agriculture and philosophy might live side-by-side, but not together.

This separation of status between the leaders and the subjects of the commune is reflected in Jean-Marie Roland's letter to Champagneux in early 1792 – by which time all had given up on the dream:

> 'I was as sure of this as my existence – to create a monument to patriotism and the useful arts, such as does not exist even in Paris [. . .] we would have made a community such as never existed before in the provinces, which could have become famous and would have rewarded our pains with either reputation or profit.'[15]

Perhaps this was not Brissot's intention, but it seems that for Marie-Jeanne's husband at least, there was a third aim, beyond self-improvement and improvement of the local peasantry: fame and wealth for the founders. Would Brissot et al. have recognized this failure to exemplify the virtue they promoted on time to save the commune? In any case, they were caught up in the Revolution almost immediately after they began to plan, and by the time they would have wanted to retire from their role in the Revolution, their fates were already sealed.

3 An American in Paris: Thomas Paine and the Girondins women

3.1 A new era of ideas and principles

Thomas Paine first arrived in France in 1787, and he moved between there and England until his arrest in December 1793, and release some months later, upon which he moved back to America. In August 1792, Paine was granted honorary French citizenship, alongside a few foreign supporters of the Revolution. Paine already had two citizenship: English, from birth, and American, also honorary. Paine was connected to the Girondins, and during his stay in Paris, met at least two of our protagonists, Sophie de Grouchy and Marie-Jeanne Roland. He may also have encountered Olympe de Gouges at the Condorcet's home or at one of the clubs she and he both frequented. But as she spoke no English and he could not converse in French, their acquaintance must have been very limited.

The same was somewhat true of his acquaintance with Marie-Jeanne. During Roland's ministry, Paine visited Jean-Marie and Marie-Jeanne at their Paris home. Marie-Jeanne reports on his character in her usual style:

> I have already named the most notable of the people I entertained, but I must also mention Paine. He had been given French citizenship as one of the celebrated foreigners whom the nation felt proud to adopt, being noted for his writings, which had played a large part in the American Revolution and might have helped to bring about a similar revolution in England. I cannot form an absolute judgment of him because he could speak no French though understood it, and I was in much the same position with English; so that although I could follow his conversation with others, I could hardly engage him in one myself. But I did form the impression that, like so many authors, he was not worth so much as his writings.
>
> [. . .]
>
> The daring of his opinions, the originality of his style, his audacious way of casting unpleasant truths in the faces of those he was exposing naturally caused a great sensation. But I would judge him more adept at setting things alight than at preparing the foundations of government. He can illuminate a revolution but hardly helps to construct a constitution.[16]

Marie-Jeanne Roland was not the only person to think that Paine's enthusiasm we perhaps superior to his policy-making capacities. Sophie de Grouchy's friend and correspondent, Etienne Dumont, had taken quite violently against Paine, having journeyed with him from Paris to London.

> I had met Paine five or six times, and I was ready to forgive an American for his prejudices against England. But I was put off him by his incredible pride and presumptuous smugness. To hear him, he had done everything in America. He was like a caricature of the vainest Frenchman. He believed that his *Rights of Man* could take the place of all the books in the world, and he told us quite sincerely that were it in his powers to annihilate all the libraries, he would not hesitate to do so in order to destroy all the errors they held and to begin again, with the *Rights of Man*, a new era of ideas and principles.[17]

Elsewhere in his *Memoirs*, Dumont recalls his sense of Paine as an unbearable braggart, who held himself responsible for the American Revolution and had come to France to 'start another one'.

Did Paine, in fact, think he was responsible for either Revolution or was Dumont incredibly unfair? Paine did hold some rather strong views on his part in the events that led to the French Revolution. In his *Rights of Man*, he wrote that it was the consequence of 'a mental revolution previously existing in France [. . .] a spirit of political inquiry [which] began to diffuse itself through the nation at the time the dispute between England and the then colonies of America broke out'. Conveniently, these intellectual beginnings coincided with the publication in France of Paine's *Common Sense*, a book in which he explains and encourages the revolutionary spirit. So Paine did probably see himself as partially responsible for the French Revolution.

More perhaps than the violence of the Revolution, Paine saw himself as responsible for the republican ideas that grew alongside it. At the time when the Girondins, Brissot, the Rolands and the Condorcets were discussing the founding of a republican society and journal, Paine was spending much of his time at the Condorcets' home. He could not, he told them, write for the journal regularly, as he could only write in English, and his works would have to be translated. But he could provide the leading ideas for the project; he could define republicanism and offer arguments for why the French should opt for this form of governance.

But even then, Marie-Jeanne Roland was right that he did better in terms of enthusiasm than careful thought. His exchanges with the Abbé Sieyès, author of the pamphlet that inspired the creation of the Assembly and perhaps even the beginning of the revolution 'What Is the Third Estate', suggest that he could be stubborn and refuse to understand an argument made in opposition to his. Sieyès was a republican too and an ardent revolutionary. He had been instrumental in the three estates to gathering in Versailles. But Sieyès was also cautious and did not think it would be wise to attempt to change everything about the structure of the French government all at once. Inspired by classical republicanism, and Montesquieu's take on it, he believed that a republic was a nation governed by laws, not men. Good laws guaranteed freedom if all were equal in its eyes. The government was simply the organ in charge of making sure the law was established, taught and respected. But it did not really matter who was in charge of the government, provided they agreed to the rule of law. A king who was willing to accept a constitution could do it just as well as a representative government, and in the case where a monarchy was already in place, then it would be less onerous to keep the monarchy and institute the rule of law through it. Paine, however, did not see things in this way. As monarchy always means the absolute power of one individual, Paine said, it was also always potentially tyrannical, as it depended on the unknown character of the individual in question.[18] He did not engage with Sieyès's distinction – borrowed from Montesquieu – between mode and principle of government, which meant that a constitutional monarchy could guarantee liberty and be a republic. For Paine, the very presence of a monarch jeopardized all attempts at forming a republic. Perhaps he regarded Montesquieu's *Spirit of the Laws*, where this possibility was spelt out, as one of the books that should have been burned when *The Rights of Man* came out!

Paine's friendship with the Condorcets was certainly one of the reasons why they saw America as a model. And it was also a cause of Dumont's impatience with Paine. Dumont admired the Condorcets and the British Constitution. The fact that Paine was turning his friends against England was, therefore, a major irritant:

> Paine had given them very false ideas about England. I often fought them but in vain. America struck them as the model of right government, and it seemed easy to them to transplant the federation system to France.[19]

It is true that the Condorcets agreed with many of Paine's ideas about republicanism and the American model. They gave Paine's 'Letter to the Editors' pride of place in their journal, *Le Républicain*, and used another one of his pieces (but signed by Achilles Duchatelet) to advertise the journal in placards and in Brissot's paper, *Le Patriote François*. On the other hand, it can hardly be the case that it was Paine who planted the seed of republicanism in Condorcet and Grouchy's head. Dumont believed that he did and that Condorcet became a true republican at the time the king ran away, that is, at the time Paine was his guest. However, we know that Sophie was already a firm republican then and that she had been from her early twenties, so it is not likely that she and Condorcet needed the extra push from Paine. Dumont also believed that it was due to Paine being their guest that the Condorcet's home became the homestead of republican ideas. Although Paine may indeed have attracted more republican visitors, Brissot, Cabanis, and others were already well established in the Condorcet's salon, and their republican convictions too predated Paine's visits.

Dumont's exchanges with Sophie in 1792 tell us a bit more about the nature of their disagreement. In May 1792, the English government decided to make an example of Paine, and he was summoned to court that month. The summons was moved to December, but Paine did not go, and he was tried and convicted in absentia. But the news of the deferral had not yet reached Paris when Sophie wrote to Dumont, who was then in England with Jeremy Bentham:

> I have learned with much sadness of the Paine affair. Is it true that he is in prison? Is there nobody who will save him from tyranny, this man who has done so much good for other men? It is not to you that I address this question, but to Lord Lansdowne. Find out for me, please, what state his affairs are in and what consequences they may have. I hope that to stop me worrying, you will come off your laziness and reply.[20]

Sophie was well aware, it seems, that Dumont would and could do nothing for Paine. But she hoped that for her sake, he would find out what was happening. She was perhaps also wary of asking a favour of him as he had failed to reply to her previous letter asking for feedback on her draft of the *Letters on Sympathy*.

Sophie concludes the letter by denouncing the inertia of the Assembly and wishes that she could join him for a rest in his 'fresh pastures'. But she then further marks her disagreement with him over Paine by adding that the Paine affair put her off travelling to England this year. The nation Dumont wants her to admire is responsible for causing harm to a person that she admires (and Dumont does not).

A few months later, in August 1792, the topic of England came up again as Sophie wrote to inform Dumont of how her friends were faring in the government (Condorcet had been elected to the Assembly). She deplored the fact that the Revolution is not well seen in England and blames those aristocrats who escaped there. But she conceded that were the English to hear of the extent of the 'popular vengeance' that was exerted in Paris that month (the 10 August massacre of the Swiss guards), and that true patriots deplored, he would probably feel that the English were justified.

3.2 Running headlong into atheism

Although Olympe de Gouges did not know Paine, she had something in common with him that Marie-Jeanne Roland and Sophie de Grouchy did not: she was not an atheist. And one important way in which Paine, as an American by adoption and a Quaker by birth, sought to influence the French was by attempting to direct them away from atheism into a form of rational Deism. He did not wish them to return to the Catholic Church but thought it was a grave mistake to deny the existence of God and the way it revealed itself in creation. He described the French of that period as 'running headlong into atheism' and saw his role in writing *The Age of Reason* as diverting them from that path, showing them that one could be reasonable and defend the values of the Enlightenment and of the Revolution while believing in God.[21]

Atheism was indeed, if not rife, at least significantly present among Paine's revolutionary friends and acquaintances. Without supporting the abuses perpetrated during the Revolution on convents and monasteries, they did not, for the most part, seek to find a more rational religion. Gouges was unusual in her Deism, as was her enemy, Robespierre. Condorcet, Brissot and Madame Roland were openly atheist.

One reason why one might expect the Girondins to reject religion is the fact that many of them were scholars or writers who had read and thought about the texts of the Enlightenment. Condorcet, in his last work, the *Sketch of the Progress of Human Reason*, presents religion as the antithesis of Enlightenment, based on lies and the enemy of reason and independent or critical thought. While he saw that the institutions of religion had in some sense helped the growth of knowledge by encouraging priests to study, it had also halted it by forcing the rest of the population to remain in the state of ignorance that was most conducive to their uncritical obedience.[22] This view of religion was very much shared by his wife, Sophie de Grouchy, whose *Letters on Sympathy* say little about religion, but what it says agrees with Condorcet's views. Grouchy saw religion not only as a system of oppression but also as a false system, based on an incoherent set of principles and dismissible by the proper use of reason. Religious leaders' appeal to authority relied on a poor understanding of the notion of rights and even poorer use of reasoning:

> As if reason could approve of leaving a sovereign (who may sometimes be a tyrant) unchecked, except by his remorse, the progress of the Enlightenment, or the despair of his victims? As if reason allowed that the merit of fathers was anything more than prejudice in favour of children! As if it authorized a religious leader (should a true religion exist) to possess oppressive riches and to let intolerance be the result of his

ministry! Last, as if it could allow that any power originally established for the interest of those submitted to it should become a source of tyrannical privileges and impunity for its custodians! How did it come to be, however, that the sacred title of right, which has been used everywhere to hide and disguise the power of might, became a mask inscrutable for the multitude, in spite of the fact that it is in their interest to tear it off? For a long time, no doubt, those governing men calculated that they could easily master the people by keeping their reason oppressed under the weight of need; that they could enchain the great by giving them the people, and entertain their vanity with rattles; and that all they had to fear was, from the former, excessive misery, and from the latter, general Enlightenment.[23]

The Girondin's critique of religion was always based on the oppressive behaviour of institutions, and the dogmatic teachings of the church, rather than personal faith. Both Marie-Jeanne Roland and Sophie de Grouchy lost their faith in part through reading Rousseau during their adolescence – despite the fact that Rousseau himself was not an atheist. While Rousseau sought to retain a sense of the divine and moved from one religion to the other, seeking a better fit for his belief and perhaps more possibilities for reform, Sophie and Marie-Jeanne saw only the oppressive institutions and gave up altogether on religion. In doing so, they also avoided Rousseau's distinctions between private and public religion, a distinction which played an important role in the spiritual progress of the Revolution.

Rousseau argued, in the final chapter of the *Social Contract*, that there were two kinds of religion: religion of man and religion of citizen. The first is private, without any official or public worship, a cult of moral duty. Rousseau calls it the religion of the Gospel, or old Christianity and gives it the title of true theism. The second spells out rights within a nation and promotes allegiance to the laws of that nation in accordance with spiritual dictates. Rousseau characterizes this sort of religion as bad because it is based on lies but at the same time useful in drawing support for the nation and promoting patriotism. Rousseau also says that there is a third 'bizarre' kind of religion, which gives citizens a second government, forcing them into contradictory allegiances. He cites Roman Catholicism (the religion to which he converted in early adulthood) as an example.

The difference between a purely civic code, such as was advocated by the Cult of Reason in the early days of the French Revolution, and a civic religion, such as proposed by Rousseau and exemplified by Robespierre's Cult of the Supreme Being, is that the latter is grounded in the existence of a real (private) religious sentiment. Robespierre instituted the Cult of the Supreme

Being after abolishing the earlier Cult of Reason in 1794. The Cult of the Supreme Being followed Rousseau's recommendation for a civic religion, one that served a different purpose from, but was not incompatible with, a private religion.

A nation of atheists is less likely to be moved to obey a civic religion than a nation of theists. But obeying a civic religion does not count as an act of faith in the same way that obeying one's private religion does. The purely civic religion, Rousseau argued, helps set up the laws of the nation as grounded on a sentiment of sociability without which it's impossible to be a good citizen or faithful subject. It utilizes religious virtues to create citizens who care about the good of their nation:

> There is, therefore, a purely civil profession of faith, the articles of which it is the business of the Sovereign to determine; not exactly as religious dogmas, but as social sentiments of sociability, without which it is impossible to be either a good citizen or a loyal subject. Although it cannot force anyone to believe them, it can banish from the State whoever does not believe them; he can be banished, not for impiety, but for being unsociable, and for being incapable of cherishing the laws and justice sincerely, or of sacrificing, at need, his life to his duty.[24]

Rousseau's civic religion just falls short of Plato's noble lie – used in the *Republic* to ensure subjects accept the social and political order as both natural and necessary. Civic religion does not exclude citizens having a private religion, which grounds the religion of the state by applying the sentiments personal religion dictates to pious allegiance to one's community. There is no doubt lies are involved in the foundation of a civic religion – especially in the case of a political ruler claiming to be descended from or appointed by God. But these lies need not impact directly on people's private beliefs – they merely help their behaviour become more beneficial to the society they live in.

The first civic religion of the French Revolution was the Cult of Reason, instituted in 1794. It was the natural conclusion of what the Girondins had believed but enforced with the Jacobins' iron hand. The Cult of Reason was presented as a way of securing freedom by defeating ignorance – reason replacing the lies of religion with eternal truths and the virtues that seek and preserve them.[25]

The purpose of a civic religion is to unite a people in defence of their nation, to help them put the nation before their own needs. The Cult of Reason was, in that sense a civic religion, declaring the people to be the only God and reason the source of all virtues. But Rousseau's civic religion did have theistic elements: including among its dogmas the existence of a benevolent and intelligent God, an afterlife, a system of divine rewards and punishment and the sanctity of the law.

Although Paine started to write *The Age of Reason* before the Cult of Reason was instituted, he was responding to the conditions that eventually brought it about, that is, the idea that a reasonable, enlightened people should not and could not believe in God. His response was symmetrically opposed to the Cult of Reason: organized religion was harmful; he agreed with Condorcet and Grouchy. But this ought not to prevent us from seeing that there is a god and living one's life accordingly. Like Brissot, his preferred manifestation of religious spirit was Quakerism, which combined strong morals with private, unobtrusive practice (though they too fell short in some ways):

> The true deist has but one Deity, and his religion consists in contemplating the power, wisdom, and benignity of the Deity in his works and in endeavouring to imitate him in everything moral, scientifical, and mechanical. The religion that approaches the nearest of all others to true Deism, in the moral and benign part thereof, is that professed by the Quakers: but they have contracted themselves too much by leaving the works of God out of their system. Though I reverence their philanthropy, I can not help smiling at the conceit that if the taste of a quaker could have been consulted at the creation, what a silent and drab-coloured creation it would have been! Not a flower would have blossomed its gaieties, nor a bird been permitted to sing.

4 Conclusion

Olympe de Gouges, Marie-Jeanne Roland and Sophie de Grouchy never travelled to America, but the philosophy that influenced the American Revolution also deeply influenced their thought through the words of those who had travelled there (Brissot) or come from there (Paine). This was reflected in the sort of republicanism they accepted as well as their attitude to slavery and abolitionism. But they nonetheless retained a more French attitude towards religion, failing to be swayed by the puritan beliefs coming from the American Republic.

The abolitionist movement and the revolution

In the eighteenth century, a total of 6,548,195 African children and adults embarked on vessels to be sold into slavery. From this, 5,654,009 disembarked on the other side. Nearly a million died on the way, in terrible circumstances. Another 960,603 disembarked on French soil.[1] Some of those men and women ended up in Saint Domingue. They were put to work under harsh and cruel circumstances, to produce indigo, coffee and sugar.

Two years after the Bastille fell, the enslaved men and women of Saint Domingue revolted and organized an armed revolution. In 1792 slavery was abolished on the island. In 1801, Toussaint Louverture, one of the leaders of the Haitian Revolution, issued a constitution for the island and proclaimed himself its governor. Toussaint was captured by Napoleon's army in 1802, and Napoleon promptly reinstated slavery.

The struggles of the men and women of Saint Domingue were at the centre of several political debates in Paris. The island was the source of political dissent, because of its economic importance and its reliance on slavery. It also raised questions of racial equality. There was disagreement as to whether Black men who were not enslaved should be granted full citizen rights.

Olympe de Gouges was fully engaged in the fight for the abolition of slavery.[2] She worked to raise awareness of slavery from the mid-1780s right up to the year of her death in 1793. Neither Marie-Jeanne Roland nor Sophie de Grouchy wrote about slavery or the slave trade. But political efforts to bring slavery to an end were a crucial part of the background of their lives and thought.

1 Slavery, abolitionism and the women

The women of the Revolution, or at least the three we are concerned with here, took different degrees of interest in the abolitionist movement. All three were close to Brissot, so all three would have known about this important project of his. Olympe de Gouges was involved from the first. Her earliest play – written before the society was founded – illustrates the injustice of slavery and the horrors of the slave trade. She kept on writing against slavery throughout the Revolution. What Roland wrote during the Revolution was often closely connected to the workings of the revolutionary government and, in particular, her husband's ministry and its attempts to put republican principles into action. She almost certainly did discuss slavery with Brissot and others, but this does not come across in her writings – not even in her correspondence. In her earlier, pre-revolutionary writings, however, she did seek to reconcile her republican convictions against slavery with her belief that women should not be politically autonomous in her early writings. Grouchy did not write about slavery either. But after her husband's death, it is likely that she edited and published Condorcet's text on abolitionism, together with his last work, which she helped write. We may presume that she had had a part in creating the later texts on slavery, too, if only by discussing the ideas with Condorcet. If Sophie did prepare this edition, then the very fact that she decided to print her husband's texts on slavery in the same edition as the work she'd helped write, the *Sketch*, is significant: this is something she could stand by.

One potential source of knowledge on the voices of enslaved women of French Haiti might be the account of the history of racial prejudice in Saint Domingue written by Julien Raimond in 1791 *Préjugés des Colons Blancs*. Unfortunately, Raimond fails to recognize that the women he wrote about were dominated in one way or another by the white planters and instead chooses to explain the origin of racism as arising from them. Raimond traces the beginnings of racial prejudice to the arrival on the island of white women. Before that, he says, white colonists had been quite happy to choose lovers and partners among their enslaved workers. But once white women arrived, they instituted racial barriers out of jealousy, preventing any human interaction between white and Black.

Women, in Raimond's account, were either interfering and vicious or passive and virtuous. He does not consider the different layers of dominations that white and especially Black women in Saint Domingue were subject to. Enslaved women who were chosen as partners were, of course, dominated – an enslaved individual cannot freely choose whether or not to marry her master – and even in the best of cases, if she married her master and bore him children, she would still be under his domination, both as an eighteenth-century wife, but also as a woman without resources beyond her husband (she could not run off to her parents' home or rely on a private fortune) and friends and relatives who were still enslaved by him. A white woman who sailed to Haiti for the sole purpose of making a good marriage, because her family could not afford a dowry for her to marry in France, would also be without resources, far and isolated from anyone who might protect her, and with no knowledge of the island, she had to inhabit for the rest of her life. If we accept the eighteenth-century republican tenet that it is not possible to become or remain virtuous unless one is free, then these women had no real opportunity to lead good lives. They remained, no matter what happened, subject to the arbitrary will of a husband, or master or both.

Perhaps given their lack of opportunity to develop their character through agency, it is not surprising that Raimond portrays white women as jealous animals, incapable of humane regard towards their Black counterparts and Black women as voiceless creatures, whose virtue is determined not by their choices but by whether or not the law allows them to marry the master who rapes them.[3]

We know, nonetheless, that eighteenth-century Black women were far from passive creatures, that they had a voice and were capable of agency to the same extent as men. The Revolution in Haiti was not a man's Revolution. The Voodoo ceremony, which marked the beginning of the slave revolt of 1791 at Bois Caiman, was officiated by a man and a woman: Dutty Boukman and Cécile Fatiman. And women were involved in the revolt that followed the ceremony. Many reports describing the horrors of the slave revolt told how women took part in the tortures and executions of white planters. More women rebels were killed than men simply because they found it harder to go into hiding, not wanting to abandon their children.

Women also played a role in the Revolution led by Toussaint Louverture, which followed the Bois Caiman revolt. One such woman who is remembered in Haiti to this day was Suzanne Sanité Belair, a young free woman of colour from Verrette. In 1796, at the age of fifteen, she married Charles Belair, lieutenant, and later general under the leader of the Haitian Revolution, Toussaint Louverture.

The Belair couple worked together, and Sanité became a lieutenant in Louverture's army. The couple was captured together in 1802. The commandant Faustin Répussard of the French army described the arrest in a letter to his General:

> Following the orders of General Jablonowski, I went to the bourg of the small river to report to Dessalines. The next day my national guards were formed into two columns, and we walked to [. . .] Simmonette not far from the Grande fond, and I was put in charge of the right column. I then went towards the *corai mauger,* where I surprised Diaqoi, Belair's brother-in-law, hidden in a ravine. After questioning him to no avail, I went into the woods with my national guard, and after a short search, I found Madame Charles Belair hidden behind a patch of high

grass and I made her come out from behind it and carried on with her to find Belair who I had been told was entrenched with some brigands but seeing his wife prisoner he gave himself away.[4]

Sanité and Charles were executed on 5 October 1802. He was condemned to the firing squad, but she, as a woman, was to be decapitated. She was twenty-one. The following account was published in an issue of *La Fraternité,* a Haitian weekly journal, some ninety years later:

> On the afternoon of the 13 Vendemiaire, Charles Belair, with his wife, was taken between two squads of white soldiers behind the Cap cemetery. When he was placed in front of the firing squad, he heard the voice of his wife exhorting him to die bravely. At the moment he placed his hand on his heart, he fell, shot to the head with several bullets.
>
> Madame Sanité refused to have her eyes covered. The executioner, despite his efforts, could not force her against the block. The officer in charge was forced to have her shot. The crowds were struck by horror at the sight of this last execution.[5]

Sanité Belair was commemorated on a Haitian 10 gourdes banknote in 2004 to mark the bicentenary of her death.

Sanité Belair was not enslaved, however, and we do not have records of writings or activities from any named enslaved woman from Saint Domingue – aside from reports of anonymous women taking part in the revolts. We do know, however, that women, like men, did overcome their slave status to become writers of note. In the second part of the eighteenth century, Rosa Maria in Portugal and Phyllis Wheatley in America wrote poetry and religious texts. They were perhaps exceptions, very much as Black men who became famous for their accomplishments in that period were. But they were also proof that Raimond does women an injustice when he writes as if they had no voice or will of their own.

2 Citizenship and freedom

While I am most concerned here with recovering women's voices from the revolutionary debates surrounding slavery, I need to say a little more about the political scene and the social realities surrounding these debates as they are a necessary framework for the recovery process. What they also will allow us to see, is that women philosophers' apparent lack of concern for enslaved individuals – which is true at least in Roland's case – matched the politicking of the time. Although the Amis des Noirs were in principle working towards abolitionism, much of their actual work concerned the citizenship of free men of colour, who were often enslavers themselves.

Although women did not directly participate in the debates that took part between the two main actors of abolition in France: Brissot's group, the Société des Amis des Noirs, and the planters' group, the Club Massiac, they were certainly privy to their speeches. They could listen to them or read about them. And they could certainly engage with those who spoke at the Assembly.

The following letter from Louise-Keralio-Robert to Brissot, written in October 1791, is such an example: she berates him for not speaking at the Assembly and complains that Pastoret, who was made president of the first Legislative (the Second Assembly after the Constituante), is no better than Barnave. Both Barnave and Pastoret were members of the Club Feuillant, that is, constitutional monarchist, and Barnave had strong ties with the pro-slavery group, the Club Massiac:

> Can you tell me why you do not speak at the Assembly? Why did you not support the decree so shamelessly revoked? Tell me, if you can, by what fatality the intrigant Pastoret come to be the first president of the Second National Assembly? He perhaps sometimes speaks out of principle, but his heart is always full of corruption. [. . .] He will soon unveil his true nature and will not even enjoy, as a supposed patriot, the ephemeral reputation that Barnave usurped. [. . .] I know him and can predict his destiny.[6]

If the speeches they heard at the Assembly and Clubs were a strong factor in women's political thought, so was the society in which they moved. And while there were no enslaved individuals living in France at the time of the Revolution, there were many white planters who chose to live in France and leave the day-to-day running of their plantations to managers residing in the colony. Any information they obtained through them was, of course, very one-sided and not perhaps likely to encourage the development of abolitionist views – except insofar as the colonists were also often of a royalist persuasion, with connections to the Club Feuillant more than to the Jacobins. But colonists sometimes brought their families home to France, and it was not unusual for some family members to be the children of enslaved women. One such individual who was a well-known member of French high society before and during the Revolution was the musician Chevalier Saint-George. I will now give a short description of these social and political realities surrounding slavery in France at the time of the Revolution in the hope that it may help recover the voices of Gouges, Roland and Grouchy.

2.1 France and the colonies

There was no slavery in metropolitan France in the eighteenth century, and there hadn't been for three centuries. When Jefferson visited Paris, the enslaved men and women he brought with him became automatically free and had to choose whether they wished to remain as servant in Jefferson's household, receiving a wage for their work or seek their fortune elsewhere. This was not necessarily a real choice, and enslaved men and women could well be intimidated into staying with their owners simply because they had nowhere else to go. This was the case of Mary Prince, who came to England with the family which had bought her in 1828, and upon finding out that she was legally free, was threatened with expulsion in the streets of London. It was not until she had made contacts with abolitionists willing to help her that she was truly free to go. But even then, she remained free only while in England and was never able to travel back to the West Indies, where her husband had stayed. So despite the illegality of slavery in France, it may well have been the case that some families had enslaved workers with them and either paid them very little or, as Mary Prince's masters did, threaten to throw them out into the streets.[7]

There were also free people of African descent living in France, some who were perhaps emancipated or descendants of enslaved people, living as peddlers in poverty, some who were part of the servant and artisan classes, and some who belonged to aristocratic colonial families who had come back to France.

In the colonies themselves, the population was also mixed in various ways due to its history. Saint Domingue was invaded by French Buchaneers in the seventeenth century. It was a part of the island known as Hispagniola, which had been taken by Columbus in the fifteenth century. The natives of the island, the Taino people, had been declared extinct in the sixteenth century, but they probably were simply mixed with the Spanish invaders. Saint Domingue was the part of the island which the Spanish had not been able to cultivate. The French had first tried to populate the island of Saint Domingue with paid labourers, but the climate was too harsh, and the experiment failed early on. Saint Domingue was then parcelled out and sold to French aristocratic families for cheap (so went to younger sons), and they in turn purchased enslaved workers to cultivate their land. Enslaved Africans, weakened by the transportation in slave boats, did not find it any easier to live and work on the island than their well-fed white owners and many died in the process of making Saint Domingue a real prospect for agriculture.[8]

The white plantation owners who had only each other and their enslaved labourers to associate with began to choose wives among enslaved women. They married, had children, acquired free status and inherited their land. After one generation of slavery-economy, the population of Saint Domingue changed to accommodate a different class of people: free men of colour. French law responded to this change very quickly. Louis XIV's administration brought out an edict in 1685, the 'Black Code' which regulated commercial and legal life in the colonies but also asserted the legitimacy of inter-racial marriage and the rights of mulattos and free men of colour, as they were called in Saint Domingue at the time. Enslaved people could be freed during the lifetime of their master or in their will. They could also be given land or inherit it. The rights of those who were emancipated were to be the same as those of a white French citizen.

The Black Code made a big difference to the development of the French colonies as it allowed mixed-race children to acquire an aristocratic education, sometimes being sent to Paris for it, and come back to become successful planters or professionals in their native island. By the eighteenth century, mulatto families were established and successful. Some young men moved to France and achieved success there, such as the composer Joseph Bologne, Chevalier Saint-Georges.

Joseph Bologne was born in Basse-Terre, Guadeloupe in 1745. His father, George de Bologne, was a protestant planter, married with one daughter and his mother was an enslaved Senegalese from his father's household, Nanon. Joseph was a 'mulatto', or a man of colour of the first degree (according to the Saint Domingue classification). In 1759 he moved to Paris with his father, mother and half-siblings. There he received a first-class education and distinguished himself in fencing and music.

His musical career was both brilliant and thwarted. As a successful composer and a protégé of Marie-Antoinette, he was offered in 1775 the directorship of the Académie Royale, or the Paris Opera. But two of its leading sopranos complained that they would not work under the leadership of a mulatto, so he was not appointed. The complaint against Bologne was recorded in the gossip columns of the *Correspondance*:

> No sooner were Mesdemoiselles Arnould, Guimard, Rosalie, and others informed about the news [that Saint-Georges had been proposed as music director of the Opéra], they presented a placet [petition] to the Queen, assuring her Majesty that their honour and their delicate conscience could never allow them to submit to the orders of a mulatto.

Such an important consideration makes all the impression it is expected to make, but, after many projects and discussions regarding the matter, the question has been decided by the king, who in the end took it upon himself to have the Opéra managed on his behalf by the Intendants and Treasurers of the *Menus Plaisirs*.[9]

As well as composing and playing, Bologne was invested in the theatre. He was the manager for Madame de Montesson's private theatre – and in this role, he became acquainted with Olympe de Gouges.

During the Revolution, Bologne put his musical – and theatrical – career on hold in favour of the military. He was made the first captain of the National Guard in Lille, and later colonel of the Légion Nationale du Midi, also known as the Black Legion, where he commanded over 1,000 men of colour, among whom Alexander Dumas (the father and grandfather of the novelists of the same name). Bologne's connections with the Duke of Orleans and General Dumouriez, who both fell foul of the Revolution, caused him to be suspended and imprisoned for eighteen months.

Once he was freed, Bologne travelled to Haiti to observe the Revolution there. He was disappointed – for one reason or another, he did not think the Revolution was going well. Perhaps he was wary of independence jeopardising the move towards emancipation. Many planters of colour were still in favour of slavery. We know little about Saint-Georges's involvement with the abolitionist movement. In 1790 he spent some time in London with Philippe Egalité, the son of the Duke of Orleans. There he was reportedly attacked in the streets, but we have no evidence that this had anything to do with his anti-slavery beliefs or activities. He died in 1799 in Paris of bladder disease.

2.2 Amis des Noirs and Massiac: Clubs fighting at the Assembly

Even before the foundation of the Société des Amis des Noirs, the men who became its members, such as Mirabeau, Condorcet and the Abbé Grégoire, had already denounced slavery in their speeches and writings, claiming that as slavery was illegal in France and went against the new constitution, there was really no justification for allowing it to go on in French colonies. Despite this evident enthusiasm for abolition, much of the political debates surrounding the colonies during the revolutionary period were not aimed at abolishing slavery. Instead, revolutionary politicians argued for and against granting free men of colour full citizenship.

The dispute is documented in a doctoral dissertation presented at the Sorbonne by Anna Julia Cooper in 1925. Cooper, who was herself born into slavery in the United States in 1859, and was one of the two first African-American women to obtain a master's degree, went on to receive a doctorate on the French attitude to slavery during the Revolution. Her thesis contains a trove of details about the speeches that were pronounced at the Assembly and the various disputes between the Société des Amis des Noirs and the Club Massiac, the group of white planters who met at the Hotel Massiac in Paris.

The white planters wanted the number of deputies for Saint Domingue to be proportionate to the population of the French part of the island. Mirabeau retorted that if they wanted the entire population to count towards representation, they needed to grant the whole population citizenship. They could not have things both ways: either those who were enslaved were citizens and could choose their own representative, or the number of deputies could not take them into account.[10]

The Club Massiac began to petition the Assembly against granting people of colour full or active citizenship – that is, they did not want them to be able to vote or to be represented. On 3 July 1789, Mirabeau reinforced his point to include free men of colour, who were, like the colonists, taxpayers and whose number was roughly equal to that of the white colonists. Mirabeau concluded: do the white colonists think they will not defend the cause of the Freemen of colour?

The free men of colour in question, many of whom were planters and enslavers who had enjoyed equal status with the white colonists since the Black Code, were now in danger of being relegated to a lower status that is, the white planters did not want them to represent themselves in the Assembly or to be able to vote for white representatives. Many white colonists were based in France and had easy access to the Assembly. But the same was not true of the would-be elected representatives of the free men of colour. Eventually, several travelled to Paris to take part in the debates, and they found support from Brissot and the Société des Amis des Noirs. Among them were Vincent Ogé and Julien Raimond.

Although the Société des Amis des Noirs had first wanted the abolition of slavery, as early as 1789, partly because they found themselves working with Ogé and Raimond, the question that was debated in the National Assembly was whether free people of colour should be granted active citizenship. What the Assembly eventually settled on was that only those men of colour who could pass as white, and for whom a number of generations of legitimate whiteness (that is, marriage, not just union, between white and Black ancestors) could be proved should be given active citizenship.

It is also useful to give an apercu of the arguments presented by white colonists against granting free people of colour full rights of citizenship. They were, of course, appalling, both in their content and their logic. I will present three examples here.

The first text, 'Motifs de la motion faite à l'Assemblée nationale le 4 mars 1791', was presented to the Assembly by a M. Arthur-Dillon, Deputy of Martinique in the spring 1791. Arthur-Dillon (1750–94) was an English-born aristocrat who had inherited leadership of a French regiment and fought for American and French revolutions before marrying a planter heiress and settling in the colonies. In 1791 Arthur-Dillon was back in Paris and deputy of Martinique.

In the speech he presented at the National Assembly, Dillon talked about the dangers of the opinions of the Société des Amis des Noirs.

> They have no knowledge of the place and want to destroy at once political ties that only time and a long period of calm could weaken. Allowing men of colour to be represented at the Assembly would result in an immediate insurrection of the colonies against France.[11]

His argument: 'you don't know what it's like there' was one most commonly used by white colonists. It appealed in part to the French deputies' reluctance to travel to the islands and find out for themselves what it was like. It reminded them that they, the white colonists, had done the work of uprooting themselves, far from their home, and that they had to deal with the daily troubles of managing the plantations, and thereby ensuring both the nation's economic health and a supply of exotic products that the French had rather not do without.

The thought that giving free men of colour the vote would present a risk to the colonies' economic value was made much more clearly two months later by an anonymous petitioner, who called himself an 'American planter'.[12]

The anonymous planter argues that a decree that men of colour born of free mothers and fathers should enjoy civil and political right 'will bring about the subversion of the colonies because the prejudices which keep slaves in bondage will be certainly destroyed by this act as politically flawed as it is contrary to the principles of humanity properly understood'.[13]

He goes on to explain:

> The prejudices of slaves are precious; we must preserve them carefully. We can even say that each time we touch them, we will accelerate the subversion of the colonies in proportion to the gravity of the attempt against them. [. . .]

They believe themselves to be bound to servitude because they are black and because they came, or their parents did from a foreign land where slavery exists. Thinking of themselves as men, as it were, or a different species, they have become familiar with the superiority of the white, in whom they see benefactors who free slaves and better the lives of those who are not white. Last, their state, made sweeter by habit, is only bitter for a few markedly bad individuals.[14]

He also notes, more sensibly, perhaps, if only because this is an argument that can be engaged with:

There is nothing as dangerous as an excessive population of free men in a country where only slaves cultivate the earth, and which is fed mostly from outside, and whose near totality of production is not edible.[15]

This argument was often cited, not only by colonists but also by the abolitionists who recognized that this was an economic consideration worth taking into account. Some abolitionists, including Condorcet and Olympe de Gouges, responded that emancipated individuals would be more willing to cultivate the earth once they had a stake in it.

A third author, also anonymous, writing in November 1791, blamed the revolts in Saint Domingue (Haiti) on the Société des Amis des Noirs and specific members he refers to only by their initials.[16] There was, of course, some truth there: the leader of the October 1790 revolt, Vincent Ogé, was a member of the Club, and it was presumably with its approval, that, having failed to persuade the Assembly to listen, he had travelled first to England, where he received support from Clarkson, then to Louisiana, where he is said to have purchased firearms, and finally back to Haiti, where he led 300 men in a revolt. The revolt was quashed in less than a month, and Ogé was condemned to die on the Catherine wheel.

As well as attacking the abolitionists, the anonymous author of the 'Réponse' argues that the true friends of Black people are 'all men who are just and humane, all planters who work to sweeten, through their goodness, the necessary dependence of the laborious and faithful negro, and only punish the guilty negro regretfully'. This went directly against what Condorcet had written in 1781 – there is no friendship, he had said, and no virtue in being a gentle master. Any true friend or virtuous person would see immediately that owning another human being was contrary to everything good. Nonetheless, the rhetoric of the kind masters was a powerful one. Not only the French whites but also the free men of colour who were, incidentally, also enslavers, could console themselves with such myths, believing that the enslaved Blacks were better off with kind masters than they would have been by themselves.

The view that Black people are not to be seen as human in the same way as white people are was actually shared by the National Assembly in 1791, who granted the colons that Black people were as if frozen in childhood, in a state of prolonged minority, and that the state ought to act towards them as a parent, making decisions on their behalf.[17] The Société des Amis des Noirs, perhaps because they chose to fight only for the free people of colour at first, or perhaps because they were embarrassed by the role they had played in the Ogé Revolt, did not argue against this. Only Grégoire, the sole original member of the society to have survived the Terror, did not abandon the cause of abolitionism and remained very close to the events in Haiti until his death in 1831.

3 Marie-Jeanne Roland: Slavery as a republican trope

French republican thinkers of the Revolution were greatly influenced by Roman political thought, especially the Roman conception of republican liberty. It is defined in opposition to the condition of slavery. When the Romans spoke of the evil of slavery, they most often did not mean that they thought slavery should not exist. The idea, instead, was that slavery was something to be avoided. To be free, in the Roman republican sense, literally meant not to be enslaved, that is, not being owned by someone else. But it could also be taken metaphorically: life under any kind of arbitrary power was, for the Romans, tantamount to slavery. Quentin Skinner explained this as a way of defining slavery as 'belonging to someone else' being 'under someone else's rule', in someone else's sovereignty and 'dependent on the good-will of someone else'. Recent neo-Roman republicans talk of liberty as non-domination or liberty as independence. To be free, they say, is not to depend on the goodwill of someone else.[18]

Many republican thinkers of the revolutionary period embraced this Roman way of thinking about freedom and slavery. This means that in some cases, slavery is spoken of without any consideration for actually enslaved individuals. Those who are described as 'enslaved' are the subjects of a monarch, or women, subjected to husbands or fathers. In some writers, such as Mary Wollstonecraft, the description of women as slaves goes hand in hand with concern for enslaved people. In others, like Marie-Jeanne Roland, we are missing any discussion of contemporary slavery. This seems a little callous when slavery was such an essential part of the European economy. This republican way of thinking about freedom, however, was also adopted by writers who spoke of actual slavery, including the African writer Olaudah Equiano, whose narrative clearly illustrates the neo-Roman way of thinking about liberty.

3.1 Marie-Jeanne and the Spartan

Marie-Jeanne Roland was definitely among those republican thinkers who used the Romans as a model for understanding liberty. And although she used the concept of slavery as a trope for defining liberty, she also saw slavery as a real threat, which manifested itself not only through the withholding of political freedom for the subjects of a monarch and wives dependent on their husbands but also actual slavery. In her 1777 essay for the Academy of Besançon, she wrote even a republic is corrupt if it permits slavery, and that the existence of the Helots in Sparta meant that the city-state failed to defeat the despotism they meant to combat 'the rust of barbarity covers their proud masters and ruins them together. The poisoned breath of despotism destroys virtue in the bud'.

Liberty, Roland argued, in agreement with Brissot, and many other revolutionary republican thinkers, was guaranteed by virtue, and the loss of liberty in any part of the nation would mean corruption could set in:

> The rule of the general will is the only one that can maintain public happiness: from the moment power grants independence to some parts of the state [but not others], corruption is introduced and will manifest itself by enslaving the oppressed.[19]

Even when despotism is not actually active, the slightest deviation from the rule of the people, she says, could lead to enslavement. This is the converse of what she wrote in the Besançon essay, and it is clear that she believed both: corruption leads to slavery and slavery to corruption. Unfortunately, she does not seem to have written about actual slavery other than that mention of the Spartan Helots. Any mention of slavery in her letters is usually metaphorical or referring to the condition of living under a despotic government. In one letter that Brissot published in *Le Patriote Français* in April 1791, which she wrote standing during one of the sessions of the National Assembly, she announces the imminent enslavement of the French people:

> Throw your pen in the fire, o generous Brutus! And go cultivate your lettuces. For that is all that honest folk can do now. Unless a general

insurrection saves us from death and slavery [. . .] The Assembly is but
the instrument of corruption and tyranny.[20]

Those members of the Assembly that Roland is blaming for this state of affair
– the Assembly she says, has become 'Hell itself, with all its horrors' – are
the aristocratic members who wanted to reform the monarchy in accordance
with their own interest, not abolish it. Ironically, these were known as the
'Black aristocrats', so that in the letter, Roland is blaming 'the Blacks' for
wanting to enslave France. This disconnect is reinforced in the version of
the letter published by Brissot, as he introduces the author as '*une Romaine*',
a Roman woman. That Brissot himself was at the time engaged in fighting a
subset of the very same aristocrats on behalf of enslaved Africans shows that
there must have been two parallel trains of thought in revolutionary mind –
one concerned with freeing enslaved Black men and women in the colonies,
and one enflamed by Roman ideals of liberty. And whereas those who were
part of the first group were also part of the second, it is not clear that the two
were connected in their joint discourse. At least, this is how it appears from
reading Roland's Roman rhetoric, written at the same time as real slaves were
fighting for their liberty.

Nonetheless, the same rhetoric that Marie-Jeanne apparently obliviously
deployed in her letter to Brissot was also a theoretical framework favoured
by those who fought for abolition, including some who had been enslaved,
such as Olaudah Equiano, whose narrative includes many of the same tropes
Marie-Jeanne used.

3.2 Equiano

Olaudah Equiano, who had been enslaved and bought his own freedom,
made his mark on the world by spreading knowledge about the slave trade
and slavery. The book, published in 1789, told the story of his life from his
birth in Africa to the time he wrote it and denounced many of the practices of
slavery and the slave trade. Equiano also toured England in the 1780s to help
defend the abolitionist cause by spreading the word about the evils faced by
the victims of the slave trade.

One of the places where he spoke was the Dissenter village of Newington
Green, at a time when Mary Wollstonecraft lived there. When in 1789,
Equiano published his *Interesting Narrative of the Life of Olaudah Equiano,
or Gustavus Vassa, the African*, Wollstonecraft reviewed it for the *Analytical
Review*. She was, on the whole enthusiastic but felt the discussion of his
religious beliefs at the end was rather dull. Equiano, when describing
his enslavement, and arguing for his freedom, used the same republican

arguments Wollstonecraft did when she later defended the French Revolution and the rights of women.[21]

Equiano had been kidnapped as a small child, transported to the Americas and then sold to an English navy officer. When they were not at sea, he lived in his master's London house, where he was taught to read and write. The officer's daughter, who was a little older than Equiano, had him baptized and taught him the Bible. Because he was treated kindly and accepted as one of the family by his master's daughter, Equiano developed a sense of security, thinking of himself as something other than an enslaved person:

> For though my master had not promised it to me, yet, besides the assurances I had received that he had no right to detain me, he always treated me with the greatest kindness and reposed in me an unbounded confidence.[22]

And yet, one day, after months of fighting alongside each other, the lieutenant sold him. Equiano was told to board a barge from where he would join a ship sailing to Montserrat in the Caribbean:

> I made an offer to go for my books and chest of clothes, but he swore I should not move out of his sight; and if I did, he would cut my throat, at the same time taking his hanger. I began, however, to collect myself, and, plucking up courage, I told him I was free, and he could not by law serve me so. But this only enraged him the more.[23]

The ship captain introduced himself as his new master, leaving no doubt, this time, as to what the relationship would be:

> 'Then,' said he, 'you are now my slave.' I told him my master could not sell me to him, nor to anyone else. 'Why,' said he, 'did not your master buy you?' I confessed he did. 'But I have served him,' said I, 'many years, and he has taken all my wages and prize-money, for I only got one sixpence during the war; besides this, I have been baptised; and by the laws of the land no man has a right to sell me. The captain retorted that he had a method on board to make me. I was too well convinced of his power over me to doubt what he said; and my former sufferings in the slave-ship presenting themselves to my mind, the recollection of them made me shudder.'[24]

Equiano's story would have resonated with Wollstonecraft, not just because it was a story of horror and inhumanity and one that was true for so many

Africans, but also because it illustrated perfectly a point that Wollstonecraft and other republican philosophers were making again and again: to be free does not just mean to be able to do as one chooses. It means that no one should be in a position to cancel out another person's will for an arbitrary reason, to dominate, to tyrannize over them.

Equiano's story is a clear example of someone who thought they were free because they were allowed to educate themselves and work for money (even though Equiano gave his wages to his master, he seemed to have been under the illusion that it was for his upkeep, and he managed to retain enough to buy books). The lieutenant did not interfere with his efforts to better himself; he encouraged him by letting him be educated with and by his daughter. He acted kindly and generously. And yet, at a moment's notice, with no explanation, he sold him off to a violent man, to an uncertain (but certainly miserable) fate. And even then it took young Olaudah a while to realize that he had not been, at any point, free, that his sense of freedom had been but an illusion and that all along he had been *under the power* of his master, *depending on his goodwill* (or laxity). As soon as that goodwill was exhausted, simply because the master needed money, the lack of freedom became painfully apparent.

At the same time, the fact that slave narratives fitted in so well with the fashionable republican rhetoric meant that there was a risk that these narratives would become just that – sources of rhetorical devices used by white men and women to defend their political views. Even Wollstonecraft has the tendency to do just that sometimes when she describes women's subordination to men as a form of slavery.

4 Sophie de Grouchy and Condorcet's political arguments

Condorcet's first self-standing piece of writing against slavery, *Réflexions sur l'Esclavage des Nègres*, was published in 1781 under the pseudonym Joaquim Schwartz. Before that, he had written against slavery in his 'Remarques sur Les Pensées de Pascal' in 1776, arguing that any distinction between the rights of Black and white came from a 'false principle of conscience'. *Réflexions* was reprinted first in 1788, with an added Postscript from the editor, that is Condorcet himself, in which he offers a list of anti-slavery reforms conducted in America. Over the next two years, Condorcet wrote several letters to the electorate and speeches to be read at the Assembly and later published on behalf of the Société des Amis des Noirs and of the Paris Commune. Some of these texts were reprinted together in the same volume as the *Esquisse* in 1822 by an unknown editor. The text of the *Esquisse* was the one that Sophie de Grouchy had established in 1795, for the edition published under hers and Daunou's name.[25] Though it is possible that Sophie had prepared the text herself for a re-edition and that she had collected the texts on slavery to add to it, it is unlikely that she saw the edition through as she died in March 1822, the year in which the book was published. However, the fact that the text of the 1781 book was reprinted in 1788 and that the speeches were written in 1789 suggests that it is likely that husband and wife, who worked closely together on anything relating to revolutionary politics, acted as a team in some respect at least, and that the ideas offered in Condorcet's texts on slavery reflect at least in part Sophie's own.

Following a discussion of Condorcet's texts, in which I outline his arguments for the abolition of slavery, is a discussion of a text the Condorcet couple would have been familiar with, as it was discussed among the Amis des Noirs -indeed dedicated to Brissot. This text is by a writer introduced earlier, Julien Raimond, and offers a defence, not of abolition, but of granting free men of colour citizenship, a cause that Condorcet took up in his speeches to the Assembly.

4.1 Condorcet's texts

Condorcet's *Réflexions* is a difficult text. On the one hand, it contains all the ideals and sentiment that we would expect from a philosopher whose love of humanity manifested itself in all his endeavours. On the other, many of the arguments put forward, strike us as morally unacceptable. Condorcet wants abolition, but he wants it to happen slowly, so that slavery will not disappear till after seventy years of the programme he wants to put in place. Enslaved individuals will only be emancipated after twenty or thirty years, depending on their age at the time of legislation. This means that some will never be freed. Even those who are born after the laws on abolition are passed will need to remain in slavery until they are thirty-five years old.

Condorcet proposes a number of measures and sanctions to protect enslaved men and women from planters during the period of progressive abolition. Among them is the requirement that a doctor will visit them regularly and that this will help ensure that they are treated well. Condorcet argues that provided the doctors are young and principled, they will succeed in enforcing a non-violent, healthy treatment of enslaved people. Condorcet is otherwise fully aware of the extent to which slavery and the slave trade are run on principles of bribery and threats and does not trust anyone else in the colonies to perform their role with integrity. But he seems to believe that doctors will be the exception to the rule and that they will not fall against bribes and threats, at least provided their role is a temporary one only so that the rot does not set.

Waiting, and doing things progressively, according to Condorcet, will ensure the future well-being of enslaved men and women who are not, at present, capable of joining civil life and thriving because their intellectual and emotional growth has been thwarted by slavery. Those who have been enslaved have become 'incapable of fulfilling the functions of free men'.[26] Although this argument fits with Condorcet's general views on freedom and citizenship necessitating certain skills that can be educated out of human beings – he says as much in his 1789 piece on women's citizenship – here he is making a very strong assumption based on little more than intellectual speculations on what slavery will do to people. It is a great mystery how he is able to deduce that all enslaved people will have become incapable of making a life for themselves in the free world. This is especially true of those that are born after the legislation for abolition is passed – how could an infant have been habituated into servitude? But perhaps another way in which Condorcet thinks to protect the enslaved is captured by his second reason for slowing down emancipation: his concern for 'public tranquillity'.

The biggest threat to public tranquillity is, of course in part those who are enslaved themselves, who once free may seek to exact revenge on planters, or, finding themselves unable to live in the free societies established by those masters, take to 'roaming the mountains' like' 'brigands'. But Condorcet also expresses a concern for public disturbances that may arise from the planters, who, discontent at losing suddenly their labour force, decide to take revenge upon them and perhaps force them back into servitude. Whichever way it goes, it is worth noting that although Condorcet talks of abolition as a 'revolution', he fully intends it to happen without any violence whatsoever. This means that we might expect his views to change after 1789, once he has accepted that a certain amount of violence is sometimes acceptable when people need to free themselves from tyranny.

What should we make of the fact that the *Reflexions* is a difficult text? It is very tempting to try and interpret away the arguments we deem unacceptable and thereby protect Condorcet's reputation and our own beliefs about Enlightenment philosophers. But that is obviously unfair to the memory of those enslaved men and women who were told to wait and their descendants, and in a sense, it is also unfair to Condorcet himself, who surely has earned the right to be responsible for his mistake. But perhaps one point may be made that will allow us to put some of his more outrageous claims into some sort of perspective.

The *Reflections* was published anonymously, and Condorcet made an effort to present himself as someone who was not a philosopher nor a politician – merely a humble pastor with a powerful commitment to seeking justice for enslaved Africans.[27] He is not, he adds, attempting to convince those who are already enlightened, but the general public, who may well doubt whether a French philosopher or an English pamphleteer would act out of pure moral concern rather than for the sake of pursuing favours in the Academies or House of Commons. And part of the concern that this readership would have about emancipation would be the sheer practicality of it: who will cultivate the land which brings us sugar and coffee? Who will make sure that letting the enslaved live free among planters on a distant island will not result in bloodshed on both sides?

The function of the *Réflexions* is not to legislate or even influence legislation – as Condorcet's later writings were. It is to persuade the general public that some legislation towards abolition is possible and that once legislators realize that it must be done, they can trust them to find a solution that will work. And we are in the unusual position to ascertain what Condorcet might recommend to legislators in a position to legislate, as at the beginning of the Revolution, he addressed voters and the Assembly to persuade them to abolish slavery. These are the texts that we have good reason to believe Sophie de Grouchy collaborated with him on, as it was during these years that they seem to have worked most closely together.

Of the two texts included in the 1822 edition of the *Esquisse*, one was initially published in February 1789, on behalf of the Société des Amis des Noirs, and addressed to the voters choosing their representatives. The letter told voters that they had the opportunity to choose to be represented by men who would vote for the abolition of slavery. And they had a duty to do so, for

> how could they claim against the abuse perpetrated against them which have been sanctioned by laws, opposing to them the natural rights of man and the authority of reason if at the same time they approved, even though their silence an abuse so evidently contrary to reason and to the natural rights of man as slavery?[28]

Condorcet concludes that as the spokesperson of the Société des Amis des Noirs, he hopes the French will see slave trade and slavery both as an evil, the destruction of which must be *prepared*, and that they will demand of their deputies that they should turn to the question as a matter of urgency.

Note that Condorcet does not say that the French nation must abolish slavery but prepare to do so. This does not weaken the intent – preparation, here, is not to be taken as meaning that one should be ready to vote for abolishing slavery should it become necessary. Condorcet is referring to the idea already voiced that slavery cannot be abolished overnight but that it must be progressive. It is likely that he had not changed his mind in 1789 about a slow abolition, one which would leave men, women and children enslaved for many years to come.

The second of the two short pieces on slavery included in the 1822 volume concerns the demand of the planters from Saint Domingue to represent the whole population of the (half) island, including those currently enslaved. Here Condorcet anticipates to some extent Mirabeau's speeches later that year, arguing that white colonists cannot claim to represent those they do not regard as citizens. But he also goes further and questions whether those who violate human rights as the planters do should be allowed in the Assembly at all. He concludes by demanding that they stop using in their arguments the claim that enslaved individuals are happy, which goes counter to evidence received, is absurd in itself and has no bearing on the important question, which is whether they benefit from the natural rights they are entitled to.

On the whole, the 1789 speeches are much less cautious than the *Réflexions*. And this makes sense: in the winter and spring of 1789 changes were happening already, and there was hope that justice might finally find a way forward. Condorcet saw his role as including as many victims of oppression as possible in the hope for reforms.

Condorcet's text on giving women rights of citizenship, written around the same time, is often said to owe much to his wife, Sophie de Grouchy. This speculation is based on the fact that Grouchy was an intelligent woman – so exemplified what women were capable of – and an author in her own right whom we know to have actively influenced Condorcet's final pieces. But we also know about her that she was an ardent and passionate republican and that she was said to be responsible for most of her husband's most extreme views.[29] Clearly, this was unfair: Condorcet fought for justice before he met Grouchy. But it does make sense to think that she may have had a hand in the most polemical of his writings after his marriage. These were topics they both cared about, and if they were to write together at all (and we have some evidence that they did), one would expect it to be on shorter political pieces, those they hoped would have an immediate impact.

We cannot prove that Sophie de Grouchy had a hand in writing these pieces. We can only say that she almost certainly accepted the arguments made by her husband in the book she published. And these arguments are pretty clear: slavery is a crime, there are no excuses for it, nor any objections that cannot easily be refuted, it ought to be abolished immediately – even if the process of abolition will be progressive – and enslavers or any whose business depends on slavery in any way should not receive any compensation for their loss.

4.2 Raimond

By 1790, the Société des Amis des Noirs was in place, papers were being written and speeches made in the Assembly. If all French citizens were equal, and if, as Sieyès had said, rights were to be granted to all, regardless of race or sex, then slavery was obviously wrong.[30] The abolition of slavery clearly followed the principles of the Revolution and (like the emancipation of women) should have been the natural next step. However, an obstacle to this next step (which may never have been taken, as the logic of it would not have necessarily been more persuasive than prejudice or financial interests) came from the colonies themselves.

Two wealthy and influential mulattos, Vincent Ogé and Julien Raimond came to Paris to argue for their political rights under the new constitutions. Under Louis XIV's edict, The Black Code, their rights were equal to those of the white men living in the colonies. However, in the four generations since the edict had been given, those rights had been questioned and slowly eroded, so that now, the white men of the colonies were arguing that men of colour should not receive full citizen rights under the new constitution, that is, they should not be granted 'active' citizenship, they should not have the right to vote, but in every other respect, they would receive equal treatment, as passive citizenship included civic but not political rights.

However, the civic rights of the men of colour had been under attack for a while now, so people of colour in Saint Domingue were no longer free to exercise certain professions, for example, surgery or hold military honours. Their dress was also regulated so that they were not allowed to wear the same cloth or the same fashions as white people. The French people were not aware of such slights, and presumably, if they thought anything, thought that the Black Code guaranteed equality between free men, whatever the colour of their skin. But as soon as white colonists started to demand that men of colour be demoted to passive citizens, Julien Raimond and the Society of the Friends of the Blacks made it their priority to respond and to make known the extent of the racial prejudice that had taken roots on the island of Saint Domingue.

Julien Raimond was a free man of colour from Saint Domingue, son of a mulatto, Marie Bagasse, and of a white planter. He was a wealthy planter who had been educated for the law and was a natural choice to represent people of colour from the colonies at the National Assembly. Raimond succeeded in becoming a member of the French National Assembly during the Revolution and later moved back to Saint Domingue to help Toussaint Louverture write the first Haitian Constitution.

In his *Préjugés des Colons Blancs*, printed in Paris in January 1791, with a preface by Brissot, Raimond deploys the argument that free men of colour ought to be granted the status of active citizens in the colonies. They deserve this status as much as the white men, he says, because, like them, they are free.

Second, Raimond argues that all men of colour, regardless of their degree of whiteness, ought to be granted the same status, as otherwise, brothers and sisters, parents and children, would be turned against each other. In order to make this argument, he says that he needs to explain what he means by 'People of Colour' and 'degree of whiteness', hoping to emphasize, no doubt, the unnatural absurdity of such distinctions which were part of everyday discourse in Saint Domingue.

> A child issued of a white man and a black woman is a mulatto (mulatre).
> A child issued of a white man and a *mulatre* is a *quarteron* or second degree.
> A child issued of a white man and a *quarteron* is a *tierceron* or third degree.
> A child issued of a white man and a *tierceron* is a *metis* or fourth degree.
> The colour of the skin of a metis, Raimond says, is indistinguishable from that of a white person. Any person belonging to any of these groups is referred to as ' 'Person of Colour'.[31]

The white colonists who were petitioning the Assembly to revoke the rights granted by the Black Code (or at least not to take account of them in adapting the constitution to the colonies) proposed that only metis or those who could pass as white should be granted full citizenship. Raimond wanted to show that this was both wrong, unmanageable and that this desire to exclude people of colour was the result of a growing prejudice in the colonies fuelled by nothing other than jealousy. Raimond's argument against granting citizenship to people of colour according to their degree of whiteness was that this would drive a wedge between families. A brother and a sister, both tierceron, that is with three generations of white men among their ancestors, would risk ending up in different classes. The sister might marry a white man, while prejudice dictates that her brother could not marry a white woman. In such cases, the sister's metis children would become citizens, and they would look down on their cousins who were not. Raimond does not note that the same principle may be said to apply to emancipation: freeing an enslaved woman because she has born children from her master, but not her brothers, will also drive a wedge between the family, sometimes to the extent that the woman's children may become their uncles' masters. But it is typical of Raimond's text that he does not address the question of slavery.

Raimond nowhere asks that enslaved individuals should be granted the status of citizens, nor indeed that slavery should be abolished. As a planter who relied on enslaved labourers himself, perhaps he shared the beliefs of his white colleagues that slavery was necessary for the economic survival of the island. Or maybe he did not think that slavery itself was problematic – slaves were not free, so they were not entitled to political rights, and hence their rights did not need fighting for. His attitude was shared by Ogé and thereby enforced on the Société des Amis des Noirs, who appointed themselves their allies.

5 Olympe de Gouges : Polemic and educating the public

Unlike Marie-Jeanne Roland and Sophie de Grouchy, Olympe de Gouges turned to the question of slavery from an early age and did not abandon it at any point in her career. In the addendum to the 1788 edition of her abolitionist play *Zamore et Mirza*, she tells us that:

> As soon as I began to acquire some knowledge, and at an age where children do not yet think, the first sight of a negro woman led me to reflect and to ask questions about colour. Those I was able to interrogate then did not satisfy my curiosity nor my reason. They called these people brutes, creatures damned by God. But as I advanced in age, I saw clearly that it was force and prejudices that had condemned them to this horrible slavery, that Nature had no part in it, and the unjust and powerful interest of the Whites had done everything.[32]

Not only was Gouges more committed to abolitionism than Roland or Grouchy, but she was one of the most vocal, prolific and perhaps influential abolitionist writer of the French Revolution. In 1783 she wrote her first play, *Zamore et Mirza, ou l'heureux naufrage*, and submitted it to the Comédie Française. The actors liked it and accepted it. Unfortunately, her later dispute with Beaumarchais over *Le Marriage Innatendu de Chérubin* meant that the Comédie just sat on her play and refused to put it on. The contract she had signed with them meant that it could not be played elsewhere in Paris. In 1786, she had the play printed for the first time.

Zamore and Mirza, or the Lucky Shipwreck, was a play destined to interest the public in the horrors of slavery, the slave trade and the treatment of Black human beings throughout the world. Gouges also put forward an argument to explain some aspects of slavery: she proposes that it is education that is to blame for this illusion of superiority that leads some human beings to enslave others. Education, she says, teaches one class to place themselves above another. The masters no longer consider themselves merely human: 'art' places them above nature and 'instruction' makes them think of themselves as gods. On the other hand, it is a lack of education that keeps those who are enslaved from rebelling against their lot. They become 'habituated' to horrendous treatment, and education would 'open their eyes' to it.

> This difference is a very small thing, it only exists in colour, but the advantages that they have over us are huge. Art placed them above nature, education made gods of them, and we are but men. [. . .]
>
> Most of those barbarous masters treat them with a cruelty that makes nature shiver; our species, too unhappy, has become habituated to such punishments. They make sure that we are not educated: if our eyes were to open, we would be horrified at the state to which they have reduced us, and we would shake this yoke, both cruel and shameful.[33]

But at no point does Gouges suggest that only educated unslaved men and women are worthy of their freedom: they would become 'horrified' and would attempt to free themselves, but not necessarily succeed, Zamore's own education is assumed by others to be a threat to the masters and is even described as unnatural.

> What crime have you committed, both of you? Ah, I see, you are too educated for a slave, and your education had disastrous consequences for he who gave it to you.[34]
>
> You do not know this wretched race: he would slit our throat without a second thought. Here is what we must always expect when we educate slaves. They are born to be savages and tamed like animals.[35]

Education for Gouges was more of a tool for oppression than it is one for progress. In the state of nature, we are equal, but education brings about a false sense of inequality, which is perpetuated by choices educators make.

The title page of the 1788 edition of the play announces that the book was printed in Paris and that it may be bought at the author's own house, rue du Théâtre Français. At the end of the book, she added a short (seven pages) essay, entitled 'Reflexions sur les Hommes Nègres'. In this piece, she gives an account of how she first became interested in the fate of enslaved Africans in the colonies and what she sees as a fundamental flaw in pro-slavery arguments: namely, there are no natural differences between human beings based on their skin colour.

Here is an extract from her argument.

> [. . .] A commerce of men! . . . great God! And nature does not tremble! If they are animals, are we not too? In which way do the Whites differ from their species? In their colour . . . So why doesn't the dull Blonde claim preference over the Brunette, who is closer to the mulatto? This sensation of difference is just as striking as that between the negro and the mulatto. Our colour is nuanced, as it is in all the animals' nature produced, as well as plants and minerals. Why does Day not compete with Night, the Sun with the Moon, the Stars with the Firmament? Everything is variety, and this is nature's beauty. Why destroy its work?[36]

Brissot, who had read the play and decided it might help disseminate some of the ideals of the Amis des Noirs put pressure on the actors and the play was finally performed at the end of December 1789. Unfortunately, the actors bore a grudge and pressure was put on them by the members of the Club Massiac, so they arranged for the play to be put on the last day of the year, after which Parisians would be returning to their family homes to celebrate the New Year. The contract required that a play make a certain amount of money in the first three days if it was to stay on the programme. The first night was a success – but a political rather than an artistic one. People came to support it and protest against it, and they were so loud about it that few could hear the actors. Fortunately, the text was in print, and reviewers at the time noted that they'd had to refer to the printed version to know how the play ended.

The play closed, as the actors had intended, after the third day, but by then, Gouges had made a number of friends and enemies. The Société des Amis des Noirs made her an honorary member (she probably could not afford the dues for full membership). Then in the early days of 1790, she received a letter from an anonymous planter imputing that she was but the tool of Brissot's society and that her play was a call for enslaved men and women of the colonies to revolt. Gouges responded in an open letter arguing, as she saw that it was she, not Brissot, who'd first given voice to abolitionism in France, and that her play did not incite Revolution, but that it enjoined the French people and the colonists to see that all men were equal and abolish slavery, and those enslaved to trust in the new laws and wait for a better future. At the time she wrote *Zamore and Mirza*, she added, there was no organized French abolitionist movement. The Société des Amis des Noirs did not yet exist. She ponders further, whether it was her play that caused Brissot and the others to create that society, or whether it was just a happy coincidence:

> I can therefore assure you, Sir, that the Friends of the Blacks did not exist when I conceived of this subject, and you should rather suppose that it is perhaps because of my drama that this society was formed or that I had the happy honour of coincidence with it.[37]

In August 1791, enslaved men and women of Saint Domingue revolted. They were joined by free people of colour, and together they set plantations on fire. The whites fought back, and the violence escalated on both sides. Either because she was actually blamed, or because she felt she would be blamed, or again because she thought that her work was relevant to what was happening and needed to be defended, Gouges brought out a new edition of her play in March 1792. Early in 1793, she sent a copy of a play to the Committee of Public Instruction, arguing that she had been calumniated and persecuted for producing a play of true republican principles, moreover one that showed the need to instruct distant populations in the ways of the Revolution. As the revised play had not been performed, she wished them to have a copy to see whether she had not been treated unjustly.[38]

In the 'Preface' to *L'esclavage des Noirs ou l'Heureux Naufrage*, the second edition of *Zamore et Mirza*, Gouges had already attempted to defend her work against its detractors: she repeated what she had said in her open letter in 1790, that she did not incite revolt, and that her motives were philanthropic and had justice on their side. She acknowledged that she prophesized the Revolution but claimed that it was 'an invisible hand' that started it and that she herself was blameless.

Rather than spending time defending herself, or even reminding the colonists that 'she told them so' and that they are responsible for what happened to them to a large extent – she thinks they have suffered enough – Gouges took a surprising turn and decided to lecture those she had previously defended: the enslaved and free men of colour.

Her admonition is in two parts. First, she blamed the Haitian revolutionaries outright for their 'ferocity and cruelty', telling them that by their actions, they demonstrated that they belonged in chains, that they were more brute than human. She acknowledged that her evidence was hearsay – she had read reports from white men of crimes committed by Black men. She was inclined to believe these reports, no doubt, because she had witnessed similar crimes being committed in Paris by revolutionaries – although the worst was yet to come.

One cannot help sensing that Gouges had placed great trust in those people she had not met, that she had seen in them something close to her own ideal of human nature – unsophisticated nature of the sort she felt was most suited to happiness. Even now, she still claimed that enslaved people and people of colour live 'closer to nature' than their tyrants, the white colonists, did. This made little sense, even if she was only addressing enslaved rather than free men and women. What did she mean by living closer to nature? Is it simply wearing fewer layers of protective clothing and spending more time outside in the heat? If so, how could she regard this as a good thing? The climate of Haiti was ill-suited for fieldwork, and the Black slaves suffered from it as much as white workers would have, the only difference being that they had no choice but to work until they dropped.

Free men of colour, whom Gouges addresses in that same text, lived lives very much like those of the white colonists. They owned property or worked in the city, and they had their own slaves. They received the same education as their white peers did, and some, who had been sent to France to learn, were indeed better educated (which created some resentment among the poorer white colonists) Gouges's own acquaintance, Joseph Bologne, Chevalier de Saint-George, was an aristocrat, a colonel in the army, and an influential musician. St George was probably living as far from nature as it was possible to do in the late eighteenth century! In the colonies themselves, many free men and women of colour were better off than some of the whites. Their ancestors had inherited lands at a time when it was plentiful, and the family wealth had had time to grow so that they were better off than newly arrived white families. There was no reason to expect them to be in any sense 'closer to nature'.

The second part of Gouges's lecture to enslaved and free people of colour was an admonition. Those enslaved should wait for the 'wise laws' to see to it that they receive just treatment. The free people of colour should count their blessings. The French nation had given them more freedom than they ever had. And both enslaved and free men of colour were better off, she said, in the colonies than they would have been in their own countries, where their own parents sold them into slavery, where human beings were being hunted like animals, and in some cases eaten too. These were similar arguments that already in 1781, white planters had offered and that Condorcet had sought to debunk.

There is something extraordinary with hindsight in Olympe's attitude to the revolutionary Haitians. She seemed very willing to take seriously the reports of those she still called the 'Odious colonists' and showed no effort to find out how much truth there is in them. The very idea, it seems, that her beloved victims had turned violent against their tyrants shocked her. Yet, even *Zamore et Mirza* showed a hero who murdered his master, and who is at the end of the play, pardoned.

Gouges probably did not have access to accurate information about the two-way violence that Saint Domingue witnessed. The revolted slaves did not travel to France or even write to describe what was happening from their perspectives. She would read accounts of plantations set on fire, white colonists and their families tortured and murdered, all these accounts designed to gain sympathy from the French nation (Figure 14).

Olympe could have read, however, Julien Raimond's book, in which he reported the story of Guillaume Labadie, wrongly accused of planning crimes and being attacked in his home. Raimond, in a letter to Brissot published in January 1791, explains how a seventy-year-old mulatto man, well-loved and respected, with a wealth of his own making, was assaulted by white colonists. There had been a rumour that men of colour had gathered at Labadie's home at the city of Aquin, and the white colonists of that city decided to send twenty-five armed men to storm the house. They found Labadie alone and shot him. Then they tied the wounded man to the tail of a horse and dragged him through the town.[39] Had Gouges not read such accounts, or had she simply decided that violence done by the enslaved Blacks against white men was a worse offence?

The preface to *L'Esclavage des Noirs* concludes with reflections on her philosophical writings pertaining to human happiness, such as her own *Le Bonheur Primitif* or Rousseau's *On Social Contract*, and unnamed but 'august' writings by Brissot. Such writings, she says, although they are admirable, can never be truly useful, as the establishment of new doctrines will always cause more evil along the way than good.

> It is easy even for the most ignorant man to start a revolution with a few exercise books.[40]

Revolutionary France, she further argues, has drawn a lot of evil from Rousseau's writings, defacing them by turning them into calls for violence. What chance, she asks, would Brissot's and her own writing stand in such a climate? Here perhaps, we see that the philosopher is offering to retract and to let the people act in whichever way they can fight for whatever happiness they can get. The philosophers' job, persuading them that they deserve happiness, is done.

By investing the philosopher with this responsibility, Gouges was going beyond many of her contemporaries, for whom the language of slavery was first and foremost a rhetorical tool. She saw that philosophers could encourage freedom, and then hope that actions follow, but without their

Figure 14 Incendie du Cap Français, engraving, BnF.

having to take on the responsibility for bad consequences. Condorcet, more cautious, wanted to avoid these responsibilities, leading him to propose a lengthy process of abolition which would have cheated many enslaved Africans of their freedom. Gouges, by refusing to accept the responsibility for the Haitian revolts, freed the philosopher to engage fully with their ideas, and promote freedom without delays.

Women in the city

Some women of the French Revolution were able to influence the course of events. Sophie de Grouchy's journalism helped make republicanism an acceptable idea in France. Marie-Jeanne Roland participated in government through letter writing and drafting state documents for her minister husband. Olympe de Gouges was at the centre of the abolitionist movement, so much so that some blamed her for the Haitian Revolution. But what did these women accomplish for themselves? How much did they care about establishing their own political rights or those of other women? And how close did they come to success?

1 The state of things in 1789 – Caution and prejudice

The French Revolution, from the start, advocated equality and recorded it in the first efforts at drafting a constitution and a bill of rights. One of the main writers of the Rights of Men, the Abbé Sieyès, had already voiced his commitment to equality in his influential pamphlet, written during the elections for the Estate-Generals in 1788, 'What Is the Third Estate':

> I like to conceive of the law as if it is at the centre of an immense globe. Each citizen, without exception, is at an equal distance from it on the circumference of the globe, and each individual occupies an equal place. Everyone depends equally upon the law; everyone offers it his liberty and property to protect. This is what I mean by the common rights of citizens, insofar as it is this that makes them all resemble one another. [. . .] If [. . .] anyone were to wish to dominate his neighbor's person or usurp his property, the common law would repress the attempt.[1]

Sieyès's commitment to equality at that point seemed universal: 'inequalities of sex, size, age, colour, etc. do not in any way denature civic equality.'[2] These, he said, like inequality of property, are incidental differences and cannot affect civic rights. Sieyès was not sufficiently powerful or influential, however, to cause the other actors of the Revolution, or even simply the members of the Assembly, to want to extend rights to citizenship to women. Nor were his arguments sufficient to guarantee that black men and women from the colonies who had been granted equality previously could retain their status, and certainly not to free slaves. Clearly, those most vulnerable were not going to benefit from this all-encompassing equality. The idea that citizens should participate equally in lawmaking was still a travesty.

In order not to grant every right to everyone, the distinction was made between active and passive citizens – the beneficiary of political and social rights. Active citizens could participate in the running of the state. Passive citizens could not, but they were to have equal social rights to the active citizens. This meant that passive citizens could not vote, but they could, for instance, be granted a divorce. They were persons in front of the law, not subsumed under someone else's rights:

> All of a country's inhabitants must enjoy the rights of passive citizenship: all have the right to the protection of their person, their property, their freedom, etc. But not all have the right to take an active part in the formation of public powers, and all are not active citizens. Women, at least in the current state of things, children, foreigners, those that contribute nothing to supporting the public establishment must not actively influence the Republic.[3]

The French remained convinced that women's nature was fundamentally different from men and that they were not suited for political life. And even if they were granted full citizenship, they would not be capable of exercising the duties this came with. Moreover, the French feared women's influence in politics, associating it with what Olympe de Gouges called the 'nocturnal administration' of Louis XV's mistresses, and worse, the imagined influence of Marie-Antoinette on French politics. Admitting women to the city was deemed, by some, dangerous.

Even those who defended women's rights were cautious and qualified their arguments. Robespierre enabled the admission of two women to the Academy of Arras in 1787: the marine biologist Marie Le Masson Le Golft and the historian, and later journalist, Louise Keralio. But in the discourse he gave on their admission, he explained that these women's presence was desirable mainly because it would help improve the men's work. The idea was that although women were not equal to men and were definitely different, they were not necessarily harmful, and, in small numbers and carefully chosen, they could actually help improve men's performances.

One of the women championed by Robespierre, the historian and editor Louise Keralio, later, Keralio-Robert, was among the first to respond to

Sieyès's suggestion that women 'in their current state' could not be active citizens:

> We don't understand what [Sieyès] means when he says that not all citizens can take an active part in the formation of the active powers of the government, that women and children have no active influence on the polity. Certainly, women and children are not employed. But is this the only way of actively influencing the polity? The discourses, the sentiments, the principles engraved on the souls of children from their earliest youth, which it is women's lot to take care of, the influence which they transmit, in society, among their servants, their retainers, are these indifferent to the fatherland? . . . Oh! At such a time, let us avoid reducing anyone, no matter who they are, to a humiliating uselessness.[4]

Keralio was clearly (and rightly) angered by Sieyès's formulation: in what sense are women not active? What is there of passivity in the work they conduct from home, nurturing republican values and giving birth to new citizens? Like Manon Roland, Keralio was a reader of Rousseau and was convinced that there was a place for women in the republic that was central to the flourishing of the nation, even if that place was in the home rather than in the Assembly. Her disagreement with Sieyès is not about the specific role that women should play in the republic: she is reconciled to the idea that women should stay home rather than participate in debates taking place in public fora. But unlike Sieyès, she believes that the home is just as important a place for the making and cultivating of the republic as the Assembly and that those whose job is to shape the character of future citizens are no less active than those who try to legislate for the current ones.

Keralio's stance on women's rights is the subject of some controversy. In her twenties, she published a history of Elizabeth of England. The fruit of ten years' research, this is a rigorous, well informed scholarly piece that relied on her own translations (for the most part). Far from indicating any sexism or misogyny on her part, Louise Keralio only showed her admiration for the queen and her reign, and in a note to her lengthy preface on the history of England, she says, quoting Virgil's 'it was a woman that led them' that she is including all those details for the sake of other women with political ambition so that they know what background is likely to lead to success.

Keralio's book on Elizabeth was published in 1786. Her next project was an anthology of women's works throughout history, with forty volumes planned but only six produced. The anthology is dedicated to women and composed, according to the preface, for the glory of her sex. The first volume containing an account of Héloise also sheds light on Keralio's own ambitions.

Héloise, she says, was a natural genius, superior in intellect to every one of her contemporaries, regardless of sex. Héloise herself was a mother, but she had not devoted her life to bringing up her son, the unfortunately named Astrolabe. Instead, she and Abélard abandoned him to relatives in Britanny before coming back to Paris to pursue their studies and love affair, and eventually both taking up a religious life. Héloise devoted her life to learning and teaching. Her students being members of a religious order, like herself, she could not even claim to be educating those who would educate future generations. Her life was lived entirely for knowledge (and to some extent religion – though Héloise was not entirely pious). Héloise, unlike Keralio, was not part of a potential and then new republic, and Keralio wrote her history before the Revolution. This suggests that even if Keralio believed that republican women were better suited to the home, this was not something she saw as essential independently of context. The republican model called for women to be civic-minded mothers, but if they agreed to take on that role, they ought not to be diminished in their citizenship.

After three years (and six volumes) of the anthology, Keralio was forced to abandon the project due to lack of funds. But by then, the Revolution had begun, and Keralio seized another writing career opportunity: she became the editor, printer and main author of a revolutionary paper: *Le Mercure National*. This journal lasted in various incarnations (merging with others in order to pay its way) until July 1791 and was one of the first publications to advocate the end of the monarchy.

In 2006, the French historian Annie Geffroy wrote a piece about Keralio in which she described her as a pioneer of republican sexism. Eight years later, the philosopher Karen Green argued that this was an unfair and unsupported conclusion to draw.[5] So was Louise Keralio a sexist or not?

A large part of what contributed to Keralio's reputation for sexism, misogyny, even, was an anonymous, violently sexist 1790 publication *The Crimes of Queens*, which we have no real evidence to believe was hers.[6] In fact, the misogyny present in that text makes it difficult to imagine that any woman who thought so badly of her sex would want to impose her own writings on the world! Geffroy does not cite this text as evidence. Her conclusion is based in great part on a different text which, although it was printed in Keralio's newspaper, *Le Mercure National*, is unsigned:

> I do not believe that women should ever take an active part in government, and I believe that the most good the constitution can do for public morality is to keep them away from it forever. Women reign in despotic states, which is tantamount to saying they will be useless in the administration of a free country. As the austerity of republican morality

will make them more attentive to their homes, the less opportunity they will have to know enough about more about public men to determine a choice that has to be the result of constant observation and complete experience. [. . .] Contented with the task of teaching their children the decrees of the Assembly, they will not have the ambition to make the decrees, nor to dictate them.[7]

This text is a part of a review of a piece by a Jacobin lawyer Armand Guffroy, in which he advocated women's active participation in the state: women, he wrote, should be admitted to primary assemblies to deliberate on the choice of municipalities and participate in the administration of the state. If they don't, there will never be a 'public spirit'. The response published in Keralio's paper is firmly against his proposal and against any form of participation by women. But the review is not signed and could therefore have been penned by any of the several journalists working for the *Mercure National* in April 1790 – all of whom, apart from Keralio, were men.

Another text which suggests that she did not want women to participate in politics is a letter to Brissot written shortly after the women's march to Versailles. Brissot had apparently written to Keralio, remonstrating against an article she had written about women and the Revolution, calling the women of Versailles 'courageous citoyennes' and 'true heroines' and the men who had wanted to push them aside when the king was delivered to the Assembly 'imprudent'.[8] For Brissot, the women's presence at the Assembly had contributed little more than unsightly chaos, and so it is likely that he wrote to Keralio questioning her own assessment. Keralio responded, writing, oddly, in the third person, by thanking him for his 'little lesson'.

Mademoiselle de Keralio is very satisfied by what [Monsieur Brissot de Warville] said today about the influence of women. It is very much part of Melle de Keralio's principles that women should not make a great spectacle of themselves. [. . .] A love of publicity is bad for modesty, from the loss of that comes a distaste for domestic work, and from idleness, principles are forgotten and from lack of morals arise all of public disorders.

We should be forced to seek women inside their homes, their presence should be hard to obtain and rare offered as a favour.

It is part of the regeneration of France, and especially Paris [. . .]; men are busy now and consequently less attentive to the frequent apparition of frivolous or useless objects. Women [. . .] must go back to the peaceful and useful work assigned them by nature. Education will change, and in the next generation there will be fewer of these little amphibious beings whose appearance so cruelly bothered Melle Keralio that she has often been called a prude and a bigot (though she is neither).[9]

One could be tempted to read her letter as sarcastic – but Brissot was far too important and well-loved in Keralio's circle, that is, the Girondins, and the revolutionary press for her to dismiss him in such a way. And she seems to show genuine distaste for women who 'make a spectacle' of themselves and those she calls 'amphibious', that is, neither wholly male nor female but moving equally in both the public and the domestic sphere. In this letter, she does also appear to have an argument for keeping women out of politics. Women's presence in the home is a guarantee of order and morality. Order and morality are necessary for maintaining public order. Therefore, the best women can do for the republic is to stay at home and look after their children.

Karen Green cites Keralio's response to Sieyès as evidence that Keralio was a precursor of difference feminism rather than sexism. Women do have political power, she seems to say, and they do matter to the Revolution but in a different way than men. Their part is played in the home, but it is an active part – they are responsible for the formation of the republican character and the development of republican virtues. This is very much what Manon Roland also believed, as she drew on Rousseau's arguments in *Julie or the new Heloise*, that a republic was built from within individual homes, at least as much as it was in the capital and government.

There is something to be said for reading Keralio as a difference feminist rather than a sexist. We tend to think that the shackles of domesticity have always held us back, that we are fighting the same gender stereotypes that our foremothers fought from prehistoric times onwards. That we are fighting stereotypes is true, just as it is true that we are fighting off male domination. But the stereotypes were not always what they are.

In the eighteenth century, women were not necessarily thought of as ideal mothers or virtuous wives. This is something that came from Rousseau, who revived the ideals of motherhood (making sure also that it couldn't reach too great heights). This, as also his claim that mothers should feed their children themselves instead of employing the services of wet-nurses, was felt as liberating by some women. They were given a role in society that they didn't have before. They were no longer just an extra pair of hands in the family business or an ornament for the rich. They were the guarantors of virtue in the home and the republic.

Brissot's own role in Keralio's retraction of her admiration for the women of 1789 is far from admirable. What did he write to Keralio to make her thank him for his 'little lesson' and assure him at length that she did not think women should do politics? Mistacco suggests that we can guess somewhat what he said from his published response to women's presence in the Assembly:

> In his accounts, Brissot essentially edits out the women's agency, even avoiding the word 'femmes' as much as possible. He describes the women's raiding of the coffers at the Hôtel-de-Ville before they marched on Versailles as 'revolting'.[10]
>
> He portrays their entry into the National Assembly as a religious transgression committed by a genderless 'on' and their speech as indecent. 'Les bons citoyens [. . .] regretteront sans doute qu'on ait violé la sainteté d'une Assemblée nationale, par des clameurs indécentes'.[11]

Brissot's sexism was particularly shocking because he was such a great supporter of individual women, an admirer of their work (Figure 15). He was close to Keralio but also to Manon Roland and had been very interested in Olympe de Gouges's work, promoting her play on slavery. He was also a great admirer of Catharine Macaulay and was responsible for bringing her work to the notice of French readers. When such an ally also argues politely and with restraint that women should not do politics openly, then it is difficult not to listen.

Figure 15 Women marching to Versailles, engraving, BnF.

We are often led to wonder why a person who is politically sound and who is apparently unthreatened by strong and talented women can turn out to hold sexist views. In most cases, we have no way of knowing. But Brissot, in the *Memoirs* he wrote in the prison de l'Abbaye (in the cell Manon Roland had just vacated, and where she'd begun her own *Memoirs*) gives us an insightful account of his own sexism. He described his attitude towards politically engaged women in 1782 when he was visiting Geneva. Because it is such a rare moment of clarity coming from someone who was sexist, I reproduce it entirely:

> [. . .] politics seemed a heavy and boring science, unsuitable for a pretty woman. To please and to entertain was the great art that women were to learn their entire life. And if the philosophy I professed forced them to take up other studies, it was of the virtues that could render a wife or a mother's company useful and pleasant for her spouse and children. In a word, a woman given to politics seemed to me a monster, or at least, a new kind of 'précieuse ridicule'.
>
> There is no doubt that, had I thought through my opinions, I would soon have discovered their absurdity and would have turned the ridicule against myself instead of against political women. But in most of my life's external circumstances, carried by a whirlwind, I was more the slave to public prejudices than the apostate of truth.[12]

Brissot recognized the absurdity of his sexist position – he might have also recognized that it was harmful, dangerous, even. In an attempt to understand his position, he attributes it to a weaker commitment to the truth than was needed, but also to his fashionable love for Rousseau – either way, he was carried by the whirlwind of prejudice.

2 Joining hands – Le Cercle Social, La Société Fraternelle des Deux Sexes and the Condorcet marriage

Clubs and circles – which would come to be known as 'salons' in the nineteenth century – were actively preparing the Revolution since at least 1787. Many of the aristocrats or bourgeois who took part in the events of the summer and fall of 1789 used to frequent the circles of the Palais Royal, run by the anglophile Madame Genlis, the ex-lover of Philipe d'Orléans, and tutor to his children, or Suzanne Necker, the wife of the finance minister and mother of Germaine de Stael. But soon after the fall of the Bastille, revolutionary clubs sprung up, such as the Club Breton, the Club de 1789, the Cordeliers, the Friends of the Constitution (renamed the Jacobins in 1792), the Société des Amis des Noirs, the Club des Amis de la Vérité and the Société Fraternelle des Deux Sexes. Two of these, the Club des Amis de la Vérité and the Société Fraternelle, founded in 1790, explicitly admitted members of both sexes from the very start. Others are known to have admitted women as honorary members, such as the Société des Amis des Noirs who welcomed Olympe de Gouges in 1789. Most of the others allowed women to assist to meetings: Manon Roland went to the Jacobins regularly, even though she did not speak there, and Théroigne de Méricourt was a frequent visitor at the Cordeliers.

The Société Fraternelle des Deux Sexes met in the convent of the Jacobins – later, they swapped places with the Friends of the Constitution whose quarters were then in the adjoining church. They met by the light of a single candle, illuminating a bust of Jean-Jacques Rousseau at 4.00 pm every Sunday and holiday and every Tuesday and Thursday. New members had to be introduced by another member and vouched for by two more members of either sex. The members voted for a president, two secretaries, a treasurer and, according to the regulations, two female secretaries (who may not have been as important to the running of the club as their male counterparts as their names do not figure on the last page of the regulations). The main purpose of the society was to protect the constitution against ignorance, and once a month, before elections, the Rights of Man was read out loud.

Le Cercle Social, also known as the Société des Amis de la Vérité, welcomed female members and allowed them to speak. Although they did not come as close to inviting parity between the sexes as the Société Fraternelle des Deux Sexes, they did form a women-only offshoot – le Club des Amies de la Verité, founded by Eta Palm d'Aelders in 1791, and dedicated to the furthering of women's education and rights. More generally, the Cercle Social encouraged the development of feminism and invited speakers to talk about women's political participation or divorce law. The piece by Guffroy, which Keralio's journal attacked for defending women's rights was published in the Cercle's periodical: *La Bouche de Fer*.

Louise Keralio and Eta Palm d'Aelders were both members of the Société Fraternelle, and the latter also spoke at the Cercle Social. We have reason to believe that both Manon Roland and Olympe de Gouges also belonged to both clubs, and certainly, Sophie de Grouchy would have attended some of the meetings of the Cercle Social, as her husband was one of its founding members.

In 1790, Condorcet published a paper in which he argued that women ought to be included in the proposals to turn subjects into citizens.[13] If only men accede to the status of citizenship, he argued, then only half the population will be granted liberty – women will be left behind. It didn't take a famous mathematician to do the sums here, and one might wonder why so few people seemed to notice that half the population was left out of the new rules. But then that was hardly the point. No one, including Condorcet, thought that children ought to be given rights of citizenship. And women, like children, were not deemed fit to govern themselves, hence could not be trusted with the status of citizens.[14]

What prompted Condorcet to defend women's rights to citizenship? According to his biographers, Elisabeth and Robert Badinter, Condorcet did not know many women but was very much in awe and appreciative of the few he did know. His mother brought him up alone, and he lived with her until her death, two years before his marriage to Sophie de Grouchy. His second close female acquaintance was Julie de l'Espinasse, the lover of his friend and mentor d'Alembert. Condorcet and Julie were so close that he was the only person she admitted to her side as she was dying. The third, Amélie Suard, a married friend of Julie's, became his close friend and confidante when they were both in their mid-twenties.[15]

But how much should we read in these friendships? Elisabeth Badinter, a philosopher who writes about motherhood and the way gender conflicts shape society, seems to think they denote a tendency to compartmentalize women as mothers or sisters and suggests that his closeness to his own (overbearing) mother may have made it difficult for Condorcet to have sexual relationships with women. A simpler conclusion to draw from what little evidence we have is that Condorcet knew that women of quality existed, that their minds, their person, were as valuable as those of men, and that they were as capable and deserving of ruling themselves as any man. Another possible influence Badinter cites elsewhere is that of Emilie du Chatelet, the Newtonian physicist and philosopher who had lived and worked alongside Voltaire for most of her life.[16] Condorcet would not have known her as she died when he was still a toddler. But her influence on Voltaire was lasting, and no doubt Condorcet, who first met Voltaire in 1770, was aware of it.

The main prompt for Condorcet to address the question of women's rights may have been a sense of justice and consistency. He defended equality; he defended it not just for the inhabitants of France, but in the colonies too, for enslaved and free men of colour. Why would he leave women out? In his 1790 piece, Condorcet denounces the absurdity of leaving them out: how can men earnestly defend political equality and simply 'forget' half of the human race? How can twelve million individuals be left out of the argument?

Condorcet's argument relied more on argument and less on moral indignation, his aim being to rebut the prejudices he knew his contemporaries to hold. First, he presented an argument for the view that to refuse women active citizenship is an act of tyranny unless it can be proved that women are not fully capable of exercising their natural rights. This cannot be claimed on account of the fact that women are occasionally incapacitated (by childbirth) because otherwise, those men who suffer from gout every winter or who are prone to catching colds should also be excluded from political participation.

Next, Condorcet lists a number of women whose capacity to govern themselves and others; he knew no one would dispute. Among them, he names Elisabeth of England, Maria-Theresa of Austria and Catherine of Russia. Then he names women intellectuals: Catherine Macaulay, the English republican historian, so admired by Brissot and Roland, Marie le Jars de Gournay, Montaigne's adoptive daughter, and the author of Stoic-inspired texts, including a defence of women's education, the Marquise du Chatelet, physicist and mathematician. Finally, he addresses an objection that women seem to be spending too much time at home and socializing to have the requisite time and skills for politics.

Condorcet argues that if peasants can find time from farming to vote, then a woman can take time off domestic tasks to do the same. As for the lack of skills, he says:

'It is just as reasonable for a woman to spend time on her appearance as it was for Demosthenes to practice diction.' Women are asked to be attractive: it is only natural that they should employ their reason to further that goal. But should they become active citizens, those same reasoning skills will turn into political goals. Condorcet argued not that women's intelligence was indeed more focused on home life than the political, but that it was a sign of their adaptivity that they did. Out of necessity, and as soon as they were called to act as citizens, their malleable intelligence would shape themselves to the tasks at hand.

Did Sophie de Grouchy have anything to do with this text? At least indirectly, she must have: Condorcet would not have been much of a practical philosopher had he not noticed that his own partner was as able a thinker and as deserving of self-government as he was. But why did Grouchy not write the piece herself in that case? Her husband would no doubt have supported her: he supported another woman writer, Etta Palm d'Aelders when she argued in favour of women's citizenship. Condorcet secured her a talk in a club and helped print the paper for the club's proceedings. The men at the club had been so impressed that they decided to give copies of the talks to their wives so that they too would awaken to their duties of citizenship.

So why Palm D'Aelders but not his own wife? For one thing, Etta was forty-seven years old in 1790 and had behind her a successful career as a diplomat. She also had, by leaving behind that career and embracing the French Revolution, despite being a foreigner, proven her allegiance. And she was Dutch, so she came from a republican background. Sophie, in 1790, was twenty-six. She was an aristocrat and already had a reputation as a thoughtless firebrand who would lead her husband into trouble. The last thing either she or Condorcet would have wanted was for their arguments to be dismissed as an inconsequential caprice. They might have thought that the issues deserved the sort of gravitas that would not be apparent if they came from a mouth of a young aristocratic wife. But this is speculative as we have no record of a conversation on that topic. Condorcet valued his wife's advice and her philosophical productions, but nowhere mentions that she wrote on the question of women's rights.

3 Speaking out: Women in the city

In the summer of 1791, Etta Palm D'Aelders, Dutch citizen, and long-term resident in Paris, member of the Cercle Social and the Société Fraternelle des deux Sexes, was the recipient of 'atrocious calumnies' from the revolutionary paper *La Gazette Universelle* run by Louise Keralio-Robert and her husband.[17] The couple accused her of being a Prussian spy and a counter-revolutionary. Etta had, in fact, been a spy. When she'd settled in Paris, she'd been tasked, discreetly, with finding out what her countrymen felt about the Revolution. But she was also very attached to France and the republic. When the accusations came, she felt that the best way to prove her innocence would be to publish the speeches she had given and the ensuing correspondence with various regional revolutionary clubs. The collection was titled 'Appeal to French Women on the Regeneration of Morals and the Necessity of Women's Influence in a Free Government'.

Etta's first contribution to the Cercle Social had been a speech given at the end of 1790 and defended women's rights of citizenship. She had been invited because a month earlier, she had stood up and defended another speaker, Charles-Louis Rousseau, who'd argued in favour of women's political rights. 'Women!' He'd said. 'Until now, you were only mothers. Now you must be citizens too!'[18]

But the audience jeered, and Rousseau hesitated, so Etta took over. A short while later, she received the invitation to talk about women's citizenship. She did not mince her words. Men were just doing things 'by half' when they made laws in their favour and against women simply because the power was in their hands. Women were fated through marriage to 'painful and awful slavery', their husbands were despots and women's existence was secondary. None of this was deserved, she argued, refuting a common objection that women were suited to slavery. Women were, she granted, physically more 'delicate' than men, but they made up for it through moral strength. She cited famous political women: Elizabeth I, Catherine II and Joan of Arc. She asked men to look to their wives and daughters and ask themselves whether they were not just as capable as they of patriotism and courage.

Her talk was printed and shared with regional branches of the Amis de la Vérité, who in turn shared it with their wives and invited them to join them in their clubs. A few months after her resounding success, Etta petitioned for and was granted the right to found a new society, a branch of the Amis de la Vérité, but for women only. The purpose of the *Société Patriotique et de Bienfaisance des Amies de la Vérité* (Patriotic and Charitable Society of the Female Friends of Truth) was to plan and enact humanitarian projects, especially towards indigent women, widows or young women who had come from the country to work as wet-nurses and found themselves alone and abused, or putting up a school for young women of poor families.

Etta succeeded in rebutting the Roberts's accusations, but when four years later, France went to war with the Netherlands, she was imprisoned in The Hague. She was released after three years but weakened by the ordeal. She died a few months later at the age of fifty-five.

Two years after Sieyès wrote 'What Is the Third Estate', and when it had become clear that sex would count against equality, after all, Olympe de Gouges tried to reopen the debate and, in order to do so, published her 'Declaration of the Rights of Woman', which included seventeen clauses, mirroring the clauses of the 'Declaration of the Rights of Man', showing both that it would be easy and natural to include women in the Declaration and that doing so would help show some of the shortcomings of the existing document and ways in which it might be improved. For instance, Article III of the 'Rights of Man' states that sovereignty belongs to the nation. The 'Rights of Woman' adds that the nation consists of the 'union of man and woman', thereby offering an argument for its unity and leading to the following claim of the article that no individual may seize power for themselves. The nation as a concept was new to revolutionary France, and some may have wondered what it was that made a group of people a united body, rather than simply a group of individuals. Gouges's reminder that individuals are already tied to each other through marriage and family makes it easier to understand what the nation might be and whence its power may come. A family has a greater interest to serve than an individual – so does a nation.

Article IV of the Rights of Man states that liberty 'consists of doing anything which does not harm others: thus, the exercise of the natural rights of each man has only those borders which assure other members of the society the fruition of these same rights. These borders can be determined only by the law'.

Gouges turns this around in Article IV of the Rights of *Woman*: 'Liberty and justice exist to render unto others what is theirs; therefore the only limit to the exercise of the natural rights of woman is the perpetual tyranny that man opposes to it: these limits must be reformed by the laws of nature and reason.' The limits of liberty are no longer thought of as what one might do to harm others, but as what others do to harm us, and how liberty is still impeded in a world where men have rights but not women. The law, representing justice, should not simply be seen as drawing circles around individuals to prevent them from harming those outside. It should instead actively prevent domination and pursue those who engage in it. The principle is the same, no doubt, but the perspective is different. Gouges shows us that the nation, even sovereign, is not starting with a clean slate, where individuals are free as long as they do not harm each other, but that tyranny is still embedded in the fabric of human society and that placing sovereignty in the hands of the people rather than the king will not suffice to free one-half of the population from the tyranny of the other.

Following Sieyès's original suggestions that equality could only grow out of the suppression of criminal law privileges for the aristocrats, Gouges also argued that for women to have equal status as citizens would mean, in the first instance, equal status in the face of criminal law:

> **Article VII** – No woman may be exempt; she must be accused, arrested and imprisoned according to the law. Women, like men, will obey this rigorous law.

> **Article VIII** – The law must only establish punishments that are strictly necessary, and none can be punished other than by a law established and promulgated prior to the offence and legally applied to women.

> **Article IX** – The law will vigorously pursue any woman found to be guilty.

> *Rights of Woman* 1791.

Articles VII and VIII of the 'Rights of Woman' follow the 'Rights of Man' closely:

> **Article VII** – No man can be accused, arrested nor detained but in the cases determined by the law, and according to the forms which it has prescribed. Those who solicit, dispatch, carry out or cause to be carried out arbitrary orders, must be punished; but any citizen called or seized under the terms of the law must obey at once; he renders himself culpable by resistance.

Article VIII – The law should establish only penalties that are strictly and evidently necessary, and no one can be punished but under a law established and promulgated before the offence and legally applied.

But the ninth article differs significantly in Gouges's version and the original. The original states that presumed innocence means that treatment of suspects during arrests should be gentle as far as possible:

Article IX – Any man being presumed innocent until he is declared culpable if it is judged indispensable to arrest him, any rigour which would not be necessary for the securing of his person must be severely reprimanded by the law.

Gouges's Article IX, on the other hand, simply states that a woman, if guilty, should be pursued rigorously. These two versions of Article IX are not incompatible, but there is a significantly different focus. What matters to her here is not that women should be treated gently by the law before it has been determined that they are guilty, but that once found guilty, they should receive the full harshness of the law.

It may seem a little relentless of Gouges to demand that women be punished harshly. One might think that emphasizing other, more positive aspects of women's civic rights might be more of a priority in helping end their domination. However, there are relevant and perhaps mitigating factors here. Like Sieyès, Gouges realized that the first step to be taken towards equality in front of the law was to claim equal treatment by the criminal law. The criminal law – although it does not touch every citizen in the way that property law or marriage law does – is highly visible, especially as executions were public, and when it does touch citizens, it does so dramatically, possibly ending in torture and death. It is also a way of reforming the legal treatment of all, which does not require too much rethinking of social relations. Punishing a woman as one would punish a man does not take anything away from men aside from a sense that they are superior and ought to be treated differently in every way. Reforming property or marriage laws would, on the other hand, take away something from them. So in a sense, demanding that women be treated equally by the criminal law is a plausible first step.

Second, making it clear that women are to answer the law in the same way as men is a way of preventing the domination of wives by husband. If women were to answer to the law, Gouges implies, they would not need to be punished by their husbands. The state, not the family, would be responsible for punishing their infractions. At least in terms of criminal behaviour, husbands would no longer be masters of their wives. If, as Article VII states, a woman must be accused, arrested and imprisoned according to the law, she cannot be accused and have punishment inflicted upon her by a private individual. That, as stated by Article VIII, punishment can only be inflicted by law and only when it is strictly necessary precludes additional private punishment. Clause IX makes it clear that women who commit crimes will be not let off easily by the law so that there is no need for private correction. The strength of the law is meant both to prevent private punishment and show that it is redundant. It is therefore significant that Gouges, like the authors of the first constitution and Declaration of the Rights of Man, chose to focus on criminal law.

4 When the private is political

Keralio, and Roland, when they argued that a republican woman's place was in the home, were far from exceptional. Nor was that view considered by most to take women out of the political domain. The idea that the family, the home, were the heart of the republic, the place where republican virtues were nurtured, where new generations of citizens were formed, was in itself revolutionary. For the first time, French women were considered useful, not just as servants for their families but useful to the nation. They had a greater purpose.

This general attitude is visible everywhere in revolutionary France and not merely in the writings of a few educated Parisian women who had access to the men of the Assembly. One group of women, les Dames Citoyennes de Marseilles, invoked their duty to speak out (against an envoy of the king) in the autumn of 1789 calling it: 'the obligation to make their voice heard, by stealing a few moments from their domestic duties'. To be a politically engaged woman did not – could not – mean that one neglected one's home. On the contrary, a woman had to emphasize that speaking publically was time stolen from her domestic work, for only then could she be taken seriously as a citizen.

A year later, on 7 November 1790, another woman was invited to talk to the Marseilles branch of the Jacobins' club. Her speech was published under the title of 'Le Patriotisme des Dames Citoyennes'.

> Happy those who, giving the nation children, and holding in the arms the tender fruit of conjugal love, offer to suckle with their milk, the great principles of equality, a passionate love for the nation, for liberty, and an inviolable attachment to the constitution.[19]

The republican mother is not just a milk bottle, but she has the sacred duty, at the same time as she feeds her children, to imbue them with the values that she herself must embody – for just as one's diet influences the quality of milk one produces, it's necessary to be virtuous oneself in order to transmit virtue. Nor is the mothers' role purely ideological: she must transmit values, but more than that, she must make sure that future generations are entirely committed to the constitution, that is, to the way in which the Assembly decided that the values of liberty and equality had to be embodied. In that way, it is up to mothers to ensure that future generations will not renege on these values and that they will continue to uphold the choices made in 1789.

In the ancient regime, a French marriage could only be annulled through a special dispensation from the pope. In 1792, divorce became legal. It was possible to divorce in two ways. First, a couple could decide they simply no longer wanted to be married. In this case, they simply had to wait six months after submitting a demand for divorce, and the divorce would be finalized after that period. One spouse could also ask for divorce for cause of cruelty, desertion and infidelity. Until the Napoleonic period, divorce was reasonably easy to obtain. Napoleon made it harder, and by 1816 it was no longer legal.

The first divorce laws were drafted after 10 August 1792, when the republic was proclaimed. This was in spite of the Constitutional committee having decided that the Constitution of 1791 would remain, only with amendments pertaining to the king's role (which would be deleted). But divorce was very much on everybody's minds and had been since 1789 when the freeing of France from despotism was likened to the freeing of a woman from marriage to a tyrannical husband. One defender of the Revolution wrote that France, 'a nation for so long oppressed by despotism and its laws, all of a sudden becoming mistress of its own destiny, aspires for liberty'.[20]

From the beginning, then, the French saw strong connections between the state and the family, the public and the private. As soon as the Revolution started, the public debate on marriage laws, which had already existed but been contained by the laws and the all-powerful clergy, amplified. Women's clubs throughout France discussed divorce, and the Cercle Social in Paris, and its women-only offshoot, Le Club des Amis de la Vérité, led by Etta Palm d'Aelders, spearheading the discussion. There were some who still defended the indissolubility of marriage, but, at least in print, they were outnumbered by pro-divorce pamphlets and articles five to one.[21]

It is not clear what Manon Roland thought about divorce. As a member of the Cercle Social and the Société Fraternelle des Deux Sexes, she was at least open to the discussion of divorce.[22] It was not something she considered in her own marriage, even when she fell in love with Francois Buzot, but perhaps that was because although she did not love her husband anymore, she was still strongly attached to him and did not think he had done anything to deserve desertion. Her strong sense of duty would have meant that the marriage contract could not be dissolved except for some very good reasons.

But we do have writings by both Gouges and Grouchy on divorce.

Gouge published her views on divorce in the same pamphlet which contained her Declaration of the Rights of *Woman*, in the last paragraph of the postscript:

> Marriage is the tomb of trust and love. A married woman can, with impunity, give bastards to her husband and a fortune that is not theirs. The unmarried woman only has the feeblest rights; ancient and inhuman laws forbid her the right to the name or wealth of the father of her children, and no new laws have been devised to address this matter. If trying to give my sex an honourable and fair substance seems, at this time, paradoxical on my part, like attempting the impossible, then I will leave the glory of treating on this matter to the men to come but, while we wait, we can pave the way through national education, the reestablishment of morals, and by addressing conjugal conventions.[23]

Her first claim, that marriage is 'the tomb of love', corresponds to the general public attitude at the beginning of the Revolution. The Comte d'Antraigue, who had compared the Revolution to a woman being finally free from her husband, also decried the laws that allowed parents to force marriage on their children: 'that sentiment and love are not even heard . . . it is not a marriage, it is a sacrifice, it is a sacrilege'. Marriage was no longer thought of as a commercial union, but people were beginning to demand that love should have a part in it.

Gouges also wrote about marriage in her *Bonheur Primitif*. There she wrote that a marriage contract ought to be based on love and trust and not imposed by others but freely chosen by both parties. But she quickly turns to another problem that arises from marriage laws. Women, she says, only derive social status from their married state. That status is not substantial and allows women to live respectably in appearance only while behaving immorally as long as they do not get caught. Unmarried women, on the other hand, have no status and no rights – they cannot even inherit their family's wealth. Reforming marriage laws and education at the same time (for she understands that laws alone won't do the job unless people are in a position at least to understand them) is the only way to help women regain some sort of 'substance'.

A year after the publication of *Primitive Happiness*, one year before the *Rights of Woman* and two years before the divorce law was accepted,

Gouges wrote a play in which she treated the same questions, *The Necessity of Divorce*. In this short and humorous play, she shows how even the best marriages, those founded on both love and compatibility of character, can become an unbearable burden simply because it is not reversible. Reasonable divorce laws, she argues are the only way to safeguard marriages, and render relationships between men and women, parents and children, healthy. In that text, she emphasizes that marriage relations can quickly turn to tyrannical relations and that an unhappily married woman can become a slave to her husband.

> Repeatedly exposed to the crude insults of a tyrant who treats you as a slave, who despises everything about you, who sees your qualities as defects or vices, subjected to duties that can sow in your bosom the fatal germ of a destructive poison, you cannot be blamed for refusing these tyrannical duties.[24]

The play features a married couple and their best friend, a marriage sceptic. The couple is in difficulty and the husband is on the brink of cheating. Their friend decides to save their relationship by pretending to them that the Assembly has made divorce legal. The couple's reaction is to realize that they do not want to be apart from each other. Their friend concludes that he was right: 'With the possibility of divorce, the ties of marriage are flower chains. Without it, they are the iron chains of a slave that torment him his entire life.'

Gouges, therefore, was not against marriage as such, nor was she against the possibility of lifelong marriage. But it had to remain a possibility, not a necessity, in order to be a free union that both parties can enjoy fully, without falling into a relationship of tyranny. Sophie de Grouchy, when she touched on the question of divorce in her *Letters on Sympathy*, suggested not only that divorce should be legal but also, looking back at the Roman legal system, that temporary unions should be allowed.

> Let us suppose next that this same inequality, and the laws made in order to sustain it, were no longer reducing most marriages to nothing but conventions and pacts between fortunes, so quickly concluded that it only becomes apparent long afterwards whether personal preferences are met, and where the price of love, fixed at the same time as the dowry is calculated without knowing if it is possible to love, and especially to love each other. Let us suppose at last that man would stop imposing on his fickle heart, and his will, even more changeable, indissoluble ties which are incompatible with his nature, whose flexibility and proud independence can only be fixed by a habitual sentiment of freedom.

Let us suppose that divorce were to be allowed for all people. Let us suppose even that, as in Rome, for the sake of human weakness and the more lasting needs of one sex, and it were possible to form temporary unions that the law would not repudiate but set the conditions for.[25] From then on, we will see that most unjust acts committed in the name of love (or rather the degradation of love) will no longer be motivated. This passion will lose, through the ease of satisfaction, that dangerous strength it acquired from the obstacles it encountered. Too long has society prevented unions being formed through mutual taste and set up walls between the two sexes (under the pretext of protecting virtue) such as made it nearly impossible for hearts and souls to come to know each other, as is necessary for the creation of virtuous and lasting unions.[26]

Most crimes committed for the sake of love or sexual desire, she sad, arose from unduly strict marriage laws and the impossibility for two people to contract a temporary union without thereby becoming criminals. More importantly, she argued that a reform of marriage law that included the possibility of divorce was a necessary step towards equality. It is the desire to preserve large fortunes which makes most marriages so artificial and results in unhappiness and transgression. Should large fortunes no longer exist, and should it no longer be possible to transmit them hereditarily, then, she argued, there would be no need for the marriage contract to be anything but voluntary, and at the same time, there would not be financial impediments to the dissolution of a marriage.

In 1792, the divorce law was pronounced. Between January 1793 and June 1795, the Assembly received large quantities of petitions – two-thirds of which were written by women for divorces. Six thousand divorces were pronounced during the course of these two and a half years. Women who petitioned typically expressed their wishes in terms of oppression and tyranny. Men sometimes argued in favour of love.[27] But all those who petitioned were determined, one way or another, to free themselves from the marriage chains. Republican freedom truly took its place in the family.

The ease with which one could get a divorce during the early years of the Revolution provided Sophie de Grouchy with a safety net during the Terror, *albeit* a heart-breaking one. In January 1794, while Condorcet was in hiding at Madame Vernet's, she filed for divorce. This was a measure that both Condorcet and Cabanis had insisted on. Because of his status as an outlaw, all of Condorcet's assets had been confiscated. Divorce would allow Sophie to retain some of her personal assets, as well as protect her from being arrested as the wife of an outlaw. But to Condorcet and Grouchy, the main reason was to protect their daughter. In a letter discussing the proceedings, Grouchy told Condorcet as much:

> It would be less painful for me to lay down my life for you than to be in a position, in any circumstance, to deserve the reproach of having cut myself off from your troubles. I [?] that the visible explanation of the procedure which is causing me more unhappiness than you is the life of our child. And the date of the petition, posterior to your worst infortunes, shows clearly that its motive was maternal care and not any weakness on my part. [. . .] My soul, like yours, is torn apart and horrified by even this apparent break-up. But between myself and this shadow of lies, see the interest of our child.[28]

The petition for the divorce was recorded on 7 January 1794, and the divorce pronounced in May of the same year, with Cabanis as a witness. By then, Condorcet had disappeared, and no one knew of his whereabouts. Despite it having been mostly his idea, Condorcet was depressed by the divorce. He could no longer accept his life as a recluse, his uselessness, and the risk he posed to all around him, especially his landlady, Madame Vernet. He must have talked of running away, as Sophie wrote to him:

> I throw myself at your feet to ask that you stay. It is absolutely impossible that you should fall in the hands of your enemies . . . Give me back the little life and peace I have left by swearing that you will stay [. . .] Will you not take care of your life anymore?[29]

But Condorcet, it turns out, did not care for his life anymore, except for the sake of those he loved, and even sometimes, that was not enough:

> I am only holding on to life for the sake of love and friendship. I have said my goodbye to glory [. . .] what madness to aspire to centuries and live nothing of the present life flowing past! There is, in epistolary exchanges, a mass of ideas that we throw around without verifying or justifying them. We are ourselves, the present self, not the prepared self, made up of past selves. I will be less of a philosopher, but I will be more of an honest man.

But even such accommodations were not sufficient to keep Condorcet going: 'This is no life! There is only superficiality left in me, and the main is dead.'[30]

Condorcet finished writing the draft of his introduction for the Encyclopedic project he had started years earlier, his history of human progress, sent it to Sophie for safekeeping, and in March 1794, he left Madame Vernet's house. He walked for several days, and was arrested in the town of Bourg-la-Reine, where he died during the night, either of exhaustion, a heart attack, or because he'd ingested the poison given him by his friend Cabanis.

5 Amphibious creatures

There is no question but that the French Revolution was a hotbed of feminist thinking and concrete proposals for reforms. Women and their allies argued that they should be allowed to take their place alongside men as full, active citizens, that they too should be relieved from the tyrannical domination not only of a king but also of their husbands. They wrote books, plays, pamphlets, took to the streets and clubs, and petitioned. They obtained, at least for a few years, the right to divorce. But by the end of the century, even that was taken from them by the new regime.

Perhaps we might think that the women themselves were not entirely ready for their emancipation, that as some of their men contemporaries told them, they had not yet achieved the requisite maturity to become citizens, and like children, they needed protection until they did. But if that is what was thought, it was not followed by any serious attempt by the French government either during or after the Revolution to educate women about citizenship.

Another thought is that the resistance to feminist reform came from the women themselves who saw themselves as belonging to a different sphere than the one where active citizenship could happen. Keralio-Robert, for instance, insisted that her citizen work happened in the home, where women educated future citizens but also influenced their social circle, servants, local artisans and shopkeepers, as well as friends and family. But not all the women philosophers of the Revolution saw the domestic sphere as incompatible with political action – in fact, as much of the Revolution's politics happened within salons, hosted by the likes of Manon Roland, Sophie de Grouchy, Madame Helvetius or Germaine de Stael, it is clear that politics happened very much in the home. Feminist thinkers of the French Revolution were very much what Keralio called 'amphibious creatures' who saw their domain as the home but could breathe politics as well as domesticity and demanded to be given the official titles to do so.

Epilogue

Writing out the women: Sophie de Grouchy after the Terror

The early days of the Revolution brought hope for women that their voices would be heard. The Terror put an end to that. Several women authors and philosophers, including Marie-Jeanne Roland and Olympe de Gouges, died at the guillotine. All those that remained were strongly discouraged from speaking out. Sophie de Grouchy suffered from the consequences of this silencing. In the aftermath of the Terror, she did not produce any new writings of her own. Instead, she turned her efforts to the immortalization of her husband's philosophy. She became a salonière, hosting men in her home so they could discuss politics. Grouchy's life after the Terror is symptomatic of how the women philosophers of the late eighteenth century were wiped out of intellectual history.

1 Sophie's writing career

In the summer of 1791 Sophie de Grouchy wrote for *Le Républicain*, applying philosophical arguments to the question of whether Louis XVI should remain king. By the spring of 1792, she had drafted her *Letters on Sympathy* and started work on a philosophical novel, which she wasn't particularly happy with. Yet, the *Letters* were not published till 1798, at the same time as her translation of Adam Smith's *The Theory of Moral Sentiments* and *The Origins of Language*. After that, she edited her husband's *Works* but did not publish anything else in her name.

Why the hiatus between the productive first years of the Revolution and 1798, and why no more until her death in 1822?

The years of the Terror, between 1793 and 1795, were clearly not auspicious for philosophical writings in her case. She had to keep herself and her family safe, keep her husband's spirits up while he lived and also earn enough to feed her daughter, sister and extended family. She could not earn by writing philosophy, but she called on her other talent – painting – and set up a small studio above an underwear shop that she asked her husband's secretary's brother, Auguste Cardot, to manage. Between the painting, the shop, the trips to visit her husband and her family responsibilities, there was no time for writing. Yet, it seems that she was not completely inactive philosophically, but that she worked together with her husband on his last published work: *The Sketch of Human Progress.*[1]

While in hiding, Condorcet started to write an *Apology* which was meant to explain and justify his role in the Revolution, and show that he had been wronged by his persecutors, the Jacobins. Sophie, sensing that this work would be of little value philosophically or personally, urged him to give it up and instead to turn back to a work he had begun several decades before: a history of the progress of human nature. The unfinished manuscript of the *Apology* ends with a note in Sophie's hand 'Abandoned at my request'.[2]

Although we do not have any hard evidence that Condorcet and Grouchy wrote together, it seems likely that some of the passages in particular are hers and that others are the product of a collaboration between husband and wife. We do not have a final manuscript that corresponds to the first edition by Grouchy, which suggests that she added some paragraphs herself. The only existing manuscript, addressed to Sophie, is very messy and would have required much editing to make sense of the marginal annotations and in-text corrections. Several of the differences between the manuscript and the first edition concern women and the place of the family in human progress. Perhaps these were ideas she and Condorcet had discussed and that she knew he wanted to be included. Perhaps these were points she had suggested to him in their discussions.

In March 1794, Condorcet ran away from his hiding place in order to avoid getting Madame Vernet, his hostess, arrested. He died a few days later in a prison in the small town of Bourg-la-Reine but was not identified until several months after his death, so that his wife remained ignorant of his whereabouts. Several months after his death, he was identified from his records. Although he'd left in a hurry and carrying false papers, he had kept with him a pocket watch given him by Sophie's brother and a small book of Latin verse. Once it was established he had died in prison, the Convention, perhaps regretting having caused the death of the philosopher, however indirectly, commissioned 3,000 copies of his new book, *Esquisse d'un Tableau des Progrès de l'Esprit Humain*, from Pierre Daunou, a historian and archivist, and later an academician, who had been in prison for protesting the arrest of the Girondins. There is no evidence that Daunou did anything more than act as a go-between and Condorcet's *Sketch* does not feature in his extent bibliography of editions, commentaries and biographical notices. The fact that Daunou is listed as a contributor whenever the first edition of the *Sketch* is mentioned is a first sign of distrust of Grouchy's editorship.

Sophie de Grouchy prepared the edition, alone, and it was published in 1795. This edition was reprinted and revised at least twice by Grouchy (alone and with collaborators in 1802 and 1822), and it was translated into English the year it was first published, and John Adams owned a copy.

In 1847, the Académicien François Arago, who noted that the 1795 edition contained passages which were absent from Condorcet's final manuscript, produced a new edition with extensive revisions, which, he said, was closer to the original manuscript that he'd obtained from Grouchy and Condorcet's daughter, Eliza O'Connor, and which he thought was more accurate because in Condorcet's hand,[3] Arago's edition is now regarded as authoritative. Not only was Grouchy's name deleted from the work – where it did belong, perhaps as co-author and at the very least editor – but with it the emphasis she had brought on the role of women and the family in human development.

Condorcet was in many ways a feminist. His 'On the Admission of Women to the Rights of Citizenship' was one of the earliest published revolutionary attempts at including women in the new republic. He also facilitated the careers of other feminists and generally participated in the early revolutionary effort to include women in political debates, co-founding one of the first mixed clubs – Le Club des Amis de la Vérité. But despite his efforts and goodwill, Condorcet had been brought up as an aristocratic man and would have had found it difficult to notice the many implications of what being a woman meant in terms of everyday life and social justice. While he argued that women should become active citizens and have the same rights as men, he had little to say about their social existence and in particular their need for social and economic independence. He also did not argue that women's existing participation through the work they did in the home bringing up future citizens should be shared and valued by men. Sophie de Grouchy, as someone who had both the principles and the experience of being a woman, was able to see this and help him (partly) remedy it. This is what we see in her edition of Condorcet's last work and may go some way towards explaining why this edition was not retained by Arago.

In the 1795 edition of the *Sketch*, there are eight separate mentions of women. This is not a great deal for a text that contains ten chapters and spans over four hundred pages. But the manuscript which Condorcet sent to his wife for safekeeping, and the one Arago used as a basis for revising Grouchy's edition contains only four mentions. Condorcet's original mentions say very little and are aligned with the custom which was to mention women in discussions of humanity only when a specific trait became relevant. At the same time, Condorcet's little thought out remarks pandered to the usual prejudices about motherhood. Women are mentioned in the first chapter on first human settlements where Condorcet claims that mothers have stronger affections than fathers and that women were originally excluded from public deliberation because they were too weak to hunt. Then in the fifth chapter, he mentions that there might have been women in Constantinople who distinguished themselves in the humanities. In the seventh chapter, women have become 'ladies' and the focus is on how in the Middle Ages they benefitted from the values of chivalry. Then in the eighth chapter, he attributes part of the progress of medicine to the acknowledgement that sexual differences are key to understanding how the human body works.

Not only are there few mentions or discussions of women in the manuscript, but there are gaps in places where one might expect a mention. There is, for instance, no reference to women who contributed to the philosophical and mathematical innovations of the Antiquity – there is no mention of Hypatia of Alexandria (114) and no mention of any particular women or of the place of women in general in his discussion of the Pythagoreans (Fragment 6, 640). Gilles Ménage in his *Historia mulierum philosopharum* (1690) listed twenty women philosophers of Antiquity. Condorcet mentions not a single one. Diogenes Laertius names women in Plato's school, the Cynic Hipparchia, the Pythagorean Theano and the mathematician Hypathia of Alexandria. It seems strange that a thinker who was committed, a few years earlier, to arguing that women were as capable as men intellectually should omit to mention any of these in his survey of intellectual progress.

Yet, Condorcet was not ignorant of the existence of women who had influenced the progress of humanity. In his 1790 pamphlet arguing for the emancipation of women, he listed a number of women who were powerful and had a positive influence in politics, science and philosophy, including Catharine Macaulay, Marie le Jars de Gournay and Emilie du Chatelet.[4] The most charitable interpretation for the absence of women philosophers and scientists from the Prospectus, perhaps, is that they did not come to mind when he was not specifically thinking about them. But this makes it more interesting and more significant that there is in fact a feminist element to the text that was added after the manuscript was delivered to Condorcet's secretary.

There are fewer mentions specifically of women in the manuscript of the *Sketch* than one might have hoped from a feminist writer, what there is, which is interesting, is an emphasis on the role of the family in human progress. On the first page of the first part, 'Men Are Gathered in Tribes', Condorcet writes that human groups are always family-based and that this is because mothers and fathers have a natural tendency to form strong emotional attachments towards their children:

A family society seems to be natural to man. Its origin is to be found in the child's need for its parents and in the natural solicitude of the mother and – though to a lesser extent – of the father for their offspring. But the child's need lasts long enough to bring into existence and foster a desire to perpetuate this life together and to awaken a lively sense of its advantages. A family that lived in a region offering ready means of subsistence could increase and become a tribe.[5]

Family ties were, understandably a strong concern for Condorcet towards the end of his life. A few days before his death, he wrote a letter to his four-year-old daughter, the 'Advice to his daughter', in which he reminded her of his love for her and the fact that as a baby, she was 'comforted by my loving care'.[6]

The needs an infant has, and the love and care it receives, are also central for Sophie de Grouchy who had argued that human sympathy first arose through the relationship of an infant with its carer:

This particular dependence on a few individuals begins in the crib; it is the first tie binding us to our fellow creatures. It is the reason why an infant's first smiles, and then her more habitual smiles, are for her nurse,[7] why she cries when she is not in her arms, and why for a long time, she likes to throw herself upon the breast that satisfied her first needs, made her experience her first sensations of pleasure and where she developed and acquired her first habits.[8]

Condorcet and Grouchy were not, of course, the only republican philosophers of the time to place so much importance on family life. Those who had read and admired Rousseau tended to regard good parenthood as one of their first duties as citizens. Mary Wollstonecraft, for instance, had argued that mothers who would not breastfeed their babies did not deserve to be called citizens.[9] Marie-Jeanne Roland and her husband had spent much of their time in the few years preceding the Revolution devising educational programmes for their daughter based on Rousseau's *Emile* and *Julie*.[10] But perhaps the revolutionary thinker whose account of the family came closest to Grouchy and Condorcet's was Olympe de Gouges who, in her 1789 *Primitive Happiness* had explained how the success of any human society depended on co-operation between loving families.

Condorcet's discussion of the importance of the family for human society in these opening paragraphs does not lead, as one might expect, to further discussion of how the family develops and how it influences the progress of humanity. But in Grouchy's 1795 edition, the idea that studying families is important in order to understand human progress is reintroduced in the last pages:

> Until now, political history, as indeed, the history of philosophy and of science has always been the history of a few men. But what the human species actually consists in, the families, subsisting nearly entirely from their labour, has been forgotten.[11]

A history of families, Grouchy and Condorcet conclude (in the jointly edited *Sketch*), is what we need to study in order to truly understand human progress, as focusing on isolated individuals, exceptionally bred royalty, or heroes, whose paths are exceptional and cannot give us an accurate picture of how humanity in general changed through the ages.

If we take into account the influence of Sophie de Grouchy as his collaborator, we can interpret this framing of the work with considerations about family life as hers, and it does give the work a distinctly feminist taste of the kind that goes beyond Condorcet's well-placed principles. Focusing on the family and its importance for human development is crucial – even more then than now – to the proper integration of women into the history of humanity and to make their lives central to any plans for future progress. Not only does it allow us to look beyond the odd, isolated woman who against all historical odds succeeded in asserting herself at the top of some discipline or other, but it also reminds men that they have a life and a set of duties within the family unit, that they are not free individuals moving history along with the sheer force of their courage or intellect, but fathers who need to change a nappy and help their daughters with their homework so that they too have a chance at participating in human progress.

It's interesting that Grouchy's first philosophical activity after the Terror display some awareness that women tend to be written out of human history, and ironical that the mark of this awareness, alongside her authorship and editorship, were themselves written out half a century later when Arago published his new 'authoritative' edition of the *Sketch*.

2 The salon in Meulan

Even if Grouchy did not write philosophy after 1795, we know that she did not give it up. She kept a salon in Paris and in the countryside, first in Auteuil, in the house next to Madame Helvetius, and later in Meulan, close to the castle of Villette where she had grown up. In 1796, she took a lover, a young journalist with political connections, Mailla Garat. They lived together between her private hotel in Paris and her rented house in Auteuil. Then, when she was once more able to access some of her money, she purchased an old convent house in Meulan, close to her ageing father. The house, built in 1642 by Anne of Austria for the order of the Annonciades, was several storeys high and set in the countryside, between the town and the castle of Villette. The nuns who'd occupied it had been evicted five years previously and the house had already exchanged hands a few times. Sophie called it the 'Maisonnette' or little house, despite its generous size – she used it to host a large philosophical circle. She also set it up as a love nest for herself and Garat. There were many bedrooms on the top floors, and a small and a large meeting room on the ground floor – one for intimate company – friends, family, Garat, while the larger room was set up for her salon. Sophie's relationship with Garat lasted two years, after which he left her for one of her friends. Their correspondence survives and has been printed alongside the *Letters on Sympathy* in an edition by Jean-Paul Lagrave. The love letters make for a sad and disappointing read. Sophie comes across like an eighteenth-century version of Bridget Jones, insecure in her love for a man who was clearly not worthy of her trust or respect, who cheated on her and had little of the intellectual potential she hoped for in a partner. The relationship ended in 1800 after Sophie heard from a friend that Garat had become engaged to be married to a close friend of hers, Aymée de Coigny.

Despite the fact that it held painful memories of her failed relationship, the Maisonette remained central to Sophie's life and she carried on receiving close friends and members of her circle. Madame Vernet, who had generously hidden Condorcet in 1793 and 1794 was a frequent visitor, as was the actress and Sophie's longtime friend Julie Talma and the Girondin Pierre-Louis Ginguené. But she also invited new friends, such as Benjamin Constant, Germaine de Staël's partner, and from 1801, her new lover the poet Claude Fauriel. Pierre-George Cabanis and Sophie's sister, Charlotte Cabanis, were also frequent visitors, and in 1807, when Cabanis's health was declining, they bought a house in the neighbourhood of the Maisonnette.

The period between 1795 and the early nineteenth century was marked for Grouchy and her friends by a series of very different political events: first the end of the Terror and the brief period of domestic peace and political optimism that followed, the advent of Napoleon, his subsequent abuse of power and eventually his fall and the restoration of monarchy with Louis XVI's brother, Louis XVIII (the title Louis XVII had been given by royalist factions to the unhappy son of Louis and Marie-Antoinette after his father's execution).

At the end of the Terror, the surviving Girondins and Brissot sympathizers found themselves once more close to power, and together, they sought to rescue the Revolution by bringing it back to the ideals it started from, those of the Enlightenment. A close friend of Cabanis, Destutt de Tracy, coined the name for this new movement, the Idéologues. This group of intellectuals brought together Lockean empiricism with a French flavour (inspired by Condillac) and a trust in the Enlightenment's cult of reason. Its members were Destutt de Tracy, Cabanis, Daunou, Guingené, Garat, Fauriel and others. One of their main concerns, in line with their desire to carry through the ideals of the Revolution, was education. They founded schools – the Ecoles Normales and Polytechnique – and a learned society – l'Institut. They disseminated their ideas in print. Their intellectual programme was described by Destutt de Tracy's *Elements d'Idéologie*, and they founded a review: *La Décade Philosophique, Litéraire et Politique*.

Sophie de Grouchy was a central figure in this new circle, as she had been in the republican circle before the Terror. The Ideologists met in her salons in Paris and Auteuil, and later at the Maisonette in Meulan. But more than simply a hostess and facilitator, she was a fully fledged participant in the intellectual debates of the circle, and when she published, first, her translation of Smith and *Letters on Sympathy*, and later, Condorcet's *Works*, the *Decade* and other journals printed very enthusiastic reviews.

Her translation and edition were praised, as were her *Letters on Sympathy*, but the latter had been written several years before and while she continued editing, Sophie had given up her career as an author by that stage. Nonetheless, her works and ideas were still a topic for discussion.

On 20 May 1799, she received a letter from Madame de Staël, who had just read her *Letters on Sympathy* and was full of admiration for them. She envied, as we saw in Chapter 6, both the style and the depth of analysis of the *Letters*. But her admiration went further and she talks of Sophie's 'authoritative reason, her true sensibility, nonetheless mastered, which makes you an exceptional woman'.

It is not clear whether Sophie accepted the praise. She had not been close to Madame de Staël before. Staël had spent most of the Revolution and all of the Terror in her Swiss castle, commenting from afar, whereas for Sophie, it was a matter of pride that she had stayed in Paris and Auteuil. A short time before she sent her *Letters on Sympathy* to the publishers, she had found out that she and her husband were listed on a register of the French people who had emigrated during the Revolution. Being on that list meant that all of one's property could be confiscated. At that time Sophie was struggling to make ends meet for herself and her extended family. Their names had been added to that list after Condorcet's disappearance, following his being proclaimed an outlaw. Because Condorcet was in hiding, and because his death went unreported for several months, it was assumed that he'd left the country. On the other hand, Sophie had officially divorced him, and she was a registered occupant of a house in Auteuil, where she had been nearly arrested on more than one occasion.

On 12 Pluviose, An VI, or 31 January 1798, Sophie de Grouchy wrote a letter asking for her name and that of her deceased husband to be struck off the list.[12] In the letter, Sophie stated that she could provide ample evidence for the fact that neither she nor Condorcet had left the country. She submitted thirteen pieces, including certificates of her residence in Auteuil, a passport for her to travel to Villette to visit her father and a report on the death of Condorcet.

Sophie's letter was then forwarded to the Minister of the Police so that he could make a very prompt report. The report was indeed prompt – the decision is dated two days later – but it was not succinct: and the same dossier containing Sophie's letter also has several lengthy documents detailing the request that hers and Condorcet's name be taken off the list. The decision states that there is no need to call forward witnesses (she had provided a long list, with Cabanis listed first) and that the presence of Grouchy and Condorcet's names on the list was clearly a consequence of the persecution Condorcet had been subjected to during the Terror.

It must have helped that the Directoire was in power at the time of her request, the government in which her friends, the Idéologues, played an important role. It's also likely that this was how she eventually found out that the reason she could not reclaim her or Condorcet's property was that they were listed as immigrants and therefore in debt to the government.

Sophie's salon also played a role in facilitating others' literary careers. Karl Benedikt Hase, a Byzantine expert who was an important part of the literary world of nineteenth-century Paris, was first introduced to these circles by a chance meeting with Sophie de Grouchy. Having walked on foot to Paris from Weimar and arriving a poor student, he was recommended to various people for his knowledge of Ancient Greek and brought to Meulan by Fauriel:

> I already talked about Madame Condorcet in one of my letters. I got to know her by chance; she wanted to learn German and a certain Fauriel, private secretary to the police minister, with whom I sometimes spend the evenings, sent me to her. It was the 28th Frimaire; look up the date and underline it, it is one of the most important in the life of your friend [the writer]. I'll admit it – the clear mind of this wonderful woman, her joy in the all-pervasive progress of humanity to a marvellous goal, her knowledge of the great moments of the revolution, in which she herself played a not insignificant role (on the day before the 10th August, when Concordet, her husband, played host to 400 Marseillaise, she was the

queen of the party), perhaps also her friendly attitude towards me – for my significant progress in French pronunciation, which has astonished everyone, was thanks to my reading French tragedies aloud to her – could not fail to have an effect on me.[13]

Her attention was also sought by more established members of the French literary circles. Firmin Didot, editor, printer, and translator, wrote to her in 1820 to ask her permission to dedicate the second edition of his translation of Virgil's *Bucolic*, which was published in 1823, a year after Sophie's death.

> To Madame de Condorcet
> From the hand of a pastor with goodness accept this fruit from his garden, perhaps a little wild? I have never seen you without thinking of the homage that a pastor long ago made to beauty.

If Sophie did not write herself in the last twenty years of her life, she nonetheless took part in philosophical debates such that her ideas permeated the writings of others. This is true in particular of her relationship with her brother-in-law Cabanis, at the time he wrote his two philosophical pieces. The first, *Les Rapports du Physique et du Moral de l'Homme*, was printed in 1802. Arguing that morality was the result of reasoning about sensations, he proposed that 'moral properties were nothing but physical properties considered from certain particular points of view' and that 'It is from that point of view that the physical study of man is principally interesting: this is where the philosopher, the moralist, the legislator must direct their gaze, and where they can find at the same time new lights on human nature, and fundamental ideas on its perfectioning.'[14] Later on, in his *Lettre sur les Causes Premières*, he departed from the apparent materialism proposed in the *Rapport* and offered instead a perspective inspired by Stoic hylozoism, that is, the doctrine that everything that exists is imbued with life.

It clearly makes sense to see the *Letters* and Cabanis's *Les Rapport du Physique et du Moral* (1802) as part of an ongoing discussion between Grouchy and Cabanis on the applications of physiology to morality and the social sciences. Grouchy's *Letters* are addressed to Cabanis, and the *Rapports* take up the same theme of the links between the senses and moral development. There is a less easily detectable link between Grouchy's thought and Cabanis's *Lettre sur les Causes Premières* (written around 1805 but published posthumously in 1824), namely that both philosophers are attempting to integrate some elements of Stoicism into an otherwise sensualist philosophy. Part of what attracted Cabanis and Grouchy to Stoic philosophy was the possibility it opened for a form of atheism that nonetheless saw something divinely pleasing in all living things. Cabanis's last work is a defence of Stoic hylozoism, rather than the materialism he is known for, that is, the view that spirit, as reason, is everywhere and most especially in humans and 'higher' animals. Another reason for their Stoic predilection was the Stoic theory of human moral development (the theory of oikeiosis, a word difficult to translate but which means something like 'making oneself at home in an environment). Central to Stoic moral philosophy is the idea that infants are born with a sense of self-preservation and that their earliest development is led by that instinct but that the instinct grows into a recognition of the role played by their family and community towards this preservation and that this is how they become moral beings. This is very close to Sophie de Grouchy's own theory in the *Letters on Sympathy*: infants discover their dependence on others through their first relationship to their nurse and this is how they first develop sympathetic feelings. Later they learn to extend these feelings and the moral ideas that they derive from them to a larger group of people.

But despite their affinities with Stoicism neither Grouchy nor Cabanis can entirely embrace Stoic ethics, as their theory of the origins of moral development is a physiological one. Cabanis, in his *Letter on First Causes*, explicitly rejects the Stoic view that pains and pleasure don't matter morally, and indeed, suggests that even the Stoics did not believe this:

> We cannot possibly agree with the Stoics that pain is not bad. Perhaps pain is not always bad in its effects – it can offer useful warnings, sometimes even strengthens physical organs just as it impresses greater energy and strength of will to morality. [. . .] But if pain was not an evil it would not be so for others any more than for ourselves. We should discount it in others and in ourselves. So why this tender humaneness that characterizes the greatest stoics much more than the firmness and the constancy of their virtues?[15]

Cabanis cites the Stoics as evidence against themselves: Cato, who gave up his horse for his companion on a scorching road in Sicily, and Brutus, who gave his coat to a sick slave on a freezing winter night. The Stoics did not, he argues, countenance the view that pain should be ignored. This was both paradoxical and provocative. The Stoics are known for their beliefs that the only good is virtue. Things that neither contribute to, nor diminish virtue are known as 'indifferent'. They argue this against the Epicureans who believe that pleasure and pain contribute to virtue and therefore that a virtuous person will pursue pleasure and avoid pain.

To be fair to them, the Stoics did not believe that all 'indifferents' were interchangeable. Cato himself argued that the instinct to self-preservation of itself guaranteed that we would have reason to choose between 'indifferents' depending on how they furthered our health. But that instinct, he claimed against the Epicureans, came before any perceptions of pain and pleasure, so that we did not have to refer to pleasure and pain in order to differentiate options that were not part of virtue.

Does this mean that Grouchy and Cabanis were in fact closer to Epicureanism than Stoicism? Not if we take into account the centrality of the Stoic process of Oikeiosis in Grouchy's moral psychology and Cabanis's endorsement of the Stoics' fundamental metaphysical claim that everything in the world is imbued with reason. They are still closer to the Stoics, but their commitment to a particular sort of physiology means that they cannot, as Cabanis says very clearly in his letter, deny the importance of pleasure and pain.

There are clear links between the *Letters on Sympathy* and *Les Rapports*, but do we have evidence that Cabanis's *Letter on First Causes* was at all related to Grouchy's own work? It seems that we have at least good reasons to believe that it was still part of an ongoing conversation between Grouchy and Cabanis. The *Letter on First Causes* was written to Claude Fauriel who was by then Grouchy's lover. Fauriel intended to write a book about Stoic philosophy (the manuscript was lost before he could finish it).

The focus on Stoicism, and the question of how one can reconcile a Stoic outlook with the belief that to be good is to relieve pain and suffering, was certainly a topic relevant to Grouchy and we can imagine that Cabanis brought it up with Fauriel because it was still being discussed in Grouchy's salon at Meulan. Cabanis and Fauriel were very close – so much so that when Cabanis's widow, who was also Sophie's sister, Charlotte, corresponded with Fauriel on the subject of the person they both loved and lost, for whom they felt 'a huge, and unshakeable tenderness, which must be very deep and sweet until your last day', she meant her husband, not her sister. And when she asks for his time and affection, it is as the 'companion of the man you loved so' and not as the sister of his life partner. The few letters from Cabanis to Fauriel that survived do give this sense of a nineteenth-century 'bromance' between them, with Cabanis writing excitedly to Fauriel that Sophie's father has reserved the room next to his own for Fauriel's upcoming visit, and signing off his letters with tender embraces and assurances of everlasting love. In one of his letters, he enquires after Fauriel's project on a Greek history and promises him the notes made by Garat (not Sophie's ex but his more scholarly brother) on a similar topic. The publication of the *Letter on First Causes*, which happened towards the end of Charlotte Cabanis's life, was a cause for much concern for Fauriel and Charlotte. Charlotte had allowed the *Letter* to be published, but she had had no control over the process and only read the introduction once it was in print. She found it full of mistakes and bad interpretations, and reflected that the author of the introduction was more interested in promoting his own dualism than making Cabanis's view clear.

The last few letters exchanged between Fauriel and Charlotte Cabanis concern the publication of a bibliographical notice on Cabanis, a project that Daunou had offered to take on before he died. There is much discussion as to whom might be a good person to edit Cabanis's paper, and once the choice is made, about how much control his widow might be able to exercise over the process. At no point during the correspondence is Sophie mentioned, even though she died fourteen years after Cabanis and had thus been part of Fauriel's life much longer. The biographical notice, based on a text drafted by Cabanis himself, was written by Peisse and published alongside an edition of the *Rapports du Physique et du Moral* and the *Lettre sur les Causes Premières* by Destutt de Tracy in 1844. That same year, perhaps even before the book was out, Claude Fauriel and Charlotte Cabanis died, both in their seventies.

3 Napoleonic laws, women and divorce

While Napoleon was not a regular at Sophie's salons, either in Paris or Meulan, two of his brothers, Joseph and Lucien, were, and he himself was at first supportive of the Idéologues. A prominent member of the group, Destutt de Tracy, had fought alongside Bonaparte and supported his rise to power. Tracy, Cabanis, Garat and Volney were among the first members of Napoleon's Senate. But Napoleon never quite took the Idéologues seriously and eventually, he turned against them.

If Napoleon had some sympathy or tolerance for the Idéologues, he was never in any way supportive of women's place in politics. At Sophie's Parisian salon he informed her that he did not like women who busied themselves with politics. This was not news, as his antipathy for Madame de Staël which led to her second exile after he was proclaimed emperor, was well known. Sophie is said to have replied that while she understood his perspective, she felt that if women could die at the guillotine, they had a right to know why, echoing Olympe's famous phrase, that if women could climb the scaffold, surely they must have the right to climb the rostrum.

Napoleon's misogyny was not merely personal. In the code written by his government in 1804, women's rights are diminished from what they were during the Revolution. One of the principal aims of the new code is to free the family from the shackles of the church and the state. Marriage is a contract whereby men and women acquire certain rights and duties pertaining to each other and their children. But the rights, at least, are asymmetrical –

husbands owe wives protection, but wives owe husbands obedience (article 214) and a wife is obliged to live where her husband decides (215) and cannot plead in her own name unless she has her husband's permission (216). A woman, but not a man, must wait ten months to remarry after the dissolution of a first marriage (228). While both husband and wife can ask for divorce on grounds of adultery, a woman can only ask for it in case where her husband had moved his mistress into the common home (230). In cases of divorce, the father is given the management of the children (287) except in special circumstances decided by the court. And although many articles refer to both paternal and maternal authority over minor children, there is a whole section dedicated to paternal power.

The effect of the Napoleonic Code on patriarchy is hard to gauge. On the one hand, the code for the first time specified precisely and in one place what recourse women had to the law and what rights they had within marriage. On the other, it established for a long time the supremacy of fathers – still today, naming a child after his or her mother when the parents are married is not straightforward in France (although that is beginning to change).

4 Posterity – where they are buried, fame, pantheon

Posterity is what happens after one's death and part of it has to do with where and how the body is disposed of. Olympe de Gouges died on 3 November 1793, Marie-Jeanne Roland five days later. Both were thrown in a common pit. Sophie de Grouchy survived them and died of illness in 1822 (she didn't live much longer than the other two, but at least she died a natural death) and was buried in a Paris cemetery. Her husband, Condorcet, because he'd died under an assumed name in the village of Bourg-la-Reine, had been thrown in a communal grave there. But in 1989, as part of the bicentennial celebrations, he was symbolically transferred to a cenotaph in the Paris Pantheon. Neither his wife nor any other woman of the revolutionary period joined him there.

Sophie de Grouchy, in a testament that we can still read in Fauriel's papers at the library of the Institut, had asked for her body to be disposed like that of a pauper's and that the money saved from an expensive burial should be distributed to the poor. She was in fact buried in the Père Lachaise, then a fairly recent cemetery in the north of Paris. The Père Lachaise, which now houses the illustrious bodies of Moliere, Jim Morrison, Chopin and Oscar Wilde, and many others, was not yet a popular resting place. Its grounds were not consecrated, which made it a risky proposition for anyone but the staunchest of atheists. But in 1817, five years before Grouchy's death, the administrators of the cemetery held a public ceremony during which the purported remains of Héloise and Abélard were transferred to the Père Lachaise. This marked the beginning of the cemetery's literary history and is possibly one of the reasons why Sophie's relatives decided to have her buried there.

Her grave, while not a pauper's pit, is very simple so that probably some money was saved to distribute to the poor. Her relatives respected her atheism and she was buried without a religious ceremony.

Olympe de Gouges and Marie-Jeanne Roland's remains were not dealt with in such a respectful manner. Their bodies were dumped in a communal grave in the now-closed Madeleine cemetery. The location of the Madeleine was particularly convenient for transporting bodies from the Place du Carousel and Place de la Revolution – the guillotine's first two locations. However, it was also close to some wealthy Paris neighbourhoods, which meant that there was a strong resistance against using that space to dump the dead.

The revolutionary period, in particular the Terror, had been hard on the Paris graveyards. The people who had died in the massacres and at the guillotine had to be buried in the already full graveyards. When the body counts started to rise, the Parisians needed somewhere to pile up their dead.

The cemetery La Madeleine was closed in the spring of 1794. Its location, close to expensive houses, meant that the smell of decomposing corpses was not something to be ignored. The site of the church of Sainte Madeleine, first opened in the thirteenth century, was located roughly where n8 Boulevard Malherbes now stands. It had a very small cemetery and a slightly larger one was built in 1690, on land that was closer to the Faubourg Saint Honoré, already a posh neighbourhood. In 1720, the curé of La Madeleine sold a large tract of land to be converted to a graveyard. The graveyard was built on a large rectangle of 45 by 19 metres surrounded by a wall. It filled up slowly at first, but in 1770 it received its first mass burial. On the occasion of the celebrations of the wedding of Louis the Dauphin and Marie-Antoinette, a show of fireworks was given to the people of Paris. This was a novelty, and more scary than exciting for many. There was a crush in the crowded streets and several hundred people died. These were buried in the Madeleine. The next large-scale burial happened in August 1792, when the Paris revolutionaries, assisted by the Marseillais, massacred the king's Swiss guards. Their mutilated bodies were thrown into a common grave at the Madeleine. By then it was summer, and the smell in the neighbourhood became unbearable – someone reported it at the Assembly, but it was decided that the risk of false rumours of a plague epidemic – often associated with the smell of decay – was too great if a fuss was made, and the subject was dropped. The rich inhabitants of the quartier would just have to put up with it.

Eventually, in March 1794, the Madeleine was closed and the next victims of the guillotine were buried elsewhere. But before then, more famous bodies were interred there, including the king and the queen, many of their supporters and family members, Charlotte Corday – who benefitted from a single occupancy plot, the twenty-two Girondins (including Brissot) who died on 31 October 1793, and of course, Marie-Jeanne Roland and Olympe de Gouges. In 1815 the bones were dug out from La Madeleine and transferred to the Errancis, which had become the new depository for the victims of the guillotines. Between March 1794 and May 1795, 1,119 decapitated bodies were thrown into a common grave at Errancis and 943 were killed between March and June 1794. Among the famous dead were Danton and the Desmoulins couple: Camille and Lucille.

The Errancies cemetery was erased during Haussman's rebuilding of Paris in the middle of the nineteenth century. The bones were once again moved, this time to the Paris Catacombs. There is a plaque that marks the transfer of the Madeleine bones in the Catacombes but does not mention their stay in Errancis.

Posterity can survive the absence of a proper burial, and a grave stone does not guarantee prosperity. But it seems that the lack of care whereby Marie-Jeanne Roland's corpse was disposed of prefaced the destiny of her writing legacy.

Marie-Jeanne Phlipon Roland is remembered as Madame Roland, for her prison diary and for her influence on the Girondins. But memory has transformed the *Memoirs* into a source of malevolent gossip against the leading men of the Revolution, and her influence is portrayed not as intellectual but as what Olympe de Gouges once called 'nocturnal ministrations'. Even a respectable historian like Max Gallo portrayed her as little more than a jealous courtesan, when he called her 'an imperious seductress, who imposes her ideas on her husband, on Barbaroux, Brissot, the leaders of the Girondist party'.

Traces of her political and intellectual influence have been wiped out from the common mind, unceremoniously.

This is somewhat less true for Olympe de Gouges. She remains known – at least in France – as a victim of the guillotine, and the author of the *Declaration of the Rights of Woman*. Despite this, Gouges was more or less shelved as an amusing but ultimately unimportant detail of the French Revolution until the Bicentenary prompted more research by French scholars into the works of women during the Revolution. Olivier Blanc, in his biography, sought to reinstate Gouges as a significant political thinker and activist, against what he described as Revisionist sexist historiographers, and the thoughtless repetition of their misleading claims by writers of dictionaries and encyclopedias who perpetuated the myth of Gouges's illiteracy and lack of influence.

Gouges has yet to be transferred to the mausoleum of the Pantheon in Paris. Her name was proposed in 2014, but she lost to four heroes (two men and two women) of the resistance. Small victory for those who feel she should be remembered in public debates, her bust was placed at the National Assembly in 2016. She was the first woman to be represented there.

Sophie de Grouchy is making a comeback in academic circles, but she is yet to be recognized as a philosopher of the Revolution. A new English translation of her *Letters on Sympathy* will perhaps help rectify this.[16] In the meantime, it is well to reflect that women, once again, despite having been active participants in a set of events that helped define modern politics, have been swept under the historical carpet.

A revolutionary bookshelf

What did Olympe de Gouges, Marie-Jeanne Roland and Sophie de Grouchy read? Which authors did they consider as formative of their character? And which books influenced their own writings? What might their bookshelves have looked like at various stages of their lives? Certainly, they would have looked different from ours, which tend to be populated with works published between nineteenth and twenty-first-century novels. They would have been different from each other too, because the three women had such different upbringings. For that reason, in the sketch I draw here, I will keep separate narratives running for the books of childhood and early adulthood. But once they reach maturity (or whatever maturity they were allowed to reach) I assume Olympe, Marie-Jeanne and Sophie had access to the same books, and the narratives will merge.

The list here is far from complete. It would take a much more careful historian – a real historian, not a philosopher – to go through archives with a fine-tooth comb to find out what books were in whose libraries when, if that information is even available (which in the case of women authors, it often isn't). Even if we did find a record of a library Sophie, Olympe or Marie-Jeanne had access to, that information would be limited. Just because a book is sitting on a bookshelf doesn't mean that it has been read or that it was influential, let alone formative.

So instead of scouring archives, I have used my knowledge of Gouges, Roland and Grouchy's writings to build this list, noting what books and authors they referred to (but not exhaustively). I also made use of a catalogue of the library of their contemporary and fellow Girondin, Pierre-Louis Roederer, who, as a book reviewer during and after the revolutionary period, probably had a more than representative selection of what was available at the time. The books I draw from this list are books that they could have read, and in some instances, that it is likely they had either read or heard of in discussions with friends.

Gouges, Roland and Grouchy were voracious readers. To give a proper apercu of all the books they might have read would require a self-standing book, not an appendix. I had to be selective and I restricted this list to (some) books that were intellectually formative. This means that I have not included anything that they would have read purely for entertainment – novels and magazines.

1 Childhood books

1.1 Olympe

There was a point in Olympe's childhood where it had to be decided which of her parents would be in charge of her education. Her mother, married to a butcher, a working woman with little time or money, or her father, an aristocrat and a published writer with a large library at his disposal. Her parents fought, and her mother won. Olympe was sent to a day school run by Ursuline nuns.

The Ursulines were authorized by the church to have a selection of books printed for their pupils. Each school had its own selection of basic educational and religious texts. Olympe may have learned to read from a spelling book, such as *Syllabaire Français ou recueil des syllabes françaises pour apprendre à épeler à l'usage des écoles chrétiennes.*

Most of her reading, once she learned how to read, would have been of a religious kind. She would have been taught religious dogma through a catechism, such as the *Grand Catéchisme d'Avignon*, where she would have learned her articles of faith. Religious practice, or devotions, would also have formed part of her education, and a popular book with the Ursulines was *Le Paradis ouvert à Philagie,* by Paul de Barry. First published in the mid-seventeenth century, it had been reprinted many times. Based on the cult of the Virgin Mary, it contained 100 Marian devotions and special prayers to the mother of Jesus to be said on particular days.

Depending on what classes were on offer for day pupils, Olympe may also have had access to a book of Geography and one of Roman history, as well as a book about the history of saints.

Although she did not see her father, Jean-Jacques Le Franc Pompignan, often, she made sure to read the plays he had written, such as his *Didon* (1734), a tragedy.

1.2 Marie-Jeanne

Like Olympe, Marie-Jeanne's education began with religious books. But we know that she had access to more books as her parents had some and they did not restrict her reading. For instance, while she too had a catechism to take to Sunday school, she liked to hide her copy of Plutarch's *Parallel Lives* inside it. This would have been the translation by Anne and André Dacier, published in 1727.

1.3 Sophie

Sophie had access to more books than either Marie-Jeanne or Olympe, and more languages to read them in as she was taught Latin, Greek and English. As a child her favourite book was Marcus Aurelius's *Meditations*, in Latin. As her mother was very devout, she no doubt also read a number of Catholic books, a catechism to prepare her for her first communion and books of Christian history and devotions. Because one of her ancestors had been a tutor to Montaigne, it is to be expected that the family had a copy of the *Essays*.

2 Young adulthood

2.1 Olympe

As she moved to Paris soon after her husband disappeared, Olympe began to frequent the theatres. She became a fan of Beaumarchais. His plays *The Barber of Seville* (1772) and its sequel *Marriage of Figaro* (1778), in particular, influenced her own work. She wrote *Le marriage Inattendu de Cherubin*, in their homage.

The Paris theatres also put on operas. She may have been present at the representation of *Ernestine*, Joseph Bologne, Chevalier de Saint-Georges's first opera. The libretto was written by Pierre Choderlos de Laclos, who later became famous for his novel, *Les Liaisons Dangereuses*. *Ernestine* was performed on 19 July 1777, at the Comédie Italienne. Gouges knew Saint-George as they were both part of Madame de Montesson's private theatre. The opera was panned at the premiere, though critiques blamed its failure on the libretto rather than the music.

As part of her ongoing self-education, Gouges read Rousseau's works. She preferred him to Voltaire because Voltaire had been her birth father's personal enemy, making fun of Pompignan's religiosity. We know Olympe had read Rousseau's *Discourse on the Arts and Sciences*, and *Discourse on the Origins of Inequality*, published in 1750 and 1755, because she refers to them in her 1789 work, *Le Bonheur Primitif*. A close reading of that text suggests that she had also read his *Letter to D'Alembert*, in which he argues that theatre is morally harmful. She may further have read her own father's 'Lettre à Monsieur Racine' (1751), which offers a very Aristotelian discourse on how the theatre can elevate public morality through the correct choice of plot, language, and characters of the actors.

In order to improve her spoken and written French (she had been brought up speaking mostly Occitan), Olympe may have owned a grammar and a thesaurus. A good choice would have been the *Grammaire Raisonnée par LaHarpe, Suard, Guingené, à l'Usage d'une Jeune Personne*. La Harpe was one of the founders of the Paris Lycée, where young Parisian ladies in search of an education took classes. If she owned a thesaurus, it was likely the *Nouveaux Synonymes Français*. Its author, the Abbé Roubauld, was an abolitionist and social reformer.

2.2 Marie-Jeanne

The biggest intellectual event in Marie-Jeanne's adult life was the discovery of Rousseau. By the time she was twenty, she had read all his books save one: *Julie of the New Heloise*. This was gifted to her by a friend when her mother died, and she tells us that the book was a revelation as much as Plutarch's had been in childhood. It gave her a sense of belonging, as a woman who was also a republican.

Marie-Jeanne read a lot in her young adulthood, and we know that she started to practise her English by reading poetry in the original. She read Milton, Thomson, Pope, and Shakespeare's tragedies, her favourites *Otello*, *Hamlet* and *Lear*.

She also read works of a scientific nature, in particular botany. She was also interested in the more obscure areas of science. We know she was a fan of Johann Kaspar Lavater, who argued that physical traits corresponded to character traits. She heard his speech and read his *Essai sur la Physiognomie* when it came out in 1786.

2.3 Sophie

At a convent school in Normandie, Sophie discovered Rousseau and Voltaire. Their books would have been easy to find, so we can assume she read most of them. Like Marie-Jeanne, she also practised her languages, translating Torquato Tasso's *Jerusalem Delivered*, a romantic epic poem about the first crusades, and the English poet Edward Young's *Night Thoughts*.

3 Maturity

Once our three heroines were fully adult, we can expect that they had access to roughly the same books.

Their philosophical background, which they acquired through reading or discussion, would have been principally Descartes, Locke and Condillac. But they also read or knew the works of the atheistic and proto-utilitarian moral philosopher Claude Adrien Helvetius – all three frequented his widow's salon in Auteuil, and his status was almost as high, in that circle, as Rousseau's or Voltaire's. They would also have either read or discussed Montesquieu's works, his *Lettres Persannes* and his *Esprit des Lois*. In the early years of the Revolution, Sophie also read Adam Smith's *The Theory of Moral Sentiments*. She translated it in 1798.

As far as *scientific knowledge* was concerned, they had access to several books on botany, including Rousseau's *Letters on the Elements of Botany, written to a lady*, in which he tried to make botany fit his conception of female morality and in particular chastity. But Olympe, Marie-Jeanne and Sophie were not prudes, and while they admired Rousseau, they preferred their science unfiltered by prejudice. Olympe for whom the cult of nature was always important probably read Bernardin de Saint Pierre's *Etude de la Nature*, when it came out in 1788.

Because all were interested in *travel* (but only Marie-Jeanne succeeded in leaving France), they may well have read the *Abregé de l'Histoire Generale des Voyages* by la Harpe, which came out in 1780. Eleven years later, they would read their friend Brissot's *Nouveau voyage dans les États-Unis de l'Amérique septentrionale*.

Economics was a big concern before the Revolution. The French economy depended on agriculture, and that was stifled by very strict laws and regulations. Unfortunately, the first attempt at freeing the commerce of grain happened at the same time as several climate disasters. Books available at the time on economy would have been Adam Smith's *Wealth of Nations*, translated and very popular in France. There were also several writings by Turgot and Condorcet that Sophie would have read, and Marie-Jeanne also, to help her husband with his own research.

History: In 1788, a French translation of Gibbon's *History of the Decline and Fall of the Roman Empire* came out. This may have presented Gouges with an opportunity to fill some of her historical lacunas. The history of England was also of some importance, and Hume's *History* was available in French, as was, from 1789, Catharine Macaulay's *The history of England from the accession of James 1. to that of the Brunswick line*, in eight volumes. We know that Marie-Jeanne read parts of the latter in English, but that in prison, she had to switch to Hume.

Revolutionary texts: One book which had a great influence on revolutionary thinkers and reformers was Cesare de Beccaria's *On Crimes and Punishments*, written in 1764 and translated that same year, with an introduction by Voltaire. Beccaria had been a good friend and visitor of the Helvetius family, so all those who frequented Madame Helvetius's salon in Auteuil would have heard about the book.

Thomas Paine, who moved to Paris in 1790, was a great source of knowledge on revolutionary thought. His *Common Sense* (1776) in the original and in French translation was very popular in France, as was, later, his *Rights of Man* (1791).

The literary culture of the eighteenth century, in particular when it came to political thought, was heavily reliant on pamphlets. One highly influential pamphlet that Olympe, Marie-Jeanne and Sophie almost certainly read was Emmanuel Joseph Sieyès's 'What Is the Third Estate?' (1789).

A great concern of the time was the question of *slavery*.

The best-known book on the topic was the Abbé Raynal and Diderot's *Histoire Philosophique et Politique des Deux Indes* published in 1770. In 1781, Condorcet published his own *Réflexions sur l'esclavage des Nègres* under a pseudonym. In the late 1780s, a number of key texts were translated from the English, such as Ottobah Cuguano's *Réflexions sur la Traite de l'Esclavage des Nègres* (1788) and Clarkson's *Essai sur les desavantages politiques de la traite des negres* (1789). And in 1791, Julien Raimond, a 'free man of colour' from Saint Domingue, published his *Observations sur l'Origine et les Progrès du préjugé des colons blancs contre les hommes de couleur; sur les inconvéniens de le perpétuer; la nécessité, la facilité de le détruire; sur le projet du Comité colonial, etc.*

The question of women's rights was also beginning to attract some discussion. One of the earlier texts of the period was Condorcet's 'Sur l'Admission des Femmes au Droit de la Cité' (1790) and in 1792, Mary Wollstonecraft's Second *Vindication* was translated under the title *Defense des Droits des Femmes*.

Notes

Chapter 1

1 '"Enfants de la Patrie, vous vengerez ma mort!"!' See Groult (2014). (Although 'fatherland' would be the literal translation, it has connotations that 'patrie' does not).

2 'Women, do you want to be republicans? Love, follow and teach the laws that remind your children to exercise their rights. Take glory in the brilliant actions they may one day perform on behalf of the fatherland, because these speak well of you; be simple in your dress, laborious in your household work; never join popular assemblies with the aim of speaking there; but by your occasional presence there, encourage your children to participate; then your fatherland will bless you because you will truly have done for it what it expects of you.' In Dauban (1864: ccxlix).

3 Naish (1991: 109), and Linton (2013), Appendix.

4 See glossary.

5 I draw this narrative of the French Revolution in great part from Marie-Jeanne Roland's *Memoires*, from Gallo (2008); and Hunt's (2004) helpful chronology.

6 Although historians have made an effort to bring other names to our attention, such as Landes (1988); Hesse (2003); Scott (1997); Trouille (1997); Goodman (2009).

7 Mandement de messieurs les vicaires généraux du chapitre métropolitain de Paris, 9 Fevrier 1817. (20)

8 L'Esprit des journaux français et étrangers, Volume 468 Une Societé de gens de lettres. April 1817.

9 Hugo cites three verses of the song during Gavroche's death scene. Tome V. Jean Valjean – Livre Premier : La Guerre entre quatre murs – Chapitre 15. Gavroche dehors.

10 See Moore (2006). Her lives include Marie-Jeanne Roland, Germaine de Staël, Pauline Léon and Théroigne de Mericourt. See also Ball (2021).

11 For biographical details on Gouges, Roland and Grouchy, I used primarily the following texts (as well as archival material cited elsewhere):
   Gouges: Blanc (2003), Groult (2014), Reid (2014).
   Roland: Reynolds (2012); Roland (1799–1800, 1827, 1864, 1900, 1905, 1913); Dauban (1864). Grouchy: Grouchy (1993, 2008, 2010, 2019); Dumont (1832); Guillois (1897); Badinter and Badinter (1988); Tetard (2003).

12 Thanks to the work of historians such as Landes and Scott, and philosophers such as Karen Green, this is beginning to change, at least in academic circles.

13 See Hesse (2003) and Goodman (2009) on the changing habits of women's publishing during the Revolution.
14 Declaration of the Rights of Woman, Article X.
15 Some nineteenth-century historians, such as Michelet or Lairtulier, do portray these women as heroines, strong, intelligent, virtuous and dedicated to their nation. But even then, at least as far as Michelet is concerned, this does not render them useful, as their gender itself proves an obstacle to the flourishing of the republic as male leaders fall in love with them.
16 See Chapter 4, Section 3.
17 See Chapter 5, Section 1.2.
18 See Goodman (2009) on how letter writing contributed to Marie-Jeanne Roland's becoming a philosophical and political thinker and an influential member of the Girondins group (265, 6).
19 Guillois (1894) and Blanc 2006).
20 On the role of the Girondins during the Revolution, see Linton (2013).
21 Rossignol (2010), and 'Olympe de Gouges' Moore, Brooks and Wigginton 2012).
22 Oliver (2016).
23 See Chapter 7.
24 Anon (1874: 6).
25 See Chapter 6.

Chapter 2

1 Berville and Barriere, in Roland (1827: xxxvi) refer to the 'bloody walls' of the building, but perhaps they are being metaphorical.
2 The French 'f***' stands for 'foutre' and old fashion swear word meaning the same as the English equivalent 'fuck'. Marie-Jeanne uses 'foutre' occasionally herself. It is likely her nineteenth-century editors added the ellipsis.
3 The princess of Lamballe was a favourite of Marie-Antoinette. The queen's other close friend, the duchess of Polignac, had left France on the queen's orders in the early days of the Revolution.
4 Letter to Bancal, 9 September 1792, in Roland (1900: 436).
5 The club's website even mentions that the lowest level of the cave was used as an impromptu prison and that a guillotine had once been placed there. The evidence for the club's claim to fame is slight, as the Jacobins mostly met across the river on the Right Bank, and 'Terror' was not used as a descriptor of the government of the Commune until later.
6 Louise-Anne Lefèvre, Madame Pétion, eventually came out of Ste Pélagie and was granted a widow's pension after the Terror. See Oliver (2009: 99). Louise-Anne's mother was less lucky and was guillotined in September 1793, so that when Marie-Jeanne Roland visited with her neighbour, she was consoling her for her loss. Jerome Pétion died together with Marie-Jeanne's lover, Buzot, in a double suicide. Their corpses were eaten by wolves.

7 Beugnot (1868: 199).
8 Dauban (1864: CCXLIV).
9 See Chapter 11 of this book.

Chapter 3

1 Gascar (1989: 246, 280).
2 Underwood (1915). Eveline Groot alerted me to this slur on Germaine de Staël.
3 Martin (1931).
4 Michelet (1855: 52).
5 Michelet (1855: 36).
6 Michelet, (1855, p.: 206).
7 Michelet (1855: 324–5).
8 Michelet (1855: 328).
9 Letzter and Adelson (2004).
10 Guillois (1904: 87).
11 Guillois (1897).
12 See Chapter 4.
13 Gallo (2008: 412).
14 Gallo (2008: 420).
15 Gallo (2008: 391).
16 Israel (2014).
17 Israel (2014: 123).
18 Israel (2014: 715).
19 Israel (2014: 206, 582).
20 Israel (2014: 123).
21 Israel (2014: 122, 123, 400).
22 John Berger in the second episode of the BBC series *Ways of Seeing*, 1972.
23 Gouges (1788e), *Le Philosophe Corrigé ou le Cocu Supposé*.
24 Roland (1827: 1, 198).
25 From Sophie Grandchamp, quoted in Reynolds (2012: 284).
26 Guillois (1897: 39). The list Grouchy sent her aunt looks like it could have been taken from a fashion magazine published sixty years later, Journal des Demoiselles, (1840), which, in its winter fashion, discusses the colour of the ribbon to be worn at different times of the day as well as the shape of the belt buckle.
27 Burke 1986, pp.: 165, 169).
28 Monteyremar (1862: 14–22).
29 Gullickson 2014). It's unclear whether the 1793 engraving from a portrait from life, included in this volume, reflects her image before or after her disgrace.
30 'Cette femme qu' on a dit fort jolie, n étoit point jolie [. . .] c étoit une virago plus charnue que fraîche, sans grâce, malpropre, comme le sont presque

tous les philosophes et beaux esprits femelles. Sa figure était érésipélateuse et sans lignes. De taille et de jeunesse et une évidence fameuse: voilà de quoi être belle dans un interrogatoire. Au surplus, cette remarque serait inutile, sans cette observation généralement vraie que toute femme jolie et qui se comptait à l être tient à la vie et craint la mort.'

31 Suleau (1791: 27–8).

32 Bibliothèque Municipale du Trocadéro (Paris 75016). Fonds Parent de Rosan : 34, 186 v (6 août 1792) et 28, 307 v (4 avril 1793) : laissez- passer d'O. de Gouges délivrés à la mairie d'Auteuil.

33 Blanc (2003: 29).

34 Roland (1827: 100).

35 Guillois (1904: 17, 20).

36 Jessica Gordon-Roth and Nancy Kendrick expressed the worry that spending time on biographical details may be 'triggering our audiences to reject these women *as philosophers* and their texts *as philosophical*'. Gordon-Roth and Kendrick (2019).

37 The most authoritative source for biographical facts about Olympe, besides her own autobiographical writings, is Olivier Blanc's (2014).

38 Gouges (1788a), *Mémoires de Madame de Valmont*, 27, Blanc (2014: 22).

39 See Blanc, 31.

40 Guillois (1904: 17).

41 Blanc (2014: 32).

42 'Marriage is the tomb of trust and love.' Postscript to the *Droits de la Femme*.

43 Z is not a usual letter in Occitan so that some of her relatives back at Montauban spelt their name with a g instead, pronounced 'dj'. See Blanc (2014: 33).

44 'Ses contemporains furent unanimes pour dire qu'elle fut fanée avant l'heure et que ses charmes diminuaient d'autant plus rapidement qu'elle en avait abusé.
    Alors, lassée de ne pas trouver dans la galanterie tout le succès capable de satisfaire son ambition trop forte, elle voulut se lancer dans la littérature. [. . .] Elle veut qu'on parle d'elle. Elle se mettra donc à écrire.' Guillois (1904).

45 See Chapter 4 for more details on this anecdote. Having a secretary in the eighteenth century was no more a sign of illiteracy than it is now: writing was hard work and materials expensive, so it was important to get it right first. Manuscripts had to be copied by someone with a neat enough hand to take to the printer. They had to be corrected by someone who would check the spelling and inconsistencies. A secretary was to eighteenth-century authors what a spell checker and a copy editor are to us.

46 Preface of *l'Homme Genereux*, Gouges (1786: viii).

47 The best biographical sources for Marie-Jeanne Roland are her *Memoir*, her correspondence, published by Roland (1913) and Sian Reynolds (2012).

48 Montaigne, Essays, Book II, Chapter 4.

49 Olympe de Gouges relates this incident in her preface to the play, published in 1787.

50 For Emmanuel's own account, see his 1829 *Fragments Historiques*.

51 Havet (1878), tome 39, 522.
52 Guillois (1897: 18).
53 Grouchy (2019: 64); Guillois (1897: 21).
54 Guillois (1897: 36–7).
55 Guillois (1897: 38). Her eyes were still troubling her in her middle age, see Lagrave (1994: 143).
56 See Badinter et Badinter (1988: 16).
57 Guillois (1897: 148).

Chapter 4

1 Dinet (2011).
2 See Grégoire (1794).
3 Gouges (1788a: 7–8).
4 Gouges (1791).
5 Guillois (1904: 20).
6 For more on Saint-Georges, see Chapter 10.
7 This play is discussed in Section 4 of this chapter and in Chapter 9.
8 Beaumarchais (1958: 21).
9 Although his campaign was somewhat self-interested – his efforts only benefitted writers, but not, for instance, composers. See Geoffroy-Schwinden (2018).
10 Gouges (1786a).
11 Ibid.
12 Fleury (1837).
13 See Blanc (2014: 46).
14 Gouges (1792a: 46–7).
15 Blanc (2014: 80).
16 See Chapter 9 for more discussion.
17 Gouges (1789b), Mes Voeux Sont Remplis, ou le Don Patriotique.
18 Gouges (1789c), Action Heroique d'Une Française, ou La France Sauvee par les Femmes.
19 Ibid.
20 Gouges (1792a), Le Bon Sens Français, p. 42.
21 Between 1790 and 1795, Paris was divided into forty-eight sections, each with its own administration. This replaced the sixty 'districts' instituted in 1789 and was in turn replaced by 'quartiers' (as they were called before 1789) in 1795 under the Directoire.
22 Gouges (1792d), Olympe de Gouges, Defenseur Officieux de Louis Capet.
23 Gouges (1793a), Arret de mort que presente Olympe de Gouges contre Louis Capet.
24 Bossuet, *Sur les Devoirs des Rois*, see also Kelly (1986).
25 Gouges (1793c), 'The Three Urns'.

Chapter 5

1 Shelley (1840: 266).
2 Roland (1827). Vol. I, 222.
3 Marie-Jeanne Roland, 21 March 1789, letter to Varenne de Fenille, in Roland (1900: 43).
4 See Green (2014).
5 Roland (1913). Vol I, 540-541.
6 Roland (1799–1800). Vol III, 138–41, and 169–79.
7 Caradonna (2012: 45).
8 Roland (1913: II, 13).
9 Roland (1913: II, 83–4).
10 'Discours sur la question proposée par l'Academie de Besançon: Comment l'éducation des femmes pourrait contribuer à rendre les homes meilleurs' (1777) is in a volume of her works published by Faugeres, in 1864. (*Mémoires de Madame Roland*. Nouvelle Edition. Tome Second. Paris: Hachette, vol II, 325–49).
11 Roland (1864: II, 338).
12 Roland (1864: II, 332, 334, 344).
13 Roland (1864: II, 344).
14 Rousseau (1761, 1997: 438).
15 Rousseau (1988: 59).
16 Roland (1864: II, 333).
17 Roland (1864: II, 334–5).
18 Roland (1827: 184).
19 Roland (1799–1800: III, 170).
20 Roland (1864: II, 337).
21 Roland (1799–1800: III, 140).
22 Roland (1799–1800: III, 171).
23 Gille (1952).
24 Roland (1827: I, 198).
25 Roland (1827: I, 287–8).
26 Roland (1900: II, 307).
27 22 November 1789, Lyon, Marie-Jeanne Roland to Brissot, in Paris (Roland 1900: II, 75).
28 Roland (1900: II, 258).
29 Reynolds (2012: 142).
30 Cited in Reynolds (2012: 220).
31 Letter to Brissot, 3 August 1789 (Perroud 1900: II, 55). Reprinted in the Patriote François, 12 August 1789.
32 Roland (1900: 115).
33 Roland is talking of Decimus Brutus, not Decius the Emperor.
34 In French, this is *foutus* – so that my translation preserves both meaning and the tone.

35 Letter to Bosc, 26 July 1789, Roland (1900: II, 53).
36 Letter to Bosc, 3 August 1789, Roland (1900: II, 55).
37 Letter to Bosc, 4 September 1789, Roland (1900: II, 61).
38 Roland (1827: 200).
39 Roland (1905: 264).

Chapter 6

1 Guillois 38.
2 Another possibility would be Arthur Young, an English agricultural writer who had achieved fame for his writings on agricultural reforms and economic and social observations. His *Tour of Ireland* (1780) was very well received among French readers who had some interest in peasants' welfare and social improvement in general.
3 See Bour (2022, 2013).
4 See Chapter 7 for a discussion of Wollstonecraft's reception in revolutionary Paris.
5 For arguments attributing contributions to Grouchy, see McLean (2012), Lagrave (1989: 437) and Bergès (2015).
6 Dumont (1832: 321–2).
7 Dumont (1832: 333).
8 Martin (1931: 116).
9 Martin (1931: 116).
10 Condorcet (1849), vol. I, 609.
11 Condorcet (1991), vol 2, 20–1.
12 Condorcet (1849), vol. I, 413–37, Belhaste (1994: 127). It is perhaps significant that in his éloge, Condorcet refers to the French royalty failing to take Vaucanson's accomplishments as seriously as others did.
13 Dumont (1849: 333).
14 Condorcet (1991: 27).
15 Condorcet (2012: 204).
16 Grouchy (2019: 58).
17 Scurr (2009: 444), and Rœderer (1856: 501).
18 See Martin (1931: 121).
19 Ibid.
20 Suleau (1791: 27–8).
21 Dumont (1832: 328–9).
22 See Porret (2000).
23 Also by Montesquieu, but Beccaria's book on punishment takes in much of what Montesquieu had to say on that topic and was perhaps a more direct and universal influence of French reformers.
24 Beccaria (1995). The translation by Abbé Morellet also undertook to restructure the text, so it was perhaps not entirely accurate. But it is possible

that Grouchy read the text in Italian – as she had previously translated Tasso's *Jerusalem*.

25 Beccaria (1995: 21).
26 Beccaria (1995: 46–7).
27 Beccaria (1995: 104).
28 Dupaty was Sophie de Grouchy's uncle, and his collaboration on the case with Condorcet was the occasion for Grouchy and Condorcet to meet. Guillois (1897: 60).
29 Sieyès (1789).
30 Cabanis and Grouchy were both friends and brother and sister in law. Cabanis knew the Condorcet couple through Madame Helvetius, his 'adoptive' mother. He was for a long time in relationship with Charlotte de Grouchy, Sophie's younger sister, and after the Terror, they married.
31 Grouchy (2019: 147).
32 It may seem odd to call the theory her own when the Letters were written as a response to Smith, but as Bergès and Schliesser have argued in their introduction to Grouchy (2019), there is plenty that is original in Grouchy's theory of sympathy.
33 Cabanis and Beaubatie (2002: 24).
34 Grouchy (2019: 91).
35 Grouchy (2019: 99).
36 Grouchy (2019: 91).
37 Cabanis and Beaubatie (2002: 26).
38 Cabanis and Beaubatie (2002: 10).

Chapter 7

1 Stewart (2002), before footnote 87.
2 See Brown (2003), and Birn (2012).
3 Brissot (1910: 302).
4 O'Loughlin (2020: 7).
5 But we also have travel journals from Henrietta Liston, who went to America in the 1780s and late to the Ottoman Empire, with her diplomat husband. See Hart, Kennedy, and Petherbridge (2020).
6 Arianrhod (2012: 39, 135).
7 The eight-volume work had not been completed in 1777 when Macaulay visited Paris. But Brissot visited her in 1783, as she was completing the final volume.
8 This journal was not, unlike her Swiss travel journal, published during her lifetime. It can be read in Champagneux's edition of her works, volume 3 (Roland 1799–1800).
9 Roland (1799–1800: 219).
10 *Ibid.*

11 *Ibid.*, 251.
12 Two such establishments were run by Mary Wollstonecraft in Islington and Newington Green, and the establishment of the latter may have coincided with the Rolands's visits.
13 Green (2019: 89).
14 Brissot reports in his *Memoirs* that during her visit, she had told Turgot that she would not visit Versailles as she had no interest whatsoever in the living arrangements of tyrants.
15 Green (2019: 80). The letter is addressed to George Simon, earl of Harcourt, who opposed the war against America.
16 Green (2019: 5).
17 Donnelly (1988: 262).
18 Green (2019: 18).
19 'As a foreigner, I was snubbed except by a few individuals, the principal one being Catharine Macaulay.' Brissot (1910), vol. I, 348–9.
20 Green (2019: 218). Brissot was known, from the beginning of his career as a journalist until the early days of the Revolution as Brissot de Warville – Warville was the English spelling for the place of his birth 'Ouarville'.
21 Brissot (1910: 350).
22 Brissot (1910: 348).
23 Brissot (1910: 349).
24 February 1792, *Moniteur National*, anon.
25 Brissot (1910: 353).
26 Macaulay (1790: 4).
27 Wollstonecraft (2014: 22).
28 See Tomalin (2004: 239–40) for details of her journey.
29 Tomalin suggests that this was because of sexist interference on the part of the Montagne (2004: 264).
30 Tomalin (2004: 250).
31 The name of the translator is not noted anywhere in the translation. In an article on the reception of Wollstonecraft in revolutionary France, Isabelle Bour (2022) suggests that the translation was by Félicité Brissot, and that Jacques-Pierre Brissot had annotated it.
32 Wollstonecraft (1792: 448–9), translator's note.
33 Wollstonecraft (2014: 23).
34 Martin, 113.

Chapter 8

1 See Sellers (2003).
2 Gazette Nationale ou Moniteur Universel, 6 November 1792, Convention Nationale, Sceance du 5 Novembre.
3 Gouges (1792c).

4 Linton (2013: 37).
5 Linton (2013: 275).
6 Roland (1827), vol. I, 402.
7 Roland (1902), vol. 1, 268.
8 Tomaselli (2021: 13).
9 Wollstonecraft (2014: 210).
10 Wollstonecraft (1789), vol. I, 391.
11 Wollstonecraft (1789), vol. I, 392.
12 Oliver (2016).
13 See Anon (1790a,b).
14 Roland (1900: 529).
15 Cited in Reynolds (2012: 128).
16 Perroud (1902: 269).
17 Dumont (1832: 270–1).
18 Condorcet and Paine (1991), vol. 1, 8 and vol. 3, 52–3.
19 Dumont (1832: 269).
20 Martin (1931: 122).
21 See Claeys (1989: 180).
22 Condorcet (1795: 23).
23 Grouchy (2019: 122).
24 Rousseau (1994: 166).
25 See Burnel (1793).

Chapter 9

1 Numbers obtained from the Transatlantic Slave Trade Database 2017.
2 When writing about slavery in this chapter, I followed the guidelines presented here: https://naacpculpeper.org/resources/writing-about-slavery -this-might-help/
3 I am taking the perspective that it would have been impossible for a woman to have consensual sex with a person who owned her. Hence my choice of the term 'rape'.
4 Quoted in deYoung (1960: 454–5).
5 *La Fraternité*, 8 Juin 1893. https://gallica.bnf.fr/ark:/12148/bpt6k5569909g/ f2.item.r=sanite%20belair%20execution
6 Cote extrait, 446AP/7 Dossier 2, G - Ma, Lettres de Brissot, n34. Archives Nationales de Pierrefite.
7 'This was the fourth time they had threatened turn me out, and, go where I might, I was determined now to take them at their word; though I thought it very hard, after I had lived with them for thirteen years, and worked for them like a horse, to be driven out in this way, like a beggar. My only fault was being sick, and therefore unable to please my mistress, who thought she never could get work enough out of her slaves; and I told them so: but

they only abused me and drove me out. This took place from two to three months, I think, after we came to England' Prince (2006: 227).

8   On the climate's unsuitability for African slaves, see James (1989: 10–11).
9   *Correspondance littéraire, philosophique et critique de Grimm et de Diderot, 1772 - 1776*, vol. 8, Paris, Furne (1830).
10 Cooper (2017: 31).
11 Dillon (1791).
12 Anon (1791a).
13 Ibid.
14 Ibid.
15 Ibid.
16 Anon (1791b).
17 Anon (1791c).
18 Skinner (1998).
19 Roland (1799–1800), vol. 3, 170.
20 Letter to Brissot 28 April 1791, edited by Brissot and published in the *Patriote Français* on 30 April 1791.
21 There is also newly uncovered evidence that Wollstonecraft's work was impacted by the Haitian Revolution. See Botting (2020, 2021).
22 Equiano (1789: 56).
23 Equiano (1789: 56).
24 Equiano (1789: 57).
25 See Chapter 11 for more details on that edition.
26 Condorcet (1822: 329).
27 It may have been the case that the identity of Schwartz was, in fact, known, at least in 1788 when the *Réflexions* was reprinted. See Jurt (1992: 11) footnote.
28 Condorcet (1822: 408).
29 See Chapter 6 for a discussion of Grouchy's reputation.
30 Sieyès (1789).
31 Raimond (1791).
32 Olympe de Gouges (1788d).
33 Gouges (1792e: 6).
34 Gouges (1792e: 19).
35 Gouges (1792e: 23).
36 Gouges (1788d).
37 Gouges (1790c: 2).
38 Manuscript letter from Papiers d'Instruction Publique de la Législative et de la Convention, Cote F 17, Dossier 388. Archives Nationales.
39 Laborde, one of the men involved in the attack, and one of Brissot's fiercest opponents, presented the event as the courageous and righteous prevention of a mulatto rebellion. It was probably such one-sided accounts that led Gouges to become horrified at the Haitian Revolution.
40 Gouges (1792e: 9).

Chapter 10

1 Sieyès (2003: 156).
2 Sieyès (2003: 155).
3 Sieyès (1789: 14).
4 *Le Mercure National*, 20 August 1789.
5 Karen Green (2014: 221).
6 Geffroy (2006: 109).
7 *Le Mercure National*, 18 April 1790.
8 Mistacco (2019: 88).
9 Archives Nationales de Pierrefite. Cote extrait, 446AP/7 Dossier 2, G - Ma, 21 pièces Lettres de Brissot, 31. My translation.
10 *Patriote français* 8 October 1789, 2.
11 Mistacco (2019: 88).
12 Brissot (1910: 273–4).
13 *Journal de la Société de 1789*, 3 July 1790.
14 The same argument was used against abolishing slavery, as we saw in the previous chapter.
15 When twenty-five years later, Condorcet run away from his hiding place in Paris, it was to the Suards, he turned. But, fearful of consequences for themselves, they turned him away.
16 Badinter and Badinter (1989: 525).
17 A later name for the *Mercure National*.
18 Charles-Louis Rousseau's feminism had its limits, as we can see from the treatise he published a few months later, 'Essai sur l'éducation et l'existence civile et politique des femmes', where he argues that for women, the duties of citizenships mostly lie in the giving birth to and bringing up citizens!
19 Quoted in Lapied (2006).
20 Comte D'Antraigue, quoted in Desan (2004: 15).
21 Desan (2004: 19).
22 Evidence that she was a member is not entirely conclusive, but she speaks approvingly of a speech against the monarchy in the Cercle Social and signed up for the 'Fraternal Societies' in June and July 1791. See Reynolds (2012: 146).
23 Gouges (1791).
24 Gouges (1790b).
25 Montesquieu (1989: 430–1).
26 Grouchy (2019: 140).
27 Desan (2006).
28 Cited in Cahen (1904: 535).
29 Cahen (1904: 537).
30 Cahen (1904: 536).

Epilogue

1 Some of the material in this section is reproduced or adapted from Berges (2018).
2 All materials relating to the text of the *Sketch* can be found in Schandeler and Crépel (2004).
3 This manuscript can now be viewed at the library of the Institut, MS885.
4 Condorcet (2012: 157–8).
5 Condorcet (2012: 9).
6 Condorcet (2012: 196).
7 Note that unlike most other writers of that period who were in favour of breastfeeding (Rousseau, Wollstonecraft), Grouchy does not focus weight on the natural mother but simply on whoever happens to be in charge of feeding the infant.
8 Grouchy (2019).
9 Wollstonecraft (2014: 176).
10 Reynolds (2012: 75, 94).
11 Schandeler and Crépel (2004: 257–8).
12 https://www.siv.archives-nationales.culture.gouv.fr/mm/media/download/FRAN_0152_02291_L-medium.jpg
13 Hase (1894: 81). Trans. Liz Disley.
14 Cabanis (1802: 78, 80).
15 Cabanis (1824: 84).
16 Grouchy (2019).

References

Anon. (1790a). 'Lettre écrite par un Français émigrant au Scioto'. New York, 23–29 mai 1790. Available online: https://gallica.bnf.fr/ark:/12148/bpt6k853452c/f3.item.r=scioto#

Anon. (1790b). 'Lettre de M. de V. à M. le C. D. M. à l'occasion des observations publiées sur l'établissement du Scioto'. Available online: https://gallica.bnf.fr/ark:/12148/bpt6k109679b.r=scioto?rk=21459;2#

Anon. (1791a). 'Essai sur l'exécution du décret du 15 mai 1791, concernant les gens de couleur, par un habitant planteur de l'Amérique'. Available online: https://gallica.bnf.fr/ark:/12148/bpt6k97905830/f443

Anon. (1791b). 'Réponse d'un ami des Noirs a la lettre de M.***, habitant de Saint Domingue'. Paris, 16 Novembre 1791. Available online: https://gallica.bnf.fr/ark:/12148/bpt6k5785201j?rk=21459;2

Anon. (1791c). 'Projet d'instruction pour les colonies relativement aux Décrets des 13 et 15'. Available online: https://gallica.bnf.fr/ark:/12148/bpt6k5790151t?rk=42918;4

Anon. (1817). 'Mandement de messieurs les vicaires généraux du chapitre métropolitain de Paris'. 9 Fevrier 1817.

Anon. (1874). 'Selected Anecdotes'. Buckingham Advertiser and Free Press, 5 December 1874.

Arianrhod, Robyn. (2012). *Seduced by Logic: Emilie du Chatelet, Mary Somerville and the Newtonian Revolution*. New York: Oxford University Press.

Badinter, Elisabeth and Robert Badinter. (1988). *Condorcet (1743–1794): Un Intellectuel en Politique*. Paris: Fayard.

Ball, Patrick. (2021). 'Alternate Currents in Women's Republicanism During the French Revolution'. *Australasian Philosophical Review*, 3: 4.

Beaumarchais, Pierre Augustin Caron de. (1958). 'The Preface to "The Marriage of Figaro"'. *The Tulane Drama Review*, 2: 3–27.

Beccaria, Cesare di. (1995). *On Crimes and Punishments and Other Writings*. Ed. Richard Bellamy, Trans. Richard Davis. Cambridge: Cambridge University Press.

Belhaste, Bruno. (1994). 'Condorcet, les arts utiles et leur enseignement'. In A. M. Charlet and Pierre Crépel (eds), *Condorcet, Homme des Lumières et de la Révolution*, 121–36. Paris: ENS.

Bergès, Sandrine. (2015). 'Sophie de Grouchy on the Cost of Domination in the Letters on Sympathy and Two Anonymous Articles in Le Républicain'. *The Monist*, 98: 102–12.

Bergès, Sandrine. (2018). 'Family, Gender, and Progress: Sophie de Grouchy and Her Exclusion in the Publication of Condorcet's Sketch of Human Progress'. *Journal of the History of Ideas*, 79: 267–83.

Beugnot, Auguste-Arthur. (1868). *Memoires du Comte Beugnot, Ancien Ministre (1783–1815)*. Paris: E.Dentu.

Birn, Raimond Royal. (2012). *Censorship of Books in Eighteenth-Century France*. Stanford: Stanford University Press.

Blanc, Olivier. (2003). *Marie-Olympe de Gouge: Une humaniste a la find du XVIIIe siecle*. Paris: Editions Rene Vienet.

Blanc, Olivier. (2006). 'Cercles politiques et «salons» du début de la Révolution (1789–1793)'. *Annales Historiques de la Revolution Francaise*, 344: 63–92.

Bossuet, Jacques-Benignes. *Sur les Devoirs des Rois, sermon prêché en 1662*. Available online: http://clicetclicetphilogram.fr/Bossuet/DEVOIRSROIS.htm

Botting, Eileen Hunt. (2020). 'From Revolutionary Paris to Nootka Sound to Saint-Domingue: The International Politics and Prejudice behind Wollstonecraft's Theory of the Rights of Humanity, 1789–1791'. *Journal of International Political Theory*. DOI: 10.1177/1755088220978432

Botting, Eileen Hunt. (2021). 'Wollstonecraft in Jamaica: The International Reception of *A Vindication of the Rights of Men* in the Kingston Daily Advertiser in 1791'. *History of European Ideas*. DOI: 10.1080/01916599.2021.1898434

Bour, Isabelle. (2013). 'A New Wollstonecraft: The Reception of the *Vindication of the Rights of Woman* and *The Wrongs of Woman* in Revolutionary France'. *British Society for Eighteenth-Century Studies*, 36: 575–86.

Bour, Isabelle. (2022). 'Who Translated into French and Annotated Mary Wollstonecraft's *Vindication of the Rights of Woman?*'. *History of European Ideas*. Online first: DOI: 10.1080/01916599.2021.2022081

Brissot, Jacques-Pierre (1791). *Nouveau voyage dans les États-Unis de l'Amérique septentrionale, fait en 1788*. Paris : Buission. Available online: https://gallica.bnf.fr/ark:/12148/bpt6k82417x.image

Brissot, Jacques-Pierre. (1910). *Mémoires, tome 1 (1754–1784)*. Ed. Perroud. Paris: Alphonse Picard et Fils.

Brissot, Jacques-Pierre. Cote extrait, 446AP/7 Dossier 2, G - Ma, Lettres de Brissot, n34. Archives Nationales de Pierrefite.

Brown, Gregory S. (2003). 'Reconsidering the Censorship of Writers in Eighteenth-Century France: Civility, State Power, and the Public Theater in the Enlightenment'. *The Journal of Modern History*, 75: 235–68.

Burnel, Henri-Pierre. (1793). 'Nécessité du Culte de la Raison'. *Au Rocher-de-la-liberté*, Imprimerie Nationale chez Gaumont, an II.

Burke, Edmund. (1790/1986). *Reflections on the Revolution in France*. Hammondsmith: Penguin.

Cabanis, Pierre-Jean-George. (1802). *Les Rapports du Physique et du Moral*. 8th ed. Paris: Baillere.

Cabanis, Pierre-Jean-George. (1824). *Letter Postume et Inédite de Cabanis à M. F*** sur les Cause Premières' avec des notes par F.Bérard*. Paris: Gabon et Companie.

Cabanis, Pierre-Jean-George and Yannick Beaubatie. (2002). *Note sur le supplice de la guillotine*. Périgeux: Fanlac.

Cahen, Léon. (1904). *Condorcet et la Révolution française*. Paris: Alcan.

Caradonna, Jeremy L. (2012). *The Enlightenment in Practice: Academic Prize Contests and Intellectual Culture in France, 1670–1794*. Ithaca: Cornell University Press.

Claeys, Gregory. (1989). *Thomas Paine, Social and Political Thought*. Boston: Unwin Hyman.

Condorcet, Jean-Antoine-Nicolas Caritat Marquis de. (1849). *Oeuvres*. Ed. A. Condorcet O'Connor and M. F. Arago. Paris: Firmin Didot Freres, Libraires.

Condorcet, Jean-Antoine-Nicolas Caritat Marquis de. (1822). *Esquisse d'un tableau des progres de l'esprit humain; suivi de Réflexions sur l'esclavage des Nègres, par Condorcet*. Paris : Masson et Fils.

Condorcet, Jean-Antoine-Nicolas Caritat Marquis de. (1795/1998). *Esquisse d'un Tableau historique des progrès de l'esprit humain*. Availabler online: testi/700/condorcet/index.html, Html edition for Eliohs by Guido Abbattista, February 1998.

Condorcet, Paine. (1991). *Aux Origines de la République 1789–1792. Volume III Le Républicain par Condorcet et Thomas Paine, 1791*. Paris: EDHIS.

Condorcet, N. (2012). *Political Writings*. Ed. Steven Lukes and Nadia Urbinati. Cambridge: Cambridge University Press.

Cooper, A. J. (2017). '(Doctoral Dissertation) L'Attitude De La France A L'Égard De L'Esclavage Pendant La Revolution'. Published Materials by Anna J. Cooper. Available online: http://dh.howard.edu/ajc_published/25

Dauban, Charles Aime. (1864). *Etude sur Madame Roland et son temps*. Paris: Plon.

Desan, Suzanne. (2004). *The Family on Trial in Revolutionary France*. Berkeley: University of California Press.

Desan, Suzanne. (2006). 'Pétitions de femmes en faveur d'une réforme révolutionnaire de la famille'. *Annales historiques de la Révolution française*, 344: 27–46.

Dillon, Arthur. (1791). 'Motifs de la motion faite a l'Assemblée nationale le 4 mars 1791'. Available online: https://www.patrimoines-martinique.org/ark: /35569/a011426186902lTxP57

Dinet, Dominique. (2011). 'L'éducation des filles de la fin du 18e siècle jusqu'en 1918'. *Revue des sciences religieuses*, 85(4): 457–90.

Donnelly, F. (1988). 'Levellerism in Eighteenth and Early Nineteenth-Century Britain'. *Albion: A Quarterly Journal Concerned with British Studies*, 20: 261–69.

Dumont, Etienne. (1832). *Recollections of Mirabeau*, 2nd edn. London: Edward Bull.

Dumont, Etienne. (1832). *Souvenirs sur Mirabeau et sur les deux premières Assemblées Législatives*. Paris: Librairie de Charles Gosselin.

Equiano, Olaudah. (1789). *Interesting Narrative of the Life of Olaudah Equiano, or Gustavus Vassa, the African*, 8th edn. Norwich.

Fleury, Mémoires de Fleury de la Comédie-Française, 1757 à 1820, Paris, éditeur Ambroise Dupont, 1837.

Fonds Parent de Rosan: 34, 186 v (6 août 1792) et 28, 307 v (4 avril 1793) : laissez- passer d'O. de Gouges délivrés à la mairie d'Auteuil.

Gallo, Max. (2008). *La Révolution Française, 1. Le Peuple et le Roi.* Pocket: XO edtions.

Garrard, Mary D. (2020). *Artemisia Gentileschi and Feminism in Early Modern Europe.* London: Reaktion Books.

Gascar, Pierre. (1989). *Album Les Ecrivains de la Révolution.* Bibliothèque de la Pléiade. Paris: Gallimard.

Geffroy, Annie. (2006). 'Louise de Kéralio-Robert, pionnière du républicanisme sexiste'. *Annales Historiques de la Révolution Française*, 2: 107–24.

Geoffroy-Schwinden, Rebecca Dowd. (2018). 'Music, Copyright, and Intellectual Property during the French Revolution: A Newly Discovered Letter from André-Ernest-Modeste Grétry'. *Transposition* [Enligne], 7. Available online: http://journals.openedition.org/transposition/2057

Gille, Bertrand. (1952). 'L'Encyclopédie, dictionnaire technique'. *Revue d'histoire des sciences et de leurs applications*, 5: 26–53.

Goodman, Dena. (2009). *Becoming a Woman in the Age of Letters.* Ithaca: Cornell University Press.

Gordon-Roth, J. and N. Kendrick. 'Recovering Early Modern Women Writers'. *Metaphilosophy*, 50 (2019): 268–85.

Gouges, O. (1786a). *Le Mariage inattendu de Cherubin.* Available online: https://www.olympedegouges.eu/le_mariage_inattendu.php

Gouges, O. (1786b). *L'Homme Généreux.* Trans. Clarissa Palmer. Available online: https://www.olympedegouges.eu/homme_gen.php

Gouges, O. (1788a). 'Madame de Valmont, Preface pour les dames'. In *Oeuvres de Madame de Gouges, dediées à Monseigneur Le Duc D'Orleans.* Paris: L'Autheur. Available online: http://gallica.bnf.fr/ark:/12148/bpt6k6546469r.r =gouges.

Gouges, O. (1788b). *Lettre au people ou projet d'une caisse patriotique. Letter to the People, or Patriotic Purse Project.* Trans. Clarissa Palmer. Available online: https://www.olympedegouges.eu/patriotic_purse.php

Gouges, O. (1788c). *Remarques Patriotiques. Patriotic Observations.* Trans. Clarissa Palmer. Available online: https://www.olympedegouges.eu/patriotic _observations.php

Gouges, O. (1788d). 'Réflexions sur les Hommes Nègres'. In Clarissa Palmer (trans.), *Zamore et Mirza ou l'Heureux Naufrage, Drame Indien.* Reflections concerning Black Men, Zamore and Mirza, or the Fortunate Shipwreck, an Indian drama. Available online: https://www.olympedegouges.eu/zamore_et _mirza.php

Gouges, O. (1788e). 'Le Philosophe Corrigé ou le Cocu Supposé'. Available online: https://fr.wikisource.org/wiki/Le_Philosophe_corrigé

Gouges, O. (1789a). *Le Bonheur Primitif, ou Rêveries Patriotiques*. Amsterdam, Paris: Royer. Available online: http://gallica.bnf.fr/ark:/12148/bpt6k42599j .r=Le+bonheur+primitif+de+l'homme,+ou+les+rêveries+patriotique s.langFR. *The Primitive Happiness of Mankind, or Patriotic Reveries*. Trans. Clarissa Palmer. Available online: https://www.olympedegouges.eu/bonheur _primitif.php

Gouges, O. (1789b). *Mes Vœux sont Remplis ou le Don Patriotique*. Available online: https://www.olympedegouges.eu/hopes_fulfilled.php

Gouges, O. (1789c). *Action Héroïque d'une Française, ou la France Sauvée par les Femmes*. Available online: https://www.olympedegouges.eu/action_heroique .php

Gouges, O. (1789/2014). 'Projet Utile et Salutaire'. In Martine Reid (ed.), *Femme reveille-toi! Déclaration des droits de la femme et de la citoyenne et autres écrits*, 18–29. Paris: Gallimard.

Gouges, O. (1790a). Depart De M. Necker Et De Madame De Gouges, Ou Les Adieux De Madame De Gouges Aux Français Et A M. Necker. M. Necker and Madame de Gouges's departure or Madame de Gouges's farewells to the French and to M. Necker.

Gouges, O. (1790b). *La Nécéssité du Divorce. The Necessity of Divorce*. Trans. Clarissa Palmer. Available online: https://www.olympedegouges.eu/le _divorce.php

Gouges, O. (1790c/1993). Réponse au champion américain in Olympe de Gouges: *Écrits politiques (1789–1791)*. Tome 1, préface d'Olivier Blanc. Coll. « Des femmes dans l'histoire ».

Gouges, O. (1791). *Les Droits de la Femme, A la Reine. The rights of Woman, to the Queen*. Available online: https://www.olympedegouges.eu/rights_of _women.php

Gouges, O. (1792a). *Le Bons Sens Français Ou L'apologie Des Vrais Nobles, Dédiée Aux Jacobins. French Commonsense or the Vindication of True Nobles, Dedicated to the Jacobins*. Trans. Clarissa Palmer. Available online: https:// www.olympedegouges.eu/french_commonsense_nobles.php

Gouges, O. (1792b). *Les fantômes de l'opinion publique. The Ghosts of Public Opinion*. Available online: https://www.olympedegouges.eu/ghost.php

Gouges, O. (1792c). *Réponse à la Justification de Maximilien Robespierre, Adressée à Jérôme Pétion, par Olympe de Gouges. Response to Maximilien Robespierre's Justification, Addressed to Jérôme Pétion, by Olympe de Gouges*. Trans. Clarissa Palmer. Available online: https://www.olympedegouges.eu/ response_max.php

Gouges. O. (1792d). *Olympe de gouges, défenseur officieux de Louis Capet. Olympe de Gouges, Louis Capet's Unofficial Advocate*. Trans. Clarissa Palmer. Available online: https://www.olympedegouges.eu/defenseur _officieux.php

Gouges, O. (1792e). *L'esclavage des Noirs ou l'Heureux Naufrage, Drame en Trois Actes. Représenté à la Comédie Française en Décembre 1789*. Paris. Available online: http://gallica.bnf.fr/ark:/12148/bpt6k566870. Black Slavery, *or the Fortunate Shipwreck.* Trans. Clarissa Palmer. Available online: https://www .olympedegouges.eu/esclavage_des_noirs.php

Gouges, O. (1793a). *Arrêt de mort que présente Olympe de Gouges contre Louis Capet. Decree of Death against Louis Capet.* Presented by Olympe de Gouges. Trans. Clarissa Palmer Available online: http://www.olympedegouges.eu/ decree_of_death.php

Gouges, O. (1793b). *Testament Politique d'Olympe de Gouges. Olympe de Gouges's Political Statement.* Trans. Clarissa Palmer. Available online: https:// www.olympedegouges.eu/political_testament.php

Gouges, O. (1793c). *Les Trois Urnes. The Three Urns.* Trans. Clarissa Palmer. Available online: https://www.olympedegouges.eu/three_urns.php

Green, Karen (ed.) (2019). *The Correspondence of Catharine Macaulay.* New York: Oxford University Press.

Green, Karen. (2014). *A History of Women's Political Thought in Europe 1700–1800.* Cambridge University Press.

Grégoire, Henri. (1794). 'Rapport sur la nécessité et les moyens d'anéantir les patois et d'universaliser l'usage de la langue française'. *Convention nationale*: 1–19.

Grouchy, Emmanuel de. (1829). *Fragments Historiques à la Campagne de 1815 et à la Bataille de Waterloo Par le General de Grouchy.* Paris : Firmin Didot frères.

Grouchy, Sophie de. (1993). *Lettres sur la Sympathie suivies des Lettres d'Amour à Maillat Garat.* Ed. Jean-Paul Lagrave. Montreal: Presses de l'Universite du Quebec.

Grouchy, Sophie de. (2008). *Letters on Sympathy (1798): A Critical Edition.* Ed. Karin Brown, Trans. James McClellan III. Transactions of the American Philosophical Society, New Series 98. Philadelphia: American Philosophical Society.

Grouchy, Sophie de. (2010). *Les Lettres sur la Sympathies (1798) de Sophie de Grouchy: Philosophie morale et reforme sociale.* Ed. Marc-André Bernier and Deidre Dawson. Oxford: Voltaire Foundation.

Grouchy, Sophie de Sandrine Bergès and Eric Schliesser. (2019). *Sophie de Grouchy's Letters on Sympathy: A Critical Engagement with Adam Smith's The Theory of Moral Sentiments.* New York: Oxford University Press.

Groult, Benoîte Ainsi. (2014). *soit Olympe de Gouges.* Paris: Livre de Poche.

Guillois, Alfred. (1904). Thesis presented and passed on 12 December 1904 on Olympe de Gouges, considerations generals sur la mentalité des femmes pendant la revolution. Faculty of medicine and pharmacy in Lyon.

Guillois, Antoine. (1894). *Le Salon de Madame Helvetius, Cabanis et l.es Idéologues.* Paris: Calman Levy.

Guillois, Antoine. (1897). *La Marquise de Condorcet, Sa Famille, Son Salon, Ses Amis 1764–1822.* Paris: Paul Ollendorff.

Gullickson Gay, L. (2014). 'Militant Women: Representations of Charlotte Corday, Louise Michel and Emmeline Pankhurst'. *Women's History Review*, 23: 837–52.

Hart, Patrick, Kennedy Valerie and Dora Petherbridge (eds) (2020). *Henrietta Liston's Travels The Turkish Journals, 1812–1820*. Edinburg: Edinburg University Press.

Hase, Karl Benedikt. (1894). *Briefe von der Wanderung und aus Paris von Carl Benedict Hase*. hrsg. O. Heine. Leipzig: Breitkopf und Härtel.

Havet Julien. (1878). '*Étude sur Nicolas de Grouchy et son fils Timothée de Grouchy, sieur de La Rivière*, par le vicomte de Grouchy et Émile Travers'. *Bibliothèque de l'école des chartes*., tome 39. 522–5.

Hesse, Carla. (2003). *The Other Enlightenment: How French Women Became Modern*. New Haven: Princeton University Press.

Hugo, Victor. (1982). *Les Misérables*. Hammondsmith: Penguin.

Hunt, Lynn. (2004). *Politics, Culture and Class in the French Revolution: Twentieth Anniversary Edition*. California University Press,.

Israel, Jonathan. (2014). *Revolutionary Ideas, And Intellectual History of the French Revolution from The Rights of Man to Robespierre*. Oxford and Princeton: Princeton University Press.

James. C. L. R. (1989). *The Black Jacobins. Toussaint Louverture and the San Domingo Revolution*. 2nd edn. New York:Random House,.

Jourgniac de Saint-Méart, F. (1792). *Mon agonie de trente-huit heures, ou Récit de ce qui m'est arrivé, de ce que j'ai vu et entendu pendant ma détention dans la prison de l'abbaye Saint-Germain depuis le 22 août jusqu'au 4 septembre*. Paris: Desenne. Available online: https://gallica.bnf.fr/ark:/12148/bpt6k40949m?rk =21459;2

Jurt, Joseph. (1992). 'Condorcet et les Colonies'. *Proceedings of the FCHS*, 15: 9–21.

Kelly, G. and Man Mortal. (1986). 'Immortal Society'. *Historical Reflections / Réflexions Historiques*, 13: 24–49.

Lagrave, Jean-Paul. (1989). 'L'influence de Sophie de Grouchy'. In Pierre Crépel (ed.), *Condorcet: Mathématicien, économist, philosophy, homme politique*, 430–45. Paris: Colloque International.

Lairtulier, E. (1840). *Les Femmes Célèbres de 1789 à 1795 et leur influence dans la Révolution*. Paris: France, Librairie Politique.

Landes, Joan B. (1988). *Women and the Public Sphere in the Age of the French Revolution*. Ithaca: Cornell University Press.

Lapied, Martine. (2006). 'Parole publique des femmes et conflictualité pendant la Révolution dans le Sud-Est de la France'. *Annales historiques de la Révolution française*, 344: 47–62.

Letzter, J. and R. Adelson. (2004). 'The Legacy of a One-woman Show: A Performance History of Julie Candeille's "Catherine, ou la belle fermière". *Nineteenth-Century French Studies*, 33: 11–34.

Linton, Marisa. (2013). *Choosing Terror: Virtue, Friendship, and Authenticity in the French Revolution*. Oxford: Oxford University Press.

Macaulay, Catharine. (1763–83), *The History of England from the Accession of James 1. to that of the Brunswick Line*, 8 Vols., London: Printed for the author and sold by J. Nourse, J. Dodsley and W. Johnston. (Volumes 5–8 are titled *The History of England from the Accession of James 1. to the Revolution*. London: C Dilly).

Macaulay, Catharine. (1790). *Observations on the Reflections of the Right Hon. Edmund Burke on the Revolution in France*. London: C. Dilly.

Martin, Jean. (1931). 'Achille du Chatelet et le Premier Mouvement Républicain en France d'Après des Lettres Inédites (1791–1792)'. *La Révolution Française*, 34: 105–32.

McLean, Iain. (2012). 'The Paris Years of Thomas Jefferson'. In Cogliano, Francis D. (ed.), *A Companion to Jefferson*, 110–27. Chichester: Blackwell.

Michelet, Jules. (1855). *Les Femmes de la Révolution*. The Project Gutenberg EBook. Available online: http://www.gutenberg.org/files/18738/18738-h /18738-h.htm 2006.

Mistacco, Vicky. (2019). '"Le corps petit, mais l'âme grande": Voicing a Woman's Ambition in Louise de Kéralio'. *Women In French Studies Special Conference Issue*. Available online: http://purl.flvc.org/fsu/fd/FSU_libsubv1_scholarship _submission_1578588553_f8cde7a6

Montesquieu, Charles de. (1989). *The Spirit of the Laws*. Ed. Anne M. Cohler, Basia C. Miller, Harold S. Stone. Cambridge: Cambridge University Press.

Monteyremar, Henri de. (1862). *Charlotte de Corday : étude historique avec documents inédits*. Paris: Sartorius.

Moore, Lisa, Joanna Brooks and Wigginton Caroline (eds) (2012). *Transatlantic Feminisms in the Age of Revolutions*. New York: Oxford University Press.

Moore, Lucy. (2006). *Liberty: The Lives and Times of Six Women in Revolutionary France*. Harper Collins.

Naish, Camille. (1991). *Death Comes to the Maiden: Sex and Execution 1431–1933*. London: Routledge.

O'Loughlin, Katrina. (2020). *Women, Writing and Travel*. Cambridge: Cambridge University Press,.

Oliver, Bette W. (2009). *Orphans of the Earth: Girondins Fugitive from the Terror, 1793–1794*, Lanham: Lexington Books.

Oliver, Bette W. (2016). *Jacques Pierre Brissot in America and France 1788–1793*. Lanham: Lexington Books.

Paine, Thomas. (1776). *Common Sense*. Philadelphia: Bell.

Paine, Thomas. (1791). *Rights of Man. Being an Answer to Mr. Burke's Attack on the French Revolution*. London: J. Johnson.

Paine, Thomas. (1794). *The Age of Reason*. London: D.I. Eaton.

Paine, Thomas. (1945). *The Complete Writings of Thomas Paine*. Ed. P. S. Foner, 2 vols. Secaucus: The Citadel Press.

Porret, M. (2000). 'Atténuer le mal de l'infamie: Le réformisme conservateur de Pierre-François Muyart de Vouglans'. *Crime, Histoire & Sociétés / Crime, History & Societies*, 4: 95–120.

Prince, M. (2006). 'The History of Mary Prince, a West Indian Slave, Related by Herself'. In Joseph Black (ed.), *Broadview Anthology of British Literature, The Concise Edition, Volume B*, 263–90. Perterborough: Broadview Press.

Raimond, Julien. (1791). *Observations sur l'Origine et les Progrès du préjugé des colons blancs contre les hommes de couleur; sur les inconvéniens de le perpétuer; la nécessité, la facilité de le détruire; sur le projet du Comité colonial, etc. par M. Raimond, Homme de couleur de Saint-Domingue.* Paris, 26 Janvier 1791.

Reid, Martine. (2014). *"Femme, réveille-toi!": Déclaration des droits de la femme et de la citoyenne et autres écrits.* Paris : Folio.

Reynolds, Sian. (2012). *Marriage and Revolution: Monsieur et Madame Roland.* Oxford: Oxford University Press.

Roederer, Pierre-Louis. (1856). *Œuvres du Comte P.L. Roederer, publiées par son fils, le Baron A.M. Roederer.* Tome IV. Paris: Firmin Didot.

Roederer, Pierre-Louis. (1836). *Catalogue des livres composant la bibliothèque de feu M. le comte Roederer.* Paris: Galliot.

Roland, M. J. (1791). *Letter to Brissot 28 April 1791.* Ed. Brissot and published in the Patriote Français on 30 April 1791.

Roland, M.-J. (1799–1800). *Œuvres de J. M. Ph. Roland, femme de l'ex ministre de l'intérieur.* Ed. L. A. Champagneux. Paris: Bidault.

Roland, M. J. (1827). *Mémoires de Madame Roland, avec une notice sur sa vie, des notes et des éclaircissements historiques.* Ed. Berville, Saint-Aubin, and Jean-François Barrière, 3rd edn, Vol. I. Paris: Baudoin Frères.

Roland, M. J. (1864). *Mémoires de Madame Roland.* Ed. Faugères, François Alphonse. New edition, Vol. II. Paris: Hachette.

Roland, M. J. (1900). *Lettres de Madame Roland (1780–1793).* Ed. Claude Perroud. Paris: Imprimerie Nationale.

Roland, M. J. (1905). *Mémoires de Madame Roland. Perroud.* Vol. 1. Paris: Plon.

Roland, M. J. (1913). *Lettres de Madame Roland (1767–1780).* Ed. Claude Perroud. Paris: Imprimerie Nationale.

Roser, Max and Ortiz-Ospina Estaban. (2017). 'World Population Growth'. Available online: https://ourworldindata.org/wp-content/uploads/2013/05/updated-World-Population-Growth-1750-2100.png.

Rossignol, Marie Jeanne. (2010). 'Jacques Pierre Brissot and the Fate of Atlantic Anti-Slavery During the Age of Revolutionary Wars'. In R. Bessell et al. (eds), *War Empire and Slavery 1770–1830,* 139–56. London: Palgrave Macmillan.

Rousseau, Jean-Jacques. (1761/1997). *Julie, or the New Heloise.* Trans. and annotated by Philip Stewart and Jean Vache. Lebanon: University Press of New England.

Rousseau, Jean-Jacques. (1762/1979). *Emile, or on Education.* Trans. Allan Bloom. New York: Basic Books.

Rousseau, Jean-Jacques. (1988). *Rousseau's Political Writings.* Trans. Julia Bondanella and Ed. Alan Ritter. New York: W.W.Norton.

Rousseau, Jean-Jacques. (1994). *The Social Contract.* Trans. Christopher Betts. Oxford: Oxford University Press.

Schandeler, Jean-Pierre and Pierre Crépel (eds). (2004). *Tableau historique des progrès de l'esprit humain: Projets, esquisse, fragments et notes (1772–1794).* Paris: Institut National D'Etudes Démographiques.

Scott, Joan W. (1997). *Only Paradoxes to Offer: French Feminists and the Rights of Man*. Harvard University Press.

Scurr, Ruth. (2009). 'Inequality and Political Stability from Ancien Régime to Revolution: The Reception of Adam Smith's Theory of Moral Sentiments in France'. *History of European Ideas*, 35 (4): 441–9.

Sellers, M. N. S. Ed. (2003). 'Republican Influences on the French and American Revolutions'. In *Republican Legal Theory*, 16–25. London: Palgrave Macmillan.

Shelley, Mary Wollstonecraft. (1840). *Lives of the Most Eminent French Writers*. Philadelphia: Lea and Blanchard.

Sieyès, Emmanuel Joseph. (2003). *Political Writings*. Ed. Michael Sonenscher. Indianapolis: Hacket.

Sieyès, Emmanuel Joseph. (1789). 'What Is the Third Estate?'. Available online: http://chnm.gmu.edu/revolution/d/280 (accessed 8 February 2019).

Skinner, Quentin. (1998). *Liberty Before Liberalism*. Cambridge: Cambridge University Press.

Smith, Adam. (1759/1976). *The Theory of Moral Sentiments*. Ed. D. D. Raphael and A. L. Macfie. Oxford: Oxford University Press.

Smith, Adam. (1776/1976). *An Inquiry into the Nature and Causes of the Wealth of Nations*. Ed. R. H. Campbell, A. S. Skinner, and W. B. Todd. Oxford: Oxford University Press.

Stewart, Iain. (2002). 'Montesquieu in England: his "Notes on England", with Commentary and Translation Commentary Translation and Annotations Includes an English Translation of Montesquieu: *Notes sur l'Angleterre*'. *Oxford U Comparative L Forum* 6. Available online: ouclf.law.ox.ac.uk

Suleau, François-Louis. (1791). *Journal de la Contre-Revolution*. Neuwied sur le Rhin.

Têtard, Madeleine Arnold. (2003). *Sophie de Grouchy, Marquise de Condorcet*. Paris: Christian.

Tomalin, Claire. (2004). *The Life and Death of Mary Wollstonecraft*, Penguin Books,.

Tomaselli, Sylvana. (2021). *Wollstonecraft, Philosophy, Passion, and Politics*. Princeton University Press.

Transatlantic Slave Trade Database. Available online: http://www.slavevoyages.org/assessment/estimates

Trouille, Mary Seidman. (1997). *Sexual Politics in the Enlightenment*. Albany: State University of New York Press.

Underwood, G. A. (1915). 'Rousseanism in Two Early Works of Mme de Staël'. *Modern Philology*, 13: 417–32.

Voltaire. (2007). *Philosophical Letters (Letters on the English Nation, Letters on England) (1734)*. Ed. John Leigh and Prudence L. Steiner. Indianapolis: Hackett.

Wollstonecraft, Mary. (1789). *The Works of Mary Wollstonecraft*. Ed. Janet Todd and Marilyn Butler in 7 volumes.

Wollstonecraft, Mary. (1792). *Defense des Droits des Femmes*. Paris: Buisson.

Wollstonecraft, Mary. (2014). *A Vindication of the Rights of Woman*. Ed. and Introduction by Eileen Hunt Botting. New Haven: Yale University Press.

Young, Maurice de. (1960). 'Jean-Jacques Dessalines and Charles Belair'. *Journal of Inter-American Studies*, 2: 449–56.

Index